Sexing the Benefit:
Women, Social Security and Financial Independence
in EC Sex Equality Law

Sexing the Benefit

Women, Social Security and Financial Independence
in EC Sex Equality Law

JULIA A. SOHRAB

Dartmouth

Aldershot • Brookfield USA • Singapore • Sydney

Published by
Dartmouth Publishing Company Limited
Gower House
Croft Road
Aldershot
Hants GU11 3HR
England

Dartmouth Publishing Company
Old Post Road
Brookfield
Vermont 05036
USA

British Library Cataloguing in Publication Data
Sohrab, Julia A.
   Sexing the benefit : women, social security and financial
   independence in EC sex equality law. – (Socio-legal
   studies)
   1.Social security – Europe   2.Social security beneficiaries
   – Europe   3.Women's rights – Europe   4.Women – Europe –
   Social conditions
   I.Title
   362.8'3'094

Library of Congress Cataloging-in-Publication Data
Sohrab, Julia A.
   Sexing the benefit : women, social security, and financial
   independence in EC sex equality law / Julia A. Sohrab.
      p. cm.
   "Socio-legal studies series."
   Includes bibliographical references and index.
   ISBN 1-85521-705-8
      1. Social security—Law and legislation—European Economic
Community countries.   2. Women—Pensions—Law and legislation–
–European Economic Community countries.   3. Sex discrimination
against women—Law and legislation—European Economic Community
countries.   I. Title.
KJE3281.S67   1996
341.7'6—dc20   96-15747
                                                                   CIP

ISBN 1 85521 705 8

Typeset by Manton Typesetters, 5–7 Eastfield Road, Louth, Lincolnshire LN11 7AJ, UK.

Printed and bound in Great Britain by Hartnolls Limited, Bodmin, Cornwall

Contents

List of Tables

Abbreviations

AA	attendance allowance
AAW	Algemene Arbeidsongeschiktheidswet (General Law on Incapacity – Netherlands)
ABW	General Assistance Act (Netherlands)
AOW	Algemene Ouderdomswet (General Law on Old Age – Netherlands)
CPAG	Child Poverty Action Group
DLA	disability living allowance
DSS	Department of Social Security
ECJ	European Court of Justice
EOC	Equal Opportunities Commission
FIS	family income supplement
FLAC	Free Legal Advice Centres
HB	housing benefit
HRP	home responsibilities protection
ICA	invalid care allowance
IS	income support
IVB	invalidity benefit
LEL	lower earnings limit
NCIP	non-contributory invalidity pension
NMW	national minimum wage
SB	supplementary benefit
SDA	severe disablement allowance
SER	standard employment relationship
SERPS	state earnings-related pension supplement
SMW	statutory minimum wage
TW	Toeslagenwet (Supplements Act – Netherlands)
WAO	long-term sickness insurance scheme (Netherlands)
WW	unemployment benefit scheme (Netherlands)
WWV	Wet Werkloosheidsvoorziening (Dutch unemployment benefit scheme)
ZW	short-term employee sickness insurance (Netherlands)

Acknowledgements

This book grew out of a doctoral thesis completed in 1994 at the European University Institute, Firenze, Italy. I am grateful to all those who helped me during my research, but all errors remain my own. First, I would like to thank the two supervisors of my PhD thesis, Brian Bercusson and Linda Luckhaus (Warwick University). I am indebted to Linda, in particular, for agreeing to supervise me in addition to her numerous other research and teaching commitments. I have learnt a great deal from her.

Many other people have also read and commented on the thesis. I would especially like to thank the three other academics who examined my PhD in December 1994, Rikki Holtmaat, Christopher McCrudden and Deidre Curtin, whose comments and questions stimulated much useful further reflection in the writing of this book. Rikki Holtmaat, in particular, has given me invaluable assistance and support in my research.

I would also like to thank the following people who have been kind enough to offer constructive comments on my work: Jeanne Gregory, Katharine O'Donovan, Carol Bacchi, Sue Millns, Joanne Scott and Wade Mansell.

I owe a great deal to fellow researchers of the European University Institute with whom I have had long discussions, and who generously spared time from their own work to read and comment on my thesis; these are Sally Sheldon, Claire Kilpatrick, Kirsten Scheiwe, Judith Blom and John Stanton-Ife. Claire Kilpatrick has shone a light for me into many of the darker corners of equality law! To Mary Daly thank you for the stimulating theoretical insights into gender and the welfare state.

I was also greatly helped by the following people who provided me with material or who met with me: Penny Wood, John Darcy, Catherine Byrne of ETUC, Rosheen Callender, Sacha Prechal, Ina Sjerps, Hans Gilliams, Dominique de Vos, Dimitrios Kontizas, Chris Docksey, Orlagh O'Farrell, Mary Johnson of FLAC (Dublin), Lorraine Fletcher of the Equal Opportunities Commission (Manchester), Len Smith of the Social Security Advisory Committee (London), Christine Crawley MEP, Philip Shiner, Nick Warren, Hedwige Peemans-Poullet of the Université des Femmes (Brussels), Elaine Whiteford, and Carol Jackson of the Department of Social Security (London).

Finally, I would like to thank friends for all their support and patience during the writing of this book. To Jeanine Hickman thank you for everything, to Sally Sheldon and James Lancaster thanks for my holiday, to Hilary Mairs for the much-needed gin therapy, to Nick Dearden for diamante and glamour, to Kenneth Armstrong for the delicious dinners, to Sue Millns for the e-mails, to Laurent Gallissot for the giggles. Many thanks also to Stephen Hicks for patiently listening to me, for his practical suggestions and for finding the time, amongst other commitments, to read and comment on parts of the book.

1   Introduction

Why do women as a rule find it harder than men to establish claims to, and receive, personal benefits from social security systems? Why does it matter anyway? What, if anything, can equality laws do to redress this structural inequality? These questions encapsulate the principal themes of this book.

In the 1990s women in the EU seem to have achieved equality. Women have entered, and will remain in, the labour market in significant numbers. Many of the rules which excluded women from employment and social security have now been removed. Yet, far fewer women than men are claimants of contributory (or social insurance) benefits, and far more women are claimants of, or receive, non-contributory benefits or means-tested benefits. Why does this matter? The problem in a nutshell is that there are important qualitative, as well as quantitative, differences between types of benefits and that women are by and large worse off than men on both counts. In a society in which men still have greater access to income and resources, and thus greater power, such differences matter in very concrete terms. The missing link in this chain of inequality is caring (whether for children, the sick or the elderly), which is an important part of the emotional, social and sexual services provided by women to men. The 'price of caring' is often financial dependence on another adult, most often the dependence of women on men.

Income, whether from employment or in the form of social security benefits, which is not personal is unable to provide the capacity to make basic choices. In the words of Tove Stang Dahl, an 'independent income of one's own is a prerequisite for participation in and enjoyment of life in a number of respects, privately as well as publicly' (1984, p.137). I would be more explicit and argue that women need to achieve a greater financial independence than they currently have as part of a feminist politics of increasing their power in society and their relative power vis-à-vis men.

A number of aspects of social security systems of the four countries covered by this book (the UK, Ireland, the Netherlands and Belgium) place significant obstacles in the way of women acquiring income by way of personal benefits. One of these is the linking of access to the contributory

1

benefits system to a particular pattern of labour market participation. Another is the rule in social assistance systems which aggregates the resources and needs of heterosexual couples who live together (either as husband and wife or as cohabiting partners). Aggregation may mean that one partner is denied benefits by virtue of another's income, and it is a vehicle for the assumption that in (heterosexual) households income and resources are shared equally.

In defining the structural inequality suffered by women (and other carers), a number of operative factors emerge, which I describe by reference to three 'layers'. The first layer concentrates on rules, such as the contributions rule and the aggregation rule, and their effects on impeding women's access to personal benefits. The second layer focuses on the construction of risk provision in social security, and the qualitative and quantitative differences in the provision for feminine and masculine 'risks'. The third layer offers 'macro-level' observations on policy which reinforces women's financial dependence on men through the inadequacy of their personal entitlements to benefits. Although these three layers cover largely the same conceptual terrain, it is nevertheless useful, in my opinion, to map out into separate strata the different mechanisms by which inequality is perpetuated.

I have argued that the second layer of inequality relates to the qualitative differences between benefits accorded for 'masculine' and 'feminine' activities. What I mean by this is that qualitative differences arise because loss of income due to exit from the labour market is generally compensated by social insurance, while benefits linked to the social role of caring, where they exist at all, are predominantly of a social assistance nature.

In the conventional parlance of social security law and policy, 'risks' denote either situations giving rise to the need for income or events triggering the payment of benefits for which a person has made contributions. The 'risks' traditionally associated with exit from the labour market, such as becoming unemployed, sickness, invalidity, industrial injuries and old age, are provided for by means of social insurance (or contributory) benefits.[1] Provision for exit from the labour market for the above reasons is essentially a construction of risk provision around the experience of the male worker in the so-called 'standard employment relationship' (see Mückenberger, 1989). Despite the presence of means-tested benefits for these risks in all four countries, the fact remains that provision for 'masculine risks' represents the backbone of social insurance systems. Generally speaking, in the UK and Ireland social insurance for these risks accords higher rates of benefits.[2] These benefits, where contribution conditions are satisfied, are paid at levels which do not vary with the income of a claimant's spouse or partner. They bear positive connotations of claimants as active citizens participating in society. In the Netherlands and Belgium, social insurance benefits for employees are paid at wage replacement levels, with higher rates being given to persons with dependent spouses or partners. This brand of social insurance does take account of the income of a partner, but the benefits provided are higher than the rates under means-tested benefits or general social insurance schemes.

The central point here is that the traditional social insurance risks are constructed around a male experience of income needs, which I describe as 'masculine risks'. 'Feminine risks', on the other hand, such as caring (whether of children, the sick or elderly), maternity and widowhood are only provided for by social insurance systems to a very limited degree.

The terminology of 'masculine' and 'feminine' risks draws upon a crucial distinction made in feminist writing between 'sex' and 'gender'. In brief, the argument is that 'sex' refers to biological sex, while 'gender' describes the social role and activities carried out by men and women. In this book I draw upon generalizations of what men do (full-time work) and what women do (caring for children and others). Since, in my opinion, these generalizations relate to gender role as opposed to biological sex – that is, they are socially constructed notions of what men and women should do – I have chosen to describe social security risks as 'feminine' and 'masculine'.

There are two 'feminine risks' to which the four systems have given social insurance benefits – maternity and widowhood. Maternity benefits represent a recognition of the loss of income attendant on a withdrawal from the labour market to give birth, and widow's benefits or pensions are given in recognition of the fact that, for many women, the loss of a husband means potential poverty.[3]

Caring in its many forms, which is still predominantly done by women, is rewarded either with no benefits at all or with means-tested and non-contributory benefits. Generally speaking, these accord lower rates of benefit and are considerably more intrusive into the private circumstances of claimants. Means-tested benefits bear negative connotations of inactivity and 'dependence' on the state. Non-contributory benefits are paid at such low levels that unless claimants can share income with, and become financially dependent on, another person (often a male partner) they face a substantial poverty risk.

I have defined 'risks' as denoting situations giving rise to the need for income. It is clear from the discussion above that I include the activity of caring as a situation giving rise to the need for income. This is so for a number of reasons. First, caring is socially valuable work and those who do this work should not be consigned to poverty or financial dependence on their partners (or on the persons they care for). Further, the need to provide care often leads to exit from the labour market, either temporarily or in terms of reduced working hours, and in this sense it creates a need for income. It is not my intention, however, to link the idea of 'risks', as I use it in this book, solely to exit from the labour market, as conceptually this privileges the masculine experience of full-time, lifelong employment.

In my opinion, the concept of social security 'risks', and the argument that inequality is linked to qualitative and quantitatively inferior benefits for feminine risks, is a useful one since it yields a more 'structural' explanation of the mechanisms of this inequality. When focusing on anti-discrimination law, particularly for lawyers, it is tempting to seek inequality no further than examples of particular rules which discriminate either directly or indirectly against women. A great deal of insight can, however, be gleaned from taking a step further back to consider the role played by broader structuring principles in perpetuating inequality. In doing this, I have found an analysis of risk provision useful, as it helps to explain why women would still have less than equal access to independent income even if all rules were made sex-neutral, and it enables an appreciation of the magnitude of many of the mechanisms by which indirectly discriminatory rules operate. By this I mean that I approach, for instance, the contributions rule not only as a legal rule with particular discriminatory effects, but also as part of a structure which gives inferior provision to feminine risks. Using this approach it becomes clear that challenging this inequality requires more than tinkering with rules and in fact requires a reappraisal of the basic structures of the current system.

Financial dependence exists where all or part of a person's livelihood depends upon income that is not wholly within that person's control – that is, it is not received directly from its source, whether that source be an employer, the state or a social security body. It is income that a person may have access to, but which goes to someone else in the first instance, such as to a spouse or partner. The shorthand I use to describe this is income 'mediated' through another person.

Income that is 'mediated' through another person also includes, in my definition, derived benefits and maintenance from an ex-partner. Derived benefits do not constitute independent income, even where they are paid directly to a woman, because they are not based on personal contributions and because they perpetuate the idea of one 'dependent spouse'. Maintenance from an ex-partner, likewise, reinforces bonds of financial dependence on men even after the breakdown of a marriage or relationship.

It is my contention that financial dependence on another person is associated with (at least) three negative features, using Lister's definition, which are a lack of control, a lack of rights and a sense of obligation (1990, p.451). I argue that financial dependence on men is one factor explaining the continuing inequalities faced by women in the four countries covered in this book. Although women's financial dependence on men is rarely absolute in the contemporary Western world, my assertion is that even partial dependence lessens women's choices and their ability to determine their own lives, both in the family as well as in the wider society, as well as creating a sense of obligation, and even powerlessness, vis-à-vis a male partner.

Given the central preoccupations of this book, it might be asked how I make the jump from financial independence to equality law. In fact, the leap was in the other direction: from equality law to financial independence. Initially my research focused exclusively on one particular piece of EC legislation, Directive 79/7/EEC on the equality of treatment between men and women in statutory social security schemes. In analysing the provisions of this Directive I found myself unable to decide whether or not they represented the 'best' way of achieving equality for women. This led me to wonder whether a policy of equal rights is the best strategy for women, and whether different or specific rights represent an advance or whether they simply perpetuate 'outdated stereotypes'. These questions prompted a period of intense reading of feminist critiques of the principle of equality in law, and in particular the well known 'equal rights versus special rights debate'. In the end I felt none the wiser; this reading had not helped me towards a better critical appreciation of Directive 79/7/EEC. It occurred to me that three elements are essential to make sense of equality laws (and the feminist equal rights–special rights debate in particular) with reference to any substantive area of law. First, one cannot afford to adopt an *a priori* either/or position (either equal rights are best or special rights).[4] Second, one needs a clear understanding of the problems (or inequalities) which need to be tackled – in other words an appreciation of the complex mechanisms through which inequality is perpetuated. Third, one needs to develop a clear idea of the desired outcome or end result – that is, one must be able to spell out at, the very least, the broad principles underpinning equality of outcomes (or substantive equality). It is not enough to refer to the goal as 'substantive equality' or 'equality of outcomes' for women without being able to indicate at least partly what it would actually mean.[5]

In developing my understanding of these elements in relation to the Directive I found that it was the concept of financial independence which made the most sense in terms of answering the question, 'So what?'. So what that fewer women can build up entitlements to social insurance and are thus forced on to social assistance? So what that few benefits or aspects of social security systems give adequate value to unpaid care work? So what that Directive 79/7/EEC has a rather narrow scope of application?

The concept of financial independence has, therefore, served two purposes. First, it is the lack of independent income available to women which I see as a structural inequality in social security systems and which ought to be tackled (whether by equality laws or other instruments). Second, the advance of financial independence for women is the goal, or the evaluative standard, against which the Directive and its implementation in the four countries is measured.

Implicit in the above is a choice that has been made to adopt what I call a 'bottom-up approach' over a 'top-down approach'. A 'top-down' approach is characterized by two principal features. First, in some feminist literature on EC equality law there is a tendency to have taken an *a priori* position on EC sex equality law as a body of law. It is common to see the argument that this body of law is only about 'formal equality', that it assumes 'symmetry' between men and women, and to see it analysed primarily in terms of equality and difference and whether 'equal rights' or 'special rights' is the best strategy. This position, I argue, begins from the 'top', the level of abstract principle, which is then applied to a concrete situation.[6] In fact, the gendered social reality is often too complex to warrant this approach.[7] In certain instances, such as in the *Integrity* case,[8] the *a priori* position taken by one commentator in particular is misguided, at least from the standard of promoting financial independence. It seems to me that one is better advised to adopt a context-specific, as well as case-specific, approach, or to put it another way, to look 'bottom-up' rather than 'top-down'. This would mean identifying a problem (from the bottom) and considering whether, and how, the abstract principle (the top) could challenge it.

A second feature of a 'top-down' approach is that it neglects to consider what the implications of particular choices are – how choices will 'pan out' in practice. An example would be espousing the idea of specific rights for women without considering what their likely effect will be for women in the short and long term.[9] I do not intend to imply a rejection of a specific rights approach, any more than I would *a priori* favour an equal rights approach. Rather my contention is that, whichever approach is advocated, it needs to be considered in the light of its likely effects.

To see how choices 'pan out' in practice necessitates a 'bottom-up' approach, which is characterized by a sound understanding of the issues, and complexities, of the gendered social reality and of the laws and structures which reinforce a particular version of this gendered reality. In this book, models of equality are analysed from the viewpoint of whether or not they are likely to advance women's financial independence.

In fact, social security law is a terrain rarely explored by equality lawyers. A glance through academic literature on EC sex equality law reveals an almost exclusive concentration on the law relating to equal pay and working conditions.[10] References in the literature to the cases and issues in social security are either 'tacked on' at the end of the discussion, or treated in a less probing way than issues around equality and employment. Social security cases are cited more often for what they say about the development of

EC law in general (for instance, the early cases under the Directive on 'direct effect'), or to show that a particular view of equality is espoused by the European Court of Justice, rather than to consider what advances this specific field of EC legislation has brought for women.[11] It may be that employment equality is seen as more important, and that the greater number of legal instruments in the employment field has fuelled greater litigation. Suffice to say that this book fills two important gaps: it concentrates exclusively on social security law, and its analysis of equality law is grounded in an appreciation of some of the material issues in this area.

There are important caveats which need to be spelled out concerning the expectations that can be made of equality law. It may seem self-defeating for an equality lawyer to argue that we ought to be modest in our expectations of equality laws' potential to deliver change. The temptation is to hang expectations on equality law as it appears to be the best tool available. Nevertheless we ought to reserve some of our energies for thinking of solutions that can be proposed and effected outside of the courts. Equality laws may indeed at times achieve substantial gains, but they also contain important limitations.

The first limitation relates to the scope of most equality laws. These can tackle, and force changes to, a number of rules which discriminate against particular groups, whether directly or indirectly. However, once a number of individual rules have been modified, to produce more radical changes in outcomes there probably needs to be reforms to structures, such as the method of building up entitlements to social insurance, or indeed the availability of public childcare facilities. This kind of change does not usually fall within the ambit of equality law.

This argument has been eloquently made by Nancy Dowd, a US feminist lawyer, in an article entitled 'Work and Family: The Gender Paradox and the Limitations of Discrimination Analysis in Restructuring the Workplace'.[12] In brief, she reminds us that gender is not the only structuring principle in the workplace; there are powerful constraints of class, race and post-industrial capitalism (Dowd, 1989). With respect to what can be included within the parameters of the equality principle, she lists a number of assertions that are not covered by 'discrimination analysis', such as the assertion that any aspect of the employment structure which imposes a hardship on parents (lack of parenting leave, lack of sick leave to care for a sick child, required overtime, required travel, long hours and so on) disproportionately impacts on women because of women's primary care responsibility for children. Primarily the argument is that where there is a lack of something, such as parental leave or credits for carers towards social insurance, equality law cannot (normally) force its introduction. This may seem overpessimistic, particularly because it is common to find references to cases in which courts have been brave and imaginative.[13] On balance, however, in my opinion, Dowd's arguments apply well to EC sex equality law.

The second limitation refers to certain institutional and political factors that cannot be ignored. Courts feel themselves to be limited in many cases in what they can do, and radical changes will not normally be forced by courts. This is not even to mention the practical and financial difficulties experienced by people in bringing cases and in the length of time these normally take. There is a point then at which it is for the legislature to act.[14]

I do not wish to appear to be arguing that equality law does not have an important part to play in changing outcomes for women. After all, this is one of the principal themes of this book – that is, critiquing the law both with reference to an external evaluative standard, and showing the ways in which more generous interpretations of the Directive could be given by the courts. Yet, equality law must remain but one way to advance financial independence, and it is from a *strategic* viewpoint that I consider the law. This book therefore is not primarily an exposition of the case law on the Directive.[15]

The warning that we ought not to expect too much from within the law raises an important challenge for equality lawyers. One can observe that much academic literature on equality concentrates either on describing the law and legal developments (a 'black-letter' approach) or on critiquing decisions. Often articles or books end with an assertion that a different interpretation of equality is needed by the European Court of Justice (ECJ) or national courts, and that more needs to be done to further the aim of substantive equality. Why not begin rather than end here – that is, by starting out with what needs to be changed and then assessing whether specific equality laws can achieve these ends? This book attempts to use this type of approach, by beginning with a detailed consideration of the major obstacles facing women in acquiring personal income from social security and then evaluating the law from this standpoint. I offer indications as to how interpretations of the law could be broadened in a way helpful for women. At the end of the book I put the assessment of equality law aside and concentrate on developing a set of criteria for the evaluation of future policy.

This book considers social security systems in four member states of the EU. A breadth of analysis, I believe, enriches consideration of any area of law; quite simply, there is much to learn from a comparative approach. This is particularly so in any examination of the implementation of laws, as well as in the development of criteria for policy change. Until very recently all the references to the ECJ for preliminary rulings on Directive 79/7/EEC came from these four countries.[16] A superficial glance across the member states prompts the view that, in these four countries, the awareness of the potentialities of the Directive has been the most pronounced. While it would be interesting to explore the reasons for this, this is beyond the scope of this book. Suffice it to say that relevant factors may be the interest of women's groups in the Netherlands and Belgium in the Directive; the well developed welfare rights lobby in the UK which frequently brings test cases; and the law centre movement in Ireland which has been active in a number of areas using the Directive.

A commonly held, and expressed, view towards social security law is that it is a 'highly technical', and even 'boring'(!), area. Naturally it should come as no surprise to the reader that I do not share this view. Social security law is indeed no more technical than, say, housing law, company law or environmental law. However, an approach to the study, or indeed teaching, of law which concentrates on legal rules at the expense of examining the context in which they operate and in which they were developed does deprive the study of law of much of its richness. In this book, I focus first and foremost on the structuring principles – here, gender – of the benefits system and offer a critical examination of the relevant rules and the gendered social context in which they operate. I hope that, by the end, the reader will be convinced that a dismissal of this area as 'highly technical' obscures issues of considerable importance both for women and society.

The book is divided into seven further chapters. In Chapter 2 I examine the gendered social reality of the UK system. In Chapter 3 I offer a critique of equality models. The next two chapters focus on Directive 79/7/EEC, considering its personal and material scope (Chapter 4) and the principle of equal treatment (Chapter 5). In Chapter 6 I look at the implementation of the Directive in the Netherlands, Ireland and Belgium, and then at the UK in Chapter 7. Chapter 8 is the concluding chapter, in which I offer four normative criteria with which to assess reform proposals.

NOTES

1 I use these terms interchangeably, and likewise the terms 'means-tested benefit' and 'social assistance'.
2 However, it must be remembered that, in the UK system, contributory benefits do not in all cases offer higher rates than means-tested benefits. Persons with specific needs, such as persons with families, may have their contributory benefits 'topped up' by the social assistance system.
3 To the extent that widow's benefits and pensions are given where a husband has paid a certain level of contributions in the past, then perhaps widow's benefits are in fact just another benefit for a masculine risk – that of dying and no longer being able to support one's family. I am grateful to Mary Daly for this point.
4 I have developed this argument further in Sohrab (1993c).
5 Discussions with Claire Kilpatrick clarified this point for me and I am grateful to her.

She argues that dubbing a particular solution as pursuing substantive equality begs a further set of questions, rather than leading to the end of a discussion over the desirability and potential effectiveness of that particular solution. I take this to mean that a proposal which purports to further 'substantive equality' is not to be automatically seen as a 'good thing' and still requires critical attention.

6   This idea was partly stimulated by an article by Diana Majury, a Canadian feminist lawyer (see Majury, 1987). She has argued, in relation to the feminist equal rights–special rights debate in the USA, that both sides are striving to craft a perfect model of equality. But, says Majury, no concept of equality can ever do this, because to be a perfect fit for a range of situations is placing too heavy a burden on the concept. Rather, feminist lawyers should identify specific problems and then consider whether the equality principle, as one of a number of avenues, is (strategically) useful in challenging that problem.

7   I use the term 'gendered social reality' to describe the inequalities facing women in the social security system, the household and in the labour market, see Chapter 2.

8   See Chapter 5.

9   This is the argument I make about Fredman's (1992) assessment of the *Integrity* case in Chapter 5.

10   In a sense, the development itself of EC sex equality law may have encouraged this. Since Article 119 of the Treaty of Rome has more legal 'clout' than the Directives, because it is horizontally as well as vertically directly effective, the European Court of Justice has consistently broadened its scope of application, and therefore effectiveness, by widening the concept of 'pay'. Pay within Article 119 extends to benefits under occupational schemes, such as retirement and survivor's pensions: see the decisions of *Barber* v. *Guardian Royal Exchange* [1990] ECR I-1889 and *Ten Oever* [1993] ECR I-4879.

11   It is said that the exception proves the rule, and the exceptions in this case are the consistently excellent and perceptive articles by Linda Luckhaus (1983, 1986a, 1986b, 1987, 1988, 1990, 1992a, 1992b); Chapter 5 of Prechal and Burrows (1990); and the collection on EC sex equality law edited by McCrudden (1987).

12   I return to Dowd's (1989) arguments in Chapter 3. It is worth noting that the context in which Dowd writes is one in which there is a great deal of litigation around the equality principle against a backdrop of little public social provision and a minimalist welfare state.

13   One such tantalizing example is mentioned by Scheiwe (1995). In its judgement in the *Neue Juristische Wochenschrift* case in 1992 the German Federal Constitutional Court stated, in relation to inequalities in pensions and the recognition of childcare periods, that the legislator is obliged to compensate to a greater extent than has so far been the case for the weaknesses of the pension insurance system where childcare periods result in disadvantages in old age pensions. Further, these disadvantages, said the Court, should be reduced by the legislator step-by-step. Another tantalizing example is the Canadian case of *Brookes* v. *Canada Safeway* regarding discrimination on grounds of pregnancy, where the court stated that 'combining paid work with motherhood and accommodating the childbearing needs of working women are ever-increasing imperatives. That those who bear children and benefit society as a whole should not be economically or socially disadvantaged thereby seems to bespeak the obvious' ([1989] 1 SCR 1219, at 1243).

14   This point is eloquently made by Scheiwe (1995) and by Claire Kilpatrick (Lecturer in Law, Bristol University) in her doctoral thesis, provisionally entitled 'Can Equality

Cross National Borders?: A Comparison of Sex Equality Employment Laws in France and the UK'.

15 See Prechal and Burrow's (1990) excellent treatment of the case law until 1989 in Chapter 5 of their book. For a more recent account of the major cases, see Sohrab (1994) and Cousins (1994).

16 Currently two German references are pending judgement by the European Court of Justice. Germany has been a rich source of equality litigation before the European Court of Justice but only, until now, concerning employment equality instruments.

2 Women in the UK Social Security System: A Gendered Social Reality

Why do women, as a rule, find it more difficult than men to establish claims to, and receive, personal benefits from social security systems? Why does this matter anyway? These are two of the central questions posed by this book. The answers to these questions are rather complex, since there are numerous mechanisms through which inequality is perpetuated. My aim in this chapter is to examine the major factors causing women's structural inequality.

I characterize the structural inequality facing women as comprising three layers. The first layer considers the 'micro-level' of the gendered impact of specific rules in the social security system. The second layer looks at the qualitative and quantitative differences in the provision for masculine and feminine risks. The third layer offers 'macro-level' observations on policy which reinforces women's financial dependence on men through the inadequacy of their personal entitlements to benefits.

These three layers cannot be fully understood without reference to the inequalities facing women in the context of the other 'gendered social realities', the labour market and the household. I examine these gendered social realities in some detail in this chapter.

In order to tease out all these various strands of argument in the detail they deserve the choice was made to concentrate on one social security system in particular – the UK system. At the end of this chapter I begin to draw out some of the parallels with the Belgian, Irish and Dutch social security systems.

The first section sets out the startling differences between women and men in the types of benefits they receive. I then go on to consider women's access to independent income from the labour market and in the household. Following that, I describe the three layers of structural inequality in turn, beginning by considering the gendered effects of specific rules, and then considering risk provision. Finally I consider some aspects of how the benefit system encourages particular gender roles.

WOMEN AS CLAIMANTS OF SOCIAL SECURITY

There is no more striking way to consider women's structural inequality than to glance at a sex breakdown of benefit claimants.[1] The contrasts are very striking, and a discussion of how such a cleavage has come about forms the main subject of this chapter.

Broadly, it is clear that women are underrepresented as claimants of employment-related contributory benefits, which are generally personal benefits, whereas women are overrepresented as claimants of means-tested and non-contributory benefits. Means-tested benefits are household-based, exert strong influences on work incentives, and are strongly related to poverty, caring, disability and old age. Non-contributory benefits are paid at very low levels and offer little in the way of financial independence.

Table 2.1 presents a breakdown of the main categories of contributory benefits by sex.

Table 2.1   Breakdown of the principal contributory benefits by sex

Contributory Benefits	Men (%)	Women (%)
Industrial injury benefit	89	11
Unemployment benefit	68	32
Invalidity benefit	76	24
Sickness benefit	74	26
Retirement pensions	35	65

A stark differentiation is revealed whereby, in general, women form between only 25–30 per cent of claimants of the major contributory benefits. The breakdown of claimants of the basic state retirement pension must be read taking account of women's so-called 'derived entitlements'. A substantial number of women receive a pension based on their husband's contributions. In 1989 it was estimated that nearly 2 million married women and 2 million widows receive a retirement pension based on their husband's contributions (see Roll, 1991, p.47). The derived entitlements of women to the retirement pension still far exceed the numbers of women entitled in their own right: in 1989 less than one-third of married women of pensionable age received the basic state pension on the basis of their own contributions (Ginn and Arber, 1992, p.262).

Table 2.2   Breakdown of three non-contributory benefits by sex

Non-Contributory Benefits	Men (%)	Women (%)
Invalid care allowance	18	82
Severe disablement allowance	40	60
Attendance allowance	37	63

The sex breakdown of claimants of the invalid care allowance, shown in Table 2.2, is indicative of the scale of caring done by women and the fact there is no other discrete benefit given to carers.[2] The breakdown of claimants of the severe disablement allowance (SDA) and attendance allowance (AA) are indicative of a trend related to the sex breakdown of contributory benefits. By this is meant that the greater proportion of women claimants of this type of benefit is a reflection of many women's inability to gain entitlement to the contributory equivalent because of an inadequate contributions record.[3] Non-contributory benefits are paid at roughly two-thirds of the rate of their principal contributory counterparts, yet the incapacity conditions to be satisfied for receipt of the non-contributory benefits are more stringent than for receipt of the contributory benefit.

The breakdown for family credit, shown in Table 2.3, reflects the policy decision to pay the benefit to the female partner/mother in the household, regardless of whether or not she is a worker. The breakdown for income support is perhaps more even than would have been expected given the stark differences in claimants of contributory benefits. This may be explained by a number of factors; first, where couples claim income support, in 19 out of 20 cases it is the male partner who is the claimant (Lister, 1992, p.42). Second, in view of the steady erosion of contributory benefits for the unemployed (a trend which will only increase with the introduction of the

Table 2.3   Breakdown of two means-tested benefits by sex

Means-tested (or 'Income-related') Benefits	Men (%)	Women (%)
Income support	43	57
Family credit	1	99

jobseeker's allowance), as well as for persons incapable of work, there has been an increase in the numbers of male claimants of means-tested benefits.[4]

Child benefit is automatically paid to women, save in exceptional circumstances. The breakdown of one parent benefit, shown in Table 2.4, reflects the overwhelming proportion of lone parents who are women.

In the following two sections I consider women and financial independence in the labour market and in the household.

Table 2.4   Breakdown of two universal benefits by sex

Universal benefits	Men (%)	Women (%)
Child benefit	2	98
One parent benefit	9	91

WOMEN AND FINANCIAL INDEPENDENCE THROUGH THE LABOUR MARKET

At a superficial glance, women's position in the labour market and their ability to gain financial independence through paid work in the UK has never looked better. A projected estimate for women's labour market participation for 1995 was that 62.2 per cent of women would be employed in the UK (Pillinger, 1992, p.12). In 1987 women workers already constituted 45 per cent of workers in employment (Morris and Nott, 1991, p.54). Significant numbers of mothers are employed: some 63 per cent of women of working age with dependent children in 1990 were in paid work (Lister, 1992, p.2). It has even been estimated that there will soon be more women than men with jobs.[5] Indeed, for women with good qualifications, professional careers, status and opportunities, the employment situation has never looked better.

There are, however, a number of patterns in women's labour market participation which mean that paid work is unlikely to provide the majority of women with income at a level conducive to financial independence (Hutton, 1994, pp.36–7). These, often interrelated, patterns are part-time work, pay inequalities, job segregation and the unequal division of labour in the home, the poor availability of childcare and the organization of time. Associated patterns are the problems of women's low pay, and levels of pay in the tertiary (or 'service') sector.

Clearly, these patterns do not affect all women. Indeed, they play their part in reinforcing differences between groups of women in terms of class and occupation, as well as between ethnic groups. It is worth taking a closer look at these patterns in turn.

Part-time work

The expansion in the labour market, in terms of new jobs created, as well as in the growth in (white) women's labour market participation, has largely been accounted for by the growth in part-time work (Lister, 1992, p.60). Women account for nearly 90 per cent of part-time workers, and part-time workers now represent one quarter of the total workforce. This type of paid work is, however, associated with a number of drawbacks in the extent of financial independence which it provides. In particular, the pay of part-time workers relative to full-time workers fell in the 1980s (Hutton, 1994, p.33).

First, women in the UK (as indeed in the Netherlands) tend to work short part-time – that is, a small number of hours. The proportion of women part-timers working fewer than eight hours has risen, and the number of jobs of no more than 16 hours per week grew at twice the rate of larger part-time jobs in the 1980s (Lister, 1992, p.7). Second, overall trends in part-time working are leading towards shorter hours, lower pay, greater insecurity and increased casualization (ibid.).

As a consequence of the association between low pay and part-time work, or short working hours, part-time workers receive little, if any, state or occupational welfare benefits. Among the estimated 1.8 million people in employment who fall outside tax and national insurance thresholds, the single largest group is part-time employees who represent 75 per cent of all those workers outside the tax and social insurance systems (Hakim, 1989, p.480).

The irony is that at the very time when women's economic activity rates are increasing, the more 'flexible' labour market is decreasingly likely to offer women an adequate independent income (Lister, 1992, p.8).

Pay inequalities

Women's earnings continue to be significantly lower than men's. Women's full-time average earnings are 77 per cent of men's (EOC, 1991, p.1). This differential is caused by a number of factors – the duration of women's paid work in terms of hours, pay inequalities, low pay and the sectors in which women's employment is located. The principal reason, however, for the differences in income between men and women appears to be the failure of part-time earnings to keep pace with the earnings of full-time workers (Hutton, 1994, p.33).

Earnings differentials are, for instance, affected by the fact that men who work full-time tend to work longer hours per week than full-time working women (EOC, 1991, p.7). Men, moreover, are more likely to receive payments additional to their basic salary, such as shift premia, overtime and incentive payments (ibid.). To put it another way, only between 2–3 per cent of working men have earnings that leave them outside the contributory benefits system and the income tax net, as compared to between 14–18 per cent of working women (Hakim, 1989, p.480).

Over their lifetimes, women's earnings are significantly affected by whether or not they have had children and, in turn, whether or not they have combined paid and unpaid work. One study found the average employment interruption of a woman with two children to be eight years full-time in total, followed by 14 years of part-time work, leading to lifetime earnings of only 57 per cent of those of a woman without children (EOR, 1993, p.6). Earnings are foregone due to absence from the labour market and reduced hours of work and the lower rates of pay per hour for part-time work (Joshi, 1991, p.180). Lower rates of pay are in turn caused by loss of experience and seniority, pay inequalities and occupational downgrading on labour market re-entry (ibid.). Heather Joshi's study found that lost seniority, experience and training opportunities have a permanent effect, although it diminishes over time, on a mother's earning potential and future pension entitlements.

Job segregation

Labour markets remain segregated by sex both vertically and horizontally to the disadvantage of women (Lonsdale, 1992, p.97). Women and men are employed in different sectors, as well as in different occupations within sectors (EOC, 1991, pp.11–13). Three-quarters of all employed women, for instance, work in the service sector, in which earnings are relatively low (EOC, 1991, p.11). Employment in the service sector is, moreover, being restructured to provide predominantly part-time work for older women and low-paid full-time work for young people (Buswell, 1992, p.80).

There is also job segregation by ethnic group; black women are much more likely than white women to be in non-manual work, and are less likely to be in professional and managerial jobs (Cook and Watt, 1992, p.16). This has an important knock-on effect on the earnings of women from ethnic groups, and their entitlements to social insurance and occupational welfare benefits.

Another aspect of job segregation is that between paid and unpaid work, where women carry out the bulk of unpaid caring and domestic work. The division of labour in the home continues to be grossly unequal; as Leira puts it, 'the dual-earner family is not a dual-carer family' (1993, p.67). One study estimated that, on average, women spend 48.4 hours per week on childcare compared to an average of 14.7 hours by men (Kowarzik and Popay, 1989, p.16). Nor has this unequal division changed significantly over time (see Warde and Hetherington, 1993, p.43). In addition to childcare, an enormous amount of unpaid care for the sick, elderly and disabled is also done by women (Lister, 1992, p.11).

Few, if any, policies in the UK promote the sharing of childcare (or other forms of care) between men and women. There are, for instance, no statutory rights to paternity leave, or rights for either men or women to take time off work to care for a sick child.[6]

Availability of childcare

An important factor affecting women's labour market participation is the availability of childcare. The UK is the second worst provider of public childcare services in the EU. There was little growth in publicly funded services in the 1980s (Moss, 1990, pp.34–7). Particular groups of women such as black women, may, indeed, experience greater difficulties in gaining access to formal childcare facilities (Cook and Watt, 1992, pp.17–18).

The cost of private childcare is a problem for many women. Recently, a government-funded survey found that almost one in three lone parents spend more than 25 per cent of their take-home pay on 'buying in' childcare. The authors of the survey concluded that, after tax and travel costs, the net return from paid work must be quite low for many lone mothers.[7]

The gendered concept of time

Time is as much of a gendered concept as paid work, but is rarely specifically refered to in assessing inequalities between men and women.[8] This gendered concept can be examined through two different lenses – first, in terms of the value given to particular uses of time. Time spent in caring work is, to a substantial extent, unpaid and thereby encourages financial dependence on others. On the other hand, full-time participation in the labour market generally yields the highest levels of income and financial independence.

Second, there is the way time is organized in society. Time organization, such as opening times for certain services and activities, is relevant to men's and women's lives in so far as the organization of certain services and activities is broadly incompatible with current patterns of full-time work. Among the important elements that parents, and mostly mothers, need to 'juggle' are school hours during term-time, school holidays, and time for recreational provision, as well as times of medical and other essential services. If certain activities are largely incompatible with full-time employment, and childcare is unavailable or too expensive, a withdrawal (whether full or partial) from the labour market is the inevitable result.

Summary

Paid work provides, and no doubt will continue to provide, a partial degree of financial independence to women. However, for many women, it is a partial independence riddled with insecurities in the guise of low pay and the disadvantages of 'flexible' types of working, as well as providing little in the way of opportunities to build up personal rights to social insurance benefits. The reverse side of partial independence in the labour market is, at least partial, financial dependence upon income earned by another person, normally a male partner, or poverty. It is to the issue of financial dependence in the household to which I now turn.

WOMEN'S INCOME DEPENDENCE ON MEN IN HOUSEHOLDS

An important source of income for many women is the sharing of income earned or received by a male partner.[9] This income-sharing is founded upon the pooling of resources, including money and time, paid and unpaid work (Daly and Scheiwe, 1991, p.5). Income-sharing is also based on the provision by women of emotional and sexual support to men. The claim on income from male partners exists both when women are actually in relationships with men, as well as where couples have separated, in the form of men's legal responsibilities to maintain their families.[10]

To the extent that women share income generated by men, and have limited access to their own personal income, it may be said that they are financially dependent on men. Such dependence is, in part, associated with a lack of control over decisions and how money is spent, and a lack of rights which creates a sense of obligation towards the primary earner (Lister, 1990, p.451).

There are two significant issues to highlight in a discussion of women's income dependence on men in households. The first is the extent to which women must look to sharing the income of their male partner because their own income is insufficient to support them. The second issue is the feminist challenge to the assumption that income is, in fact, shared equally between men and women in households.

Turning to the first of these issues, there is no simple way to assess the extent to which women must look to sharing income with their partners. But one way of considering this question is to highlight the gaps which exist in women's access to independent income. These gaps can be identified by looking at sources of household income, rates of labour market participation and receipt of social security benefits.

Before considering these gaps, however, it is worth pausing to emphasize two items. The first is that research to date seems to have been concerned with married, rather than cohabiting, couples and that greater work needs to be done in relation to the latter group. The second item is the point, albeit rather banal, that there are variations in the degree and extent to which women are financially dependent on a male partner's income over their life cycle. Female financial dependence is likely to be particularly strong when their children are young, since women's labour market participation rate in the UK is very low when the youngest child is aged under 5 years.[11] Financial dependence is also likely to be a feature of periods in which women care for sick and elderly persons.

Returning to the first of the issues highlighted in relation to women's income dependence, the information which does exist is startling and rather depressing. Esam and Berthoud found that nearly a third of married women receive less than £25 per week into their own hands, and for those without earnings the great majority have a personal income of less than £25 per week (1991, p.2). It appears that child benefit is the only income that many married women receive that is not 'mediated' through a male partner (Esam and Berthoud, 1991, p.32).[12]

Another angle of investigation is to consider the gaps in male–female earnings. Even among women in employment, it has been found that only one wife in eight had an income higher than her husband's, and that the majority of married women had a personal income less than half of that received by their husbands (Esam and Berthoud, 1991, p.10).

A further hint at the extent of financial independence is the 'earnings' gap between members of couples, which can be seen by ascertaining how many women are living in households with men and what is their rate of labour market participation. In 1989 there were four common two-parent household types:[13]

- in 14 per cent of households there were two full-time employed parents;
- in 31 per cent of households the husband worked full-time and the wife worked part-time;
- in 27 per cent of households only the husband was employed;
- in 7 per cent of households both partners were unemployed or economically inactive.

In at least 58 per cent of households with two parents and dependent children, therefore, the female partner receives less earnings than the man.

Levels of labour market participation also affect the extent of women's financial contribution to the maintenance of their households and this, arguably, has an impact on the extent of women's power and ability to make a range of choices within their households. In 1989 official statistics showed that, on average, a wife's contribution to household income overall was 17.3 per cent compared to a husband's contribution of 71.6 per cent (Lister, 1992, p.21). In two-earner couples with dependent children, a wife's contribution was 25.3 per cent, and even in two-earner couples without dependent children, the equivalent figure was 29.5 per cent (ibid.). In single-earner couples, with or without dependent children, a wife's contribution was only between 7.9 per cent and 8.1 per cent of household income (ibid.).

The second issue relevant to this section is the question whether or not women actually participate equally in the income which a man brings to the household (either in the form of earnings or social security benefits). To speak of the 'sharing' of income is to imply that income is distributed equally between members of a household. Feminist work has increasingly challenged this assumption. Benefits are paid in the majority of cases – family credit being the principal exception – on the assumption that a full sharing of income and resources takes place between men and women living together. Increasingly, however, this blanket assumption is not tenable.[14]

A body of research is developing which indicates that women and children command a less than equal share of resources, while the burden of managing a budget falls harder on women, especially at the lower income levels (ibid., p.17). One study found that while the ideal of 'sharing' is widely held, only one in five couples say their resources are genuinely pooled in practice (Roll, 1991, p.12). Moreover, it is not axiomatic that an increasing labour force participation *per se* has increased, or will increase, women's access to household resources or powers of decision-making (Vogler and Pahl, 1993).

The outcome of unequal sharing is that women and children may experience 'secondary poverty' within households. This is where their standard of living is lower and where they experience poverty even though the economic head of the household has an income which is above the poverty line.

To summarize, the extent to which women must look to sharing an income with someone else, such as an emotional/sexual partner, is significant because of the insufficient nature of their own access to income. What is not known, however, is the extent to which income *is* actually shared by members of a couple. In any case, it is unlikely that income from this source – that is, income mediated through a male partner – offers women a significant degree of choice and power. Rather, it is, in my view, associated with a lack of choices, with feelings of obligation and therefore powerlessness.

The different elements of the gendered social reality have now been considered. The focus on this gendered reality forms the background to the discussion of the three layers of structural inequality, to which I now turn.

STRUCTURAL INEQUALITY: THE FIRST LAYER

A number of rules mark women's structural inequality by impeding women's access to independent income from the statutory social security system.[15] Broadly speaking, social security rules in the UK no longer differentiate directly between men and women. Yet there are striking differences between women and men as claimants of different types of benefit. In this section I consider how such a cleavage has come about in relation to three principal benefit types in turn:

1   the contributory benefit system;
2   means-tested benefits;

3   non-contributory benefits.[16]

A number of these rules find resonance in the social security systems of Belgium, Ireland and the Netherlands.

Contributory benefits

Contributory benefits, or social insurance, link entitlement and payment of benefits to paid work, by the requirement of having paid contributions ('the contributions rule'). This has strong, and complex, gendered effects on women's ability to gain entitlement to both short-term benefits, such as unemployment and sickness benefits, and in the longer-term in terms of pension entitlements.

Although it is almost too obvious to say, only contributions from paid work can form the basis of entitlement to contributory benefits under the present UK system.[17] In other words, the unpaid work of caring or domestic work, which is mainly done by women, does not form a basis for entitlement to these benefits.[18]

One aspect of the 'contributions rule' is that, to be included within the contributory benefit system, a worker's earnings must exceed the level of the lower earnings limit (LEL) which, in 1995–96, is £58 per week. The LEL immediately excludes a number of categories of workers from the social insurance system, the majority of excluded persons being women. Women are seven times more likely than men to fall outside the tax and national insurance thresholds (Hakim, 1989, p.480).[19]

Two main categories of workers are excluded from social insurance by the LEL – part-time workers and the low-paid, in which groups women are overrepresented. Official statistics show that 2.25 million working women were excluded from the contributory benefits system altogether, due to earnings below the LEL (Lister, 1992, p.27). Low earnings are particularly associated with part-time work. It has been estimated that between a quarter and a third of part-time workers have earnings under the LEL, as compared to 0.5 per cent of full-time employees (Hakim, 1989, p.478).

Eligibility for insurance benefits is also based on a requirement of having paid contributions over specific periods of time. More women than men are likely to be denied contributory benefits because of a deficient contributions record.[20] This rule presents difficulties for women both in terms of the fact that women have shorter working lives and because women's careers are frequently interrupted by periods of caring, in addition to the periods of unemployment and sickness and incapacity experienced by all workers. In addition to the 2.25 million working women who are excluded from the contributory benefits system because their earnings are below the LEL, there are a further 1.5 million women doing occasional or irregular paid work, including homeworkers, many of whom are Asian women (Lister, 1992, p.27).

Contributions which have been paid, but which are not sufficient to create entitlements to benefits are lost to a worker wishing to claim short-term benefits, affecting atypical workers to a greater extent (Dickens, 1992, p.27). Men are less likely than women to pay 'wasted' contributions (Lister, 1992, p.27).

Contributory benefits contain a number of other rules which women may find harder to satisfy than men. These embrace rules relating to proof of availability for work, or that a claimant is actively seeking work, stipulations on seeking full-time work, as well as regulations on benefit disqualification.

Women are routinely asked about their childcare arrangements in establishing their availability for work, and they must be able to satisfy Department of Social Security (DSS) officials that they can make the necessary arrangements immediately or within 24 hours (Dickens, 1992, p.27). This may lead either to women being denied benefits, or to women taking work at unsocial hours or working in less than ideal circumstances because of the need to fit their employment around times when their partners can look after the children.

The Social Security Act 1989 introduced an 'actively seeking work' test into unemployment-related benefits. In satisfying this rule it appears that 'formal' job-seeking is favoured, and this may prejudice women. Callender (1992, p.136) suggests that women are most likely to find employment through informal means, such as by word of mouth.

Claimants are furthermore expected to be available for full-time work. The many women, who for domestic and caring reasons, wish to be employed on a part-time basis may have their benefit withdrawn or reduced after the thirteen week period of grace in which claimants may impose restrictions on the nature of the work they will accept (ibid.).[21] This practice has excluded many married women from benefits (Dickens, 1992, p.28).

Lastly, claimants may be disqualified from benefits if they leave a job without 'good cause', or where they refuse a 'suitable job' without good cause. These conditions do not include leaving a job for childcare commitments, or refusing a job that would conflict with a childcare or domestic routine (Maclennan and Weitzel, 1984, p.210). Callender (1992, p.137) argues that the distinction between voluntary and involuntary unemployment may be blurred for women, particularly in circumstances where they may have to leave a job for domestic reasons or to follow a partner to a new job.

In the longer term, the difficulties women have in getting into the social insurance system, and in maintaining substantial years of contributions, affect women's pension entitlements. Women have enormous difficulties in building up personal entitlements to both the basic state pension and the state earnings-related pension supplement (SERPS).

Looking first at the basic state pension, entitlement to the full pension requires contributions over nine-tenths of a working life (in each year of which earnings were over the lower earnings limit). Ginn and Arber (1992, p.274) found that, in comparison to Germany and Denmark, the UK has the pension system most hostile to women with interrupted and part-time employment. In 1989 less than one-third of married women of pensionable age received the basic state pension on the basis of their own contributions, and of these a quarter were paid at a reduced rate (Ginn and Arber, 1992, p.262). Although home responsibilities protection (HRP) may be available to protect entitlements for a certain number of years outside of the labour market, in order to avail oneself of HRP, women still need to have actually paid contributions for at least 20 years in order to gain a full pension based on their own contributions.

Second, the effects of lower earnings and a shorter working life are prolonged by the link between former earnings and the level of the SERPS pension supplement. In the UK between 1978 and 1986 the earnings-related supplement (SERPS) to the basic state pension was constructed in such a way as to partially offset the effect of low earning years and interruptions of employment. This was done by calculating earnings over the best 20 years of a person's career (the 'twenty years rule'). However, the basis of SERPS was changed by the Social Security Act 1986 with, amongst other changes, earnings being calculated over the best 25 years. These changes have considerably lessened the opportunities offered to part-time workers and others whose earnings are not high and who have had interrupted careers to gain an adequate level of SERPS payments (Groves, 1991, p.45).[22]

Third, the rules relating to both the basic state pension and to the SERPS calculation can cumulatively disadvantage women part-time workers. Part-time work which yields income over the lower earnings limit disqualifies women from home responsibility protection, but low-paid part-time earnings will be included in the calculations for the earnings-related pensions supplement (SERPS), potentially causing SERPS entitlement to be greatly depressed. In terms of future SERPS entitlements, therefore, it could be more 'rational' for women who care for dependent children or disabled persons not to engage in paid work at all. But of course to establish entitlement to the basic state pension and to an adequate level of SERPS to begin with, women must have substantial years of contributions – that is earnings above the lower earnings limit.

Although payments of the basic amount of contributory benefits are personal – that is, paid without regard to a partner's means – there are two aspects to these benefit payments which could nevertheless exert a negative effect on women's ability to gain an (adequate) independent income. These relate to the payment of dependent additions, and to the employment incentives of dependent partners.

First, claimants of contributory benefits with dependent partners or children may be entitled to claim additions for the latter, which are paid with the claimant's benefit. Although the addition is paid for the dependent partner, normally a wife, the income for that person is mediated through the claiming partner, normally a man. In this respect, this imputes to the person entitled to the benefit the status of breadwinner or provider.[23] In 1989 some 600 000 married men (as opposed to 60 000 married women) received additions to their contributory benefits for their dependent spouses (Roll, 1991, p.47).

Second, dependent additions contain earnings rules. This means that dependent partners can earn up to the level of the addition before it is withdrawn (although the withdrawal does not affect the basic benefit). This may have the effect of encouraging the marginal labour market participation of a dependent partner. Where this happens, the marginal employment will not permit the worker to build up personal entitlements to contributory benefits because the level of permitted earnings is underneath the lower earnings limit (LEL).

To conclude, the model of the claimant at the heart of the contributory benefit system is that of the worker in a 'standard employment relationship' (SER) who loses income by being outside of the labour market. The standard employment relationship refers to stable full-time paid work as an employee on an indefinite contract (see Mückenburger, 1989). In this model, interruptions of full-time employment are unusual and short-term. There is a fundamental 'mismatch', therefore, between women's employment and caring profiles and the current model of contributory benefits.[24] Contributory benefits at present do not offer many women a source of independent income.

Although there are many problems in the current social insurance system as regards women's access to independent income, the social insurance system contains within it important seeds ready to be fertilized in the search for effective reforms. Social insurance benefits are in the nature of personal rights, paid directly to claimants, without enquiry into a partner's income. This aspect of the social insurance system, that of creating personal entitlements, has, in my opinion, the greatest potential to offer women financial independence.[25]

Social assistance benefits

Persons with insufficient entitlements to contributory benefits can claim a social assistance (or 'means-tested') benefit, such as income support, family credit or housing benefit. These benefits encompass one rule in particular – the 'aggregation rule' – which is responsible for impeding many women's access to independent income in two ways. I will first describe the aggregation rule, then consider how many people fall within its ambit, and finally describe the two ways in which it presents obstacles to women.

Means-tested benefits in the UK are based on the joint assessment of income and needs for persons who are married or living as husband and wife (the 'aggregation rule'). In practice, this means, first, that the income of either member of a couple is treated as being available to both partners, and second, that the needs of the couple are deemed to be less than that of two single persons, on the assumption that income-sharing creates economies of scale. This principle of aggregation of a couple's income and needs presupposes that one is the breadwinner and one is the dependant (for whom the other should provide).[26]

The obstacles to an independent income for women created by the aggregation rule are considered below, after the scope of this rule has been sketched out. Aggregation appears to affect a significant number of couples; it has been estimated that 3.7 million (27 per cent of all couples) were entitled in 1990–91 to at least one jointly assessed benefit (Esam and Berthoud, 1991, p.3).

This number can only realistically increase given the social security policy of the present Conservative administration. Since the 1980s an important policy objective has been that of 'targeting' resources to persons with the lowest incomes. Targeting inevitably means more means-testing, and it has been accompanied by a steady erosion of contributory and universal benefits. In recent years the erosion of the contributory benefit system was exemplified by changes to unemployment benefit and to benefits for incapacity for work.

From April 1996 contributory unemployment benefit is to be repackaged into the jobseeker's allowance. This change will slash the contributory or social insurance element of benefits for the unemployed by half, from one year down to six months, and thereby filter claimants into the social assistance system six months earlier.

In April 1995 there was a major overhaul in the system of benefits for incapacity for work. The short-term sickness benefit and the longer-term invalidity benefit have been repackaged as 'incapacity benefit', accompanied by more stringent entitlement conditions and lower benefits. This change is likely, as with the repackaging of unemployment benefit, to filter even more people into the means-tested benefit system.

Having mapped out the extent of means-tested benefits in the UK system, and therefore of the aggregation rule, I shall return to the principal focus of this section, which is the effect of this rule on women's access to independent income. There are two principal strands to the contention that the aggregation rule impedes women's access to independent income. In brief, there is the part it plays in denying women benefits and also the strong negative influence it exerts on the employment incentives on female partners of benefit claimants.

Turning, first, to the issue of how the aggregation rule prevents a number of women from claiming a social assistance benefit for themselves, there are three aspects to this assertion. In the first place, the aggregation means that an individual claim for benefit can be denied because a partner's earnings are taken into account. That is, the earnings of a claimant's partner are treated as if that claimant has access to them, whether or not this is the case. Given the differences in earnings and labour market participation between men and women, women are more likely to find their claims denied than men. Moreover, there must be doubt over whether income and resources in couples are in fact shared equally.

I have already argued that women are more likely than men to be denied benefits because their partner's income is taken into account. Combined with the rule that only one partner in a couple may claim benefits, and the strong cultural presumption that the male partner ought to be this claimant, a situation arises where women have little access to income which is not primarily mediated through a male partner. Where social assistance benefits, such as income support, are paid to couples, in 19 out of 20 cases the benefit is in fact paid to the male partner (Lister, 1992, p.42). This is peculiar to the UK system, it seems, since although in the Netherlands means-tested benefits apply an aggregation rule, benefit payments are not necessarily paid to one on behalf of the other.

In the second place, a person cannot claim income support where their partner works full-time, defined since 1992 as 16 hours or more per week (the 'full-time work exclusion rule'). Again, given the differences in male–female labour market participation, the losers are more likely to be women.

The cumulative effect of these two rules may be that where a woman enters into marriage or 'cohabitation' with a man her means-tested benefits may be withdrawn.[27] The presumption here clearly is that the male partner will support her and, indeed, is relieving the state of the burden of her support.

This brings us to the third aspect of how women can be denied benefits. Where people begin cohabiting, or as it is now officially called 'living together as husband and wife', they become subject to the aggregation rule. This means that women who cohabit may have their benefits withdrawn or will be prevented from claiming means-tested benefits.[28] This has been officially justified on the grounds that people living in marriage-like relationships should not be better off than married couples who live together.[29] This prescription clearly takes no heed of the fact that women who cohabit with men may not in fact be financially supported by them. The cohabitation rule in fact can leave women cohabitees in a precarious financial position. Not only does their household receive less benefit than twice the single person's rate, but where their male partners do not share income with them, they have fewer legal rights to enforce support than married women. Cohabitation does not accord women the same rights as marriage, including the right to derived contributory benefits, and male cohabitees are under no legal obligations, in family law, to financially maintain their partners.[30]

It could be contended that, since the aggregation rule applies equally to men and women, it cannot be more unfair to women than men. Such an assertion would, however, ignore the reality that neutral rules can have very different effects on varied groups. The impact of the aggregation rule depends, in my opinion, on its interaction with the gendered social reality – that is, with inequalities between men and women in labour market participation and in terms of access to, and control over, income in the household. Quite simply, men are more likely to be in the labour market for more than 16 hours per week than women, and thus more women than men will be denied benefit because of their partner's earnings.

To recap, the gendered effects of the aggregation rule operate both at the level of denying women a source of income which is independent of men, and, as a second strand of my argument, by negatively affecting women's employment incentives. It is to the impact on employment incentives that I now turn.

The joint assessment of income and resources in means-tested benefits in the UK means that earnings of either partner can cause a reduction or withdrawal of the entire (household) benefit. This may well cause women in couples to whom means-tested benefits are paid to withdraw from the labour market, or deliberately not to enter it, because of the potential benefit-reducing effects of even marginal earnings. Again, these rules are sex-neutral but their interaction with wage inequalities between men and women lead more frequently to a negative impact on women's, rather than men's, employment incentives.

There is a body of research which suggests that when a man becomes unemployed and claims a means-tested benefit this may often lead to his partner giving up her employment.[31] The labour market participation rate of women married to unemployed men is consistently and significantly lower than that of women with husbands in work, and this difference has grown over time (Dilnot and Kell, 1989, p.160). Almost 90 per cent of wives whose husbands were in receipt of supplementary benefit (the predecessor to income support) were not working (ibid., p.164). Where a husband is in receipt of the contributory unemployment benefit, wives are much more likely to be in full-time work and are less likely to be working part-time (Dilnot and Kell, 1989, p.161).

The low employment rate of wives of supplementary benefit claimants could be understood as resistance to the wife being the primary earner (McLaughlin *et al.*, 1989, pp. 23–5, 67–8). However, an equally significant reason appears to be the interaction between the aggregation rule and women's wage inequality. A female partner's employment will usually generate a lower income than her male partner's earnings, and while it is likely to be insufficient to support the family it may be high enough to cause a reduction in benefit, which in turn affects the whole household.

The first strategy of families coming off benefit seems to be to secure a job with a wage that can support all the family, the now rather mythical 'family wage' (Millar, 1988, p.156). The differences between male and female earnings almost inevitably ensures that this earner will be the man rather than the woman. It can be seen, therefore, that the interaction of the aggregation rule with earnings inequalities plays a part in perpetuating a particular division or 'choice' of gender roles, in which men strive to be earners and women are the carers who are financially dependent on their male partners.[32]

These disincentive effects on women's employment were not found to operate for wives of men claiming unemployment benefit. Here, although the earnings of the dependent partner may cause a withdrawal of the dependency addition to benefit, earnings do not affect the level of the basic benefit. Since the levels of dependency additions are quite low, Dilnot and Kell (1989, pp.161–3) found that there was no disincentive for a dependent partner to keep or look for a full-time job. There may, however, still be disincentives for female partners to take low income-yielding part-time work.

In the above discussion I considered the means by which the aggregation rule, combined with the differences in patterns of labour market participation and wage inequality between men and women, can deny women claims to individual social assistance benefits and can have a negative influence of their employment incentives. The household basis or joint assessment of means-tested benefits is therefore problematic, and even detrimental to, the achievement of women's financial independence. Means-tested benefits normally provide income for women, which is mediated through men or is liable to be withdrawn at any time when a male partner can be made to be financially responsible, in theory if not necessarily in fact, for a cohabitee or wife. This limits women's choices, certainly in respect of employment (given the disincentive effects associated with means-tested benefits) and ultimately in respect of their power in households. A means-tested benefit, based on any type of aggregation rule in relation to income or needs, frustrates female financial independence and can have no place as part of a strategy to tackle the income dependency of women on men (see Chapter 8).

Non-contributory benefits: paltry benefits for carers

Social security rules interact with the wider gendered social reality to deny women access or entitlement to benefits, as we have seen in relation to the contributions rule and the aggregation of resources rule. The social security system can, however, reinforce women's financial dependence even where women do gain access to benefits. This stems from the inadequacy of benefit payments and the control exerted over labour market participation. In the non-contributory and non-means-tested benefit for carers, the invalid care allowance, for instance, rules reinforce the marginal labour market participation of carers. The low wage replacement level at which this benefit is paid also plays its part in reinforcing a carer's financial dependence on another person.

The number of women in the UK engaged in forms of care other than childcare is enormous: one in five of all women aged between 40 and 60 years are estimated to be engaged in caring for elderly, sick or disabled relatives (Dickens, 1992, p.13). Carers of sick or elderly persons experience a significant poverty risk; the personal and household income of these carers is substantially below the average (Lister, 1992, p.15).

The financial dependence of carers stems partly from the inadequate financial provision given to them by the UK social security system. The invalid care allowance is meant to compensate carers for earnings losses arising from their exit from the labour market. However, the benefit is paid at such a low wage replacement level that, by itself, it could not lift a carer out of financial dependence and poverty. This encourages a gendered difference in the experiences of being a carer or a cared-for person. Graham (1983, p.24) has contrasted the experience of financial dependence for men and women in this area, contending that, for women, being a dependent is synonymous with giving care whereas, for men, it is synonymous with receiving care.

The invalid care allowance (ICA) is currently paid at the paltry weekly rate of £35.25 to carers not in full-time employment who 'regularly and substantially' provide care to a severely disabled person of at least 35 hours per week.[33] Claims to ICA are barred if a claimant has earnings of more than £50 per week. Claimants are allowed earnings of below this figure without loss of benefit (this level has been increased in recent years).[34]

Despite its inadequate level, claiming the invalid care allowance is crucial for carers because of its role in preserving entitlement to the basic state pension. For every week the ICA is paid a claimant receives a national insurance credit, and this means that a claimant's pension contribution record is not prejudiced by their lack of earnings. It used to be the case that receipt of ICA also preserved entitlement to other social insurance benefits as well but, unfortunately, this was undermined by changes made to the contribution conditions for certain short-term benefits, such as unemployment benefit, in the Social Security Act 1988. The new contribution conditions strengthened the link between entitlement to benefits and recent employment, by requiring that claimants have paid (and not only have been credited with) contributions at a set level in the two years before the claim was made. This meant, in practice, that a carer's entitlements to unemployment benefit were no longer protected once they had ceased providing care (Lister, 1992, p.32).

The person cared for must be in receipt of attendance allowance, constant attendance allowance or the disability living allowance (DLA) at the middle or higher rate. Conditions of entitlement for these benefits are stringent (see Ogus and Barendt, 1995, p.198). In fact, during the 1980s access to the attendance allowance was tightened up by means of regulations and administrative rules requiring a greater degree of care by the carer (Land, 1991, p.10). The attendance allowance presumes a need for care of between 84 and 164 hours a week (Land, 1989, p.153).

A number of informal carers do not receive ICA, either because they do not know about the benefit, because it is not financially worth claiming, or because the person they care for is not sufficiently disabled (Glendinning, 1990, p.484). Only one tenth of carers investing the requisite hours actually receive the ICA (Glendinning, 1992, p.167).

For carers not in full-time work, caring even with receipt of ICA can mean financial dependence on a (male) spouse or on the person being cared for, or it may mean living in poverty (Glendinning, 1990, p.482). Given the low level at which ICA is paid, this benefit is more in the nature of a supplement to another (or, rather, main) income. Further, ICA can be said to favour a division of household labour in which the carer only engages in a small or limited amount of (usually atypical) employment (Bieback, 1992, p.248). In practice, this tallies to a greater extent with women's labour market participation and gender role expectations and can be said to play its role in perpetuating the gendered division of labour.

The invalid care allowance is, however, at least some recognition of the value of caring work and of the importance of maintaining a pensions record for carers. It is also a personal benefit, paid without a means test, and must in a number of cases provide women with at least a degree of independent income.

Lone parents, employment disincentives and traps into poverty

The employment disincentives inherent in means-tested benefits also affect lone parents of whom the great majority are in receipt of means-tested benefits (see Millar, 1994, p.69–70). Under income support rules a claimant is allowed to earn a given sum of money which is 'disregarded' before benefit is liable to be reduced. Until April 1988 earnings disregarded under income support (at £4) were based on income net of tax and national insurance and reasonable working expenses, including travel and childcare costs. The new rule is that only £25 of gross earnings will be disregarded, without any allowable deduction for childcare costs. As a result, many lone parents are likely to be better off financially in receipt of income support than in employment once childcare costs have been paid (Land, 1989, p.146). However, the longer women remain on social security and out of the labour market, the lower their future earnings and pensions will be (Land, 1989, p.146).

There is a similar childcare costs rule in family credit (an in-work means-tested benefit) and the disability living allowance. This may be in the process of being successfully challenged under Directive 79/7/EEC, which may ultimately lead to reform.[35] The rule in income support is, however, beyond the scope of EC equality law.[36]

Summary

In this section I have analysed the different component parts of the social security system in relation to the extent to which they affect women's opportunities to gain an independent income, highlighting in particular the rules which limit women's choices, or which allow them access to income unmediated by male partners, or which limit women's incentives to take up paid work. These can be described as both inequalities of opportunity as well as inequalities in outcomes (see, further, Chapter 6). It has been argued that, although contributory benefits do currently provide few women with an independent income, an important principle in their payment is that they are personal rights. The aspect of personal rights is the key to the positive nature of contributory benefits, as well as to the negative nature of social assistance for women.

STRUCTURAL INEQUALITY: THE SECOND LAYER

The second layer to the structural inequality facing women relates to the qualitative and quantitative differences in benefit provision for masculine and feminine social security risks. My argument here is that inequality arises in a social security structure in which qualitatively and quantitatively inferior benefits are given for feminine risks. Where caring does not allow for social insurance benefits, or anything other than means-tested benefits or low level contributory benefits, then women (and other carers) will be prevented from achieving any degree of financial independence through the social security system.

In this section I present a brief comparison between the quantitative provision given for masculine and feminine risks, having concentrated until now on presenting the qualitative differences between types of benefits. I differentiate between masculine and feminine risks on the basis of the income maintenance provided for different activities or gender roles.[37] Masculine risks are associated with exit from the labour market (by reason of unemployment, sickness and old age), while caring activities, whether of the young, sick or elderly, are associated with women's social role, and are referred to as feminine risks. The quantitative and qualitative differences between the types of protection given for male and female risks can be significant, with the qualitative differences in particular relating to issues of women's power, choice and financial independence. This section will first consider masculine risks before turning to feminine risks.[38]

Benefit provision for masculine risks

The principal masculine risks are the need for income maintenance as a result of exit from the labour market due to becoming unemployed, sick or incapable of work, disabled, or injured at work, and finally due to old age. In the UK there is a contributory benefit for each of these risks. Each of these benefits comprises a basic benefit, which can be supplemented by an addition for a dependent spouse, which is subject to an earnings rule, and additions for dependent children. The basic benefit is higher if the claimant is over pensionable age, and some benefits are taxable.[39]

Long-term benefits for masculine risks offer the highest benefits of all in the contributory benefits system: £58.85 for the long-term rate of incapacity benefit and the retirement pension, and up to £95.30 for the industrial disablement pension for persons over 18 years old who are 100 per cent disabled.

Short-term contributory benefit rates are less generous, offering £44.40 for the lower rate of the short-term incapacity benefit (for the first 28 weeks of incapacity). The higher rate of the short-term benefit, for between the 29th–52nd weeks of incapacity, is paid at £52.50. Unemployment benefit is £46.45 for persons under pension age.

With all contributory benefits it is possible to receive additions for dependent spouses, defined as wives or persons looking after a claimant's child(ren) earning under the amount of the addition. The additions, as well as the earnings limits, for dependent spouses are more generous with the longer-term benefits. Levels of additions vary between £27.50 with short-term incapacity benefit and £35.25 with long-term incapacity benefit and the retirement pension. In addition, extra benefit is given for children, at £11.05 with such benefits as unemployment benefit, invalid care allowance and incapacity benefit.

The residual benefits for masculine risks, where entitlement to contributory benefits has been exhausted or where it was never acquired, are means-tested social assistance or non-contributory benefits. Means-tested benefits have, it will be recalled, traditionally played an important role in the UK system because contributory benefits have never been generous.

The role of this supposedly residual tier has been even more heavily accentuated as a result of the policies of the Conservative administration since 1979. The growing importance of means-tested benefits has been most strongly felt among the unemployed but is also increasingly evident in benefits for incapacity for work.

Social assistance benefits are available to persons whose income and resources are below specified 'applicable amounts', which are in fact calculations of notional needs. The applicable amounts are calculated on the basis of the personal allowances (and in some cases premiums) given to various categories of claimants.

Income support (IS), the main social assistance benefit, is paid to a single person who may work under 16 hours (depending on their earnings) or to a couple/family where neither partner works over 16 hours a week. The weekly personal allowance for a single person aged 16–18 is £36.80 (higher rate), for a single person aged between 18–24 it is £36.80, and for a single person aged over 25 years it is £46.50. For a couple, where both are over 18 years, the personal allowance is £73.00. Allowances for dependent children are added to the personal allowance, and on top of these allowances a number of premiums may be paid to particular client groups, such as £10.25 per child for families with at least one child, and various premiums for those over pensionable age, or disabled or severely disabled, and for disabled children. In respect of the level of 'disregarded' earnings, £10 of earnings is disregarded per claimant, and £5 for their partner.

This cursory glance at benefit provision for masculine risks shows that social insurance benefits are provided for the principal income-loss situations, and the rates of benefit (particularly for the longer-term benefits) are relatively high.

Benefit provision for feminine risks

Caring, whether for the young, the sick or the elderly, also gives rise to the need for income maintenance. This may either be because caring, in many cases, hinders labour market participation or because caring is, in my view, an activity of societal value whose performance should not lead to poverty and financial dependence. This risk is rather ambiguously integrated within the social security system.

There is no social insurance benefit which provides income for carers. Two universal benefits give money to mothers and lone parents but this is to help with the costs of children rather than to compensate carers. In the UK system there is only one benefit given directly to compensate carers of severely disabled persons for loss of earnings and this is a non-contributory benefit paid at a paltry rate. Otherwise, carers can claim income support if they are not employed and, if they are married or cohabiting, are not prevented from claiming because of their partner's hours of work or earnings. Carers in receipt of income support are exempted from the requirement of being available for work. I consider the benefits for the different types of caring in turn.

First, child benefit is a universal benefit given to help with the costs of children. The benefit is paid at low levels (at £10.40 for the first or only child, and £8.45 for any other child). Receipt of child benefit is very important, however, since this can be used to secure future pension rights by means of home responsibilities protection. A one parent benefit can be paid to lone parents on top of child benefit at a flat rate per lone parent of £6.30 per week.

Second, where a woman lives with her partner and is out of the labour market to care for a child or children, or indeed for elderly persons, she is deemed to be supported by him. If her male partner is in the labour market it is likely that his earnings or hours of work will prevent her from receiving income support. If he is not in paid work and receiving one of the contributory benefits then, in all likelihood, he will receive an addition to his benefit for her. It has been estimated that 600 000 men (as opposed to 60 000 women) receive additions to their contributory benefits for a dependent spouse (Roll, 1991, p.47). This income, whether from the labour market or in the form of social security benefits, is first mediated through the male partner, and cannot be regarded as independent income.

Where a male partner is not in paid work he may be receiving a means-tested benefit. Since, in the vast majority of cases, he will be the claimant on behalf of the household, again the money earmarked for the female partner is mediated through the man. Given the possibility of some amounts of earnings reducing the whole amount of the benefit, it may become difficult or impossible for a female partner to combine caring with some paid work. Her choices, as well as her access to independent income, have thus been limited.

The majority of lone parents in the UK are in receipt of social assistance benefits, such as income support and family credit. Income support gives a premium in addition to the personal allowance to lone parents, and exempts them (as well as some other carers) from the requirement to register as available for work. Family credit, which can be claimed by persons, with at least one child, working 16 hours per week with low earnings, now includes a £40 allowance for childcare costs.

But neither family credit at present, nor indeed income support, allow lone parents to offset childcare costs against earnings disregarded for the purposes of calculating benefit.[40] Lone parents on income support have an earnings disregard of £25 where they work less than 16 hours a week. Due to changes in 1990 and 1993 lone parents may receive their personal allowance and part of their income support benefits in the form of maintenance from the 'absent parent'.[41] It should be remembered that, where a female lone parent begins to cohabit with a male partner, her personal entitlement to benefit will be ended by the cohabitation rule.

Third, as full-time carers of severely disabled persons, women may receive the invalid care allowance (ICA), which is a non-contributory (and thus personal) benefit paid without a means test. ICA is meant to replace the earnings of persons who have left the labour market in order to care and is paid at the paltry sum of £35.25 per week, with the possibility of an adult dependant's addition of £21.10. It can be accurately described as an 'honorarium' (Baldwin, 1994, p.188). Carers in receipt of ICA are allowed to earn up to £50.00 per week before benefit is reduced, and this rule may be seen to encourage carers, if they undertake paid work at all, to work in atypical forms of employment (Bieback, 1992, p.247). Receipt of ICA does, however, safeguard pension rights since caring for a person in receipt of an attendance allowance or the disability living allowance entitles the carer to home responsibilities protection if they have paid contributions for a sufficient number of years.

Summary

Masculine risks are provided for by contributory benefits. Although, in some cases, contributory benefits do not provide higher rates of basic benefits (normally for families), they do allow dependent (female) partners greater possibilities of taking up paid work. Means-tested and non-contributory benefits allow very little earnings into a household without causing a reduction in benefit, and in this sense they exert a tight control over both partners. Feminine risks, on the other hand, are generally protected against by means-tested and non-contributory benefits. There is no social insurance benefit for the feminine risk of caring for children, the sick or the elderly. In means-tested benefits, women are subject to the joint assessment of benefit rules, and income to the household normally passes through the male partners' hands. Non-contributory benefits do not afford significant independent income since they are paid at low levels with narrow entitlement conditions. Persons experiencing masculine risks are more likely to be able to receive independent income from the social security system than persons performing the feminine social role of caring. Given the qualitative differences between the types of benefits, these observations indicate problems for women in terms of their choices and, ultimately, their power within their relationships.

STRUCTURAL INEQUALITY: THE THIRD LAYER

The UK social security system, both in terms of its structure and rules, reflects and reinforces a particular social construction of men and women's gender roles. This assertion does not deny that state policies may be ambiguous and ambivalent, or that, within different benefit schemes, there may be contradictory aims (see Roll, 1991, p.21). Neither do I wish to suggest that the social security system has a defining responsibility in the construction of gender roles in the wider society. Rather, the benefit system is but one institution, along with the labour market, which shapes the choices that individuals make about the (gendered) division of labour between paid and unpaid work.

Looking at the welfare state at its broadest, it is readily apparent that the care of children, the sick and the elderly is by and large seen in the UK as a private matter or choice, with people left in the majority of cases to find private solutions. The private solution is often for the female partner in a household, or the (female) lone parent, to do the unpaid caring work, either in addition to some form of employment or instead of employment. To the extent that benefit rules and structures (albeit not acting in isolation) encourage this division of labour, then in my view it is possible to argue that the social security system reflects and reinforces traditional gender roles. The focus of concern is that the traditional gendered division of labour leaves women (or indeed other carers) in a financially vulnerable position. To put it another way, the traditional gendered division of labour leads to outcomes which are strongly associated with financial dependence (and a consequent lack of power and choices) and poverty.

Social security systems can shape choices of the division of paid and unpaid work – and thereby reinforce traditional gender roles or not – with varying degrees of coercion. In the Beveridge Report of 1942 we see what could be described as the 'high-water mark' of a construction of gender roles in which (married) women are clearly meant to be the economic dependants of their husbands. In the contemporary UK system married women are no longer explicitly seen as economic dependants, yet current policy, at the level of changes and of discourse, reinforce women's financial dependence on men through the inadequacy of their personal entitlements to benefits.

In this section I show the construction of married women as dependants in the Beveridgean system and then make a number of observations on the contemporary UK system.

The Beveridge Report

The Beveridge Report, published in 1942, placed the insurance principle at the centre of the post-war social security system. The central assumption of the Report was that full-time paid work was, and ought to be, the primary means of distributing income (Roll, 1991, p.23). Men and single (childless) women were supposed to support themselves through the labour market, and married women were to remain outside the labour market, engaged in domestic and caring work. Beveridge argued that husband and wife should be treated as a 'team', in which married women were to be supported by their husbands rather than by the social insurance system. Within the house-hold, women traded housework, childbirth, childrearing and physical and emotional caring (and, arguably, sexual services) as 'labours of love' in return for economic support (Clarke and Langan, 1993a, p.24).

Beveridge dismissed as 'indefensible' the invisibility of women's needs in the existing social security schemes, emphasizing the value of their unpaid caring and domestic work. But Beveridge's reference to the value of caring work went beyond an acknowledgement to become a means by which married women were trapped in this role. Beveridge adopted a clearly normative stance, arguing that '[t]he attitude of the housewife to gainful employment outside the home is not and *should not be* the same as that of the single woman. She has other duties' (emphasis added).[42]

The scheme allowed married women few choices other than financial dependence on their husbands because, in Beveridge's view

... the great majority of married women must be regarded as occupied on work which is vital though unpaid, without which their husbands could not do their paid work and without which the nation could not continue.[43]

Where a married woman did take paid work, she was automatically constructed as a secondary earner. While a marriage was in existence a husband was to replace the state as a woman's first line of defence against poverty. Under the Beveridge scheme, as it was implemented, married women were treated as dependants whether they were in or out of the labour market.

In 1943 Katherine Bompass and Elizabeth Abbott criticized Beveridge for 'denying the married woman, rich or poor, housewife or paid worker, an independent personal status'.[44] Married women had to choose between either paying full contributions for a single person's pension at the age of 60 and reduced rate benefits for unemployment and sickness benefits, or, by opting to make a very small contribution for national health and industrial injuries provision and forfeiting the right to unemployment and sickness benefits, they could, at the age of 60, draw a dependent wife's pension at 60 per cent of a single person's rate (provided their husband had reached 65 and was claiming a retirement pension). Married women could therefore only 'choose' to be *full* dependants, by paying no contributions at all, or *partial* dependants receiving reduced rate benefits in exchange for full contributions.

Contemporary constructions of roles

In the 1990s the UK system no longer encourages a Beveridgean household structure in which married women are clearly constructed as full-time dependants and unpaid carers. Although the contributory benefit system still enables both members of a married couple who divide the breadwinner–carer functions to qualify for benefits through the breadwinner, in most cases this does not have to be the man (Roll, 1991, p.37).[45] Two-earner couples may now qualify for contributory benefits (that is, for masculine risks) independently of each other on more or less formally equal terms. Where they both qualify, their two contributory benefits added together will be higher than benefits to a single-earner couple, who receive 1.6 times the single person's rate (ibid.).

But, in view of the difficulties which women have in gaining personal entitlements to contributory benefits, there are few couples who achieve independence from each other by virtue of their separate personal claims to state benefits. Women and carers will not receive wholly personal benefits for feminine risks from the social insurance system, and may only receive very low non-contributory benefits. In the majority of cases these women's (and carer's) claims to personal and adequate benefits will be limited.

Inequalities in wages and employment prospects, combined with social security rules, make it a rational strategy in terms of household income for men to devote more energy to waged work, where they can obtain a higher rate of return (Taylor-Gooby, 1991, p.101).[46] Since men's earnings are higher than women's, it is also more 'rational' for the female partner in households to take flexible or atypical forms of employment and to combine this with caring work. This is encouraged by the benefit system which permits recipients of caring benefits, such as the invalid care allowance, to earn small amounts of income from paid work (Bieback, 1992, p.248).

Inequalities in men's and women's wages also interact with the aggregation rule in social assistance benefits to create disincentives for the female partners in households to enter employment, in anything but the most marginal way, since small amounts of earnings may cause proportionately large decreases in the entire benefit to a household or couple.

In discussing the construction of gender roles within the UK social security system it is worth taking a critical look at the content of certain key themes in policy. In the 1980s and 1990s an important theme of Conservative government discourse has been 'independence' from, and 'dependence' within, the social security system. The government long ago declared the aim of eradicating the so-called 'dependency culture', in which receipt of benefits is seen as dependence on the state and is clearly less preferable to 'independence' from the state. In this section I will briefly examine this discourse in terms of what it means for income relations between adults as well as between individuals and the state, and ultimately what it means for women's financial independence.

As a starting point, I take the view that a social security policy whose aim is to encourage or reinforce the financial dependence of women on their male partners will logically lead to a limiting of women's personal claims to state benefits. Conservative governments in the 1980s and 1990s have strongly attacked what they have called the 'dependency culture', which they argue has led to claimants becoming unwilling to be self-supporting. A key policy theme has therefore been the promotion of individual responsibility and the desirability of shifting from 'dependence' on the state to individual 'independence'. What this rhetoric masks is that the flipside of decreasing dependence on the state is the increase in private dependence – that is, the economic dependence of women on men.

It is interesting to consider policy towards lone mothers more closely in relation to the issue of dependence and independence. A significant proportion of lone parents are in receipt of means-tested income support and are therefore dependent on the state. Current government policy is to shift this dependence from the state to dependence on to men, by pursuing ex-partners for maintenance and child support.

Recent legislative changes have been aimed more at decreasing the numbers of lone mothers on state benefits, rather than at enabling them to achieve financial independence either from men or from the state or indeed at easing the poverty commonly associated with female lone parenthood. Lone mothers do not gain a higher income as a result of maintenance obtained from an ex-partner under the Child Support Act 1991. If lone mothers are in receipt of the means-tested income support benefit, their benefit payment will be reduced accordingly. Moreover, should lone mothers refuse to name the absent parent they may be liable to have their income support reduced: there may be a reduction of 20 per cent of the personal allowance for six months, or a reduction of the allowance by 10 per cent for twelve months (Fox Harding, 1993, p.110).

Two strands of policy are closely tied in with the notion of the shift from public dependence to private independence, both of which are likely to operate to the detriment of women with respect to gaining access to personal or independent income. The first strand is that individuals should provide for themselves, and in particular for their old age, through occupational and private provision. But, given their weaker position in the labour market, their shouldering of the majority of adult and childcare, as well as their greater longevity, women are much less likely to be able to benefit fully from occupational and private welfare provision (Alcock, 1989, p.109).

The second strand is that the 'family' (and the voluntary and private sector) should increasingly act as alternatives to the public welfare state (Fitzgerald, 1983). In this heterosexual family, gender roles are constructed along traditional lines; men are given strong incentives to work full-time (even if this is low paid) and women are to be the providers of the bulk of caring and welfare services (see Van Every, 1992, pp.65–6). This construction of gender roles is quite clearly predicated on the financial dependence of women on men even if this is dressed up as income-sharing between partners based on complementarity of roles.

Reforms to the UK social security system since 1979 have furthered this two-pronged approach.[47] First, the contributory benefit system has been eroded and greater emphasis placed on 'targeting' resources to those with the lowest income.[48] Incentives have been provided for an expansion in occupational, and particularly private, provision. The erosion of the contributory benefit system has meant that the claims of those women who could establish a contributions record to personal income have been swept away. The expansion in occupational and private social security provision is, however, unlikely to be of much benefit to a significant proportion of women in the UK.

Second, a number of cuts were made to benefits which provided, or could have provided, women with a source of independent income, such as maternity benefits and SERPS. The Fowler Reviews of the social security system in the mid-1980s proposed a number of options, which, if they had been passed, would have further increased women's dependence on men, such as the abolition of child benefit and the payment of the new family credit benefit through the (male) wage packet (Dominelli, 1991, p.70). Most recently, part of the contributory element in benefits for the unemployed is to be substituted by means-tested provision. From April 1996 the jobseeker's allowance offers only six months of contributory benefit (as opposed to one year of unemployment benefit) before filtering claimants onto the equivalent of income support. In effect, women who had succeeded in building up entitlement to a personal benefit will find themselves subject to the rules in means-tested benefits, such as aggregation, which may lead to a withdrawal of their benefits a full six months earlier than previously.

Summary

The social security system plays a part in encouraging a particular gendered division of labour by virtue of how entitlements to benefits are acquired, how and to whom benefits are paid in terms of whether they are paid to individuals or by aggregating the income and needs of more than one person, and at what level benefits are paid. This process may be in a coercive form, such as under the Beveridgean scheme for married women, or it may be more subtle, such as where there is poor provision for feminine risks. Social security policy which focuses on decreasing dependency on the state has, it has been argued, the downside of masking and encouraging the private dependence of women on men.

CONCLUDING REMARKS

In this chapter I considered the 'gendered social reality', in terms of women and their difficulties in achieving financial independence in the labour market, the household and in the social security system. The cumulative outcome of women's financial dependence on men, inequality in the labour market and social security may be poverty.[49] Greater attention has been paid to one component of the gendered social reality – the social security system.

Contemporary social security systems appear to be structured in a gender-neutral way, but in fact they have an 'unmistakeable gender subtext' (Fraser, 1989, p.149). Women experience structural inequality in the social security system vis-à-vis men: their relationship to social security is characterized by fewer personal entitlements and qualitatively inferior provision. This multi-layered inequality is related in part to the structure of social insurance, which is geared to a 'standard employment relationship', as well as to rules such as the joint assessment of income (or needs) in social assistance, which usually mean that women's access to income is mediated through a male partner. Another layer of this inequality is the qualitative, as well as quantitative, inferiority of provision given for caring or for activities related to women's social role, which have been referred to as feminine risks.

It is not implicit, however, in my argument that all men, as opposed to a few women, can easily gain an adequate income from the social security system. Such a claim would be misplaced: it would ignore the effects of such factors as class and ethnic background on paid work and men's access and entitlements to benefits, as well as the minimum nature of UK social security provision. It would also ignore, which I have not done, recent trends across the four countries towards cuts in social insurance benefits or increases in contributions, which have a significant impact on men's access to social insurance and to the types of benefits men receive.

The social insurance or contributory benefits system poses problems in terms of women's access to personal benefits and entitlements because of the link between these benefits and paid work, via the 'contributions rule', the lower earnings limit and the requirements for continuous periods of paid contributions. A similar construction poses problems for women in Ireland and the Netherlands (see Chapter 6). Caring does not entitle women to social insurance benefits in these systems, although credits may be given for periods of care. In terms of financial independence, the positive aspect of contributory benefits is that they provide personal benefits and entitlements to women claimants, giving them income which is not mediated through a male partner. In the UK and Ireland contributory benefits are paid as flat-rate benefits, rather than as percentages of past income (as in Belgium) or related to composition of households (as in the Netherlands). In Belgium a great number of women work on a full-time basis, but once into the contributory benefit system, benefits paid may depend upon the marital or cohabiting status of claimants, with greater resources being directed to primary earners with dependants (Chapter 6).

Financial dependence for women in couples appears to be an outcome of the means-tested social assistance (and non-contributory parts of the system), and this is also echoed in Belgium, the Netherlands and Ireland. This is operationalized by the 'aggregation' rule. Since, with social assistance, the earnings of both partners is so tightly controlled, this interacts with labour market inequalities to make it more likely that it is the female partner who stays outside the formal labour market.

This has a serious impact on the choices that can be exercised by women, and ultimately on their power within their relationships. Income which is mediated through another person cannot, I argue, yield the same choice and power as personal income. It is also my contention that social security systems encourage women to be at least partially dependent on their male partners. The analysis of the provision of risks in the UK system has demonstrated that, in a general sense, provision for caring is of a qualitatively different kind not only because it may be lower in terms of benefits received, but also because they can encourage financial dependence upon men.

In the next chapter I move to another area, presenting a feminist critique of the concept of equality in law, and of EC law in this field. This will help us to understand Directive 79/7/EEC.

NOTES

1   The source is Lister (1992, p.24), taken from 1990 official statistics. A number of benefits have now changed or are soon to change: sickness benefit and invalidity benefit were merged in April 1995 to become incapacity benefit; Unemployment benefit will become the jobseeker's allowance (six months' contributory benefit followed by income support) in April 1996; the attendance allowance has been replaced by the disability living allowance; the industries injuries disablement benefit is now the industrial disablement pension.

2   There are, however, other elements of the social security system which do benefit carers, either directly by means of premiums for carers on income support and family credit (see further below), or indirectly by exempting carers from the requirement of availability for work in income support.

3   In the mid-1970s a non-contributory benefit for the disabled was introduced in recognition of the poor contributions record of particular groups. This benefit was the non-contributory invalidity pension (NCIP). It contained a rule directly discriminating against married and cohabiting women, and in 1984 this discrimination was removed and the benefit was repackaged into the severe disablement allowance. See, further, Chapter 7.

4   See, in relation to the unemployed, Millar (1988, p.152). In 1961 47 per cent of unemployed men received contributory unemployment benefit alone and 22 per cent claimed means-tested benefits alone. By 1986 only 20 per cent of unemployed men claimed only unemployment benefit, while 59 per cent were in sole receipt of a means-tested benefit. This is in fact not what was intended by Lord Beveridge, whose *Plan for Social Security* envisaged that benefits would be largely social insurance-based, with means-tested benefits as a residual tier.

5   See *The Guardian*, 9 April 1994, Commentary by Victor Keegan.

6   The current Conservative administration is implacably opposed to paternity leave, and the government has successfully vetoed a proposal for an EC Directive on the right to take time off work for care for a sick child.

7   See the article in *The Guardian*, 5 August 1993, p.9 describing a report by the Policy Studies Institute.

8   Kirsten Scheiwe, a German feminist legal academic, has written extensively about gendered models of time in labour law, social security law and family law. See Scheiwe (1991, 1995).

9   Ethnic differences are relevant here. Women from certain ethnic groups have traditionally been the economic heads of their households: 32 per cent of West Indian households are female-headed as opposed to 14 per cent of white and 6.5 per cent of Asian households. See Cook and Watt (1992, pp.13–14).

10 The Child Support Act 1991 requires absent parents, who are normally fathers, to contribute to the financial maintenance of their children. The maintenance formula also contains an element of money for the maintenance of the carer parent. The latter feature was a break with the past when only husbands could be forced to contribute to the financial upkeep of their wives on relationship breakdown.

11 Although financial dependence is strongly related to the presence of children, it is not synonymous with having children. A recent study has indicated that a substantial minority of childless women working full-time are financially dependent on transfers from their partners (Ward *et al.*, 1993), although the question of whether this income is shared equally remains open.

12 A study has found that there has nevertheless been an increase in women's personal income over the last 20 years. Webb (1993, p.32) found that £1 in every £4 that came into UK private households went into the hands of a woman in 1971, and in 1991 this proportion had risen to £1 in every £3. Webb argues that the single most important reason for this trend has been the growth in female part-time work (1993, p.35).

13 EOC, 1991, p.29.

14 See Pahl (1984, 1989, 1991) and Vogler and Pahl (1993). For a review of the literature, see Lister (1992, pp.16–23).

15 Women are also at a substantial disadvantage in terms of occupational welfare, despite the increase in their labour market participation, which is particularly due to women's part-time employment. See Ginn and Arber (1992, 1993, 1994) and Groves (1983, 1987, 1991, 1992). Women are also at a disadvantage regarding personal pensions – a trend which has been encouraged by the current Conservative administration. See, generally, Davies and Ward (1992).

16 For obvious reasons I do not consider universal benefits here; these benefits, such as child benefit, are paid regardless of income and means and are not linked to the payment of contributions. A commentary as to their adequacy, and the linked issue of qualitative risk provision, is to be found in the discussion of the second layer of inequality in the following section.

17 It is possible to be credited with contributions, for instance by home responsibilities protection (see note 18 below) or during periods of receipt of other benefits, such as incapacity benefit. But, in relation to the latter, receipt of incapacity benefit is itself a consequence of having paid contributions from paid work and establishing entitlement to this contributory benefit. In 1988 contribution conditions for some benefits were narrowed so that paid contributions were required in the previous two years, whereas, before, paid or credited contributions had been acceptable. See Ogus and Barendt (1995, p.78).

18 Unless this caring has been associated with substantial years in the labour market, which entitles a person claiming a retirement pension to use home responsibilities protection (HRP), which was introduced in 1975. HRP is given to persons who can show that, having made contributions for at least 20 years, in all the remaining contributory years they were precluded from regular employment by responsibilities at home. A worker will satisfy this requirement if (a) she or he was receiving child

benefit for a child under 16 years of age, or (b) was regularly caring for at least 35 hours per week for someone receiving attendance allowance, the care component of the disability living allowance, or the constant attendance allowance under the War Pensions or Industrial Injuries Scheme, or (c) was in receipt of income support and was exempted from the requirement to be available for work in order to look after an elderly or incapacitated person. See Ogus and Barendt (1995, p.231).

19   For a discussion of this phenomenon in relation to access of part-time workers to social insurance benefits in several European countries, including the UK, the Netherlands and Belgium, see Maier (1991).

20   In relation to unemployment benefit, see Micklewright (1990).

21   A 13-week period of grace is allowed so that persons can seek employment in their usual occupation. See Ogus and Barendt (1995, p.108).

22   Some positive news is the government's intention of extending home responsibilities protection to the SERPS scheme to cushion the entitlements of persons who have left the labour market to look after a child or a sick or elderly person.

23   I am grateful to Linda Luckhaus for this point.

24   There is a more general critique of the mismatch between the structure of contributory benefits and more general employment patterns, such as the prevalence of so-called 'atypical working'. See, generally, Bradshaw (1985), Kravaritou-Manitakis (1988), Hakim (1989), Chamberlayne (1991), Maier (1991), Luckhaus and Dickens (1991), Dickens (1992), Hewitt (1993), Bieback (1993b) and Blackwell (1994).

25   I return to this theme, in the context of possible future policy directions, in Chapter 8.

26   I am grateful to Linda Luckhaus for this point.

27   A stark description of the impact of the cohabitation rule on some women's financial independence and economic wellbeing was given by Beatrix Campbell:

> ... when a man lives in, a woman's independence – her own name on the weekly giro is automatically surrendered. The men become the claimants and the women their dependant. They lose control over both the revenue and the expenditure, often with catastrophic results: rent not paid, fuel bills missed, arrears mounting. (Quoted in Pascall, 1986 pp.221–2)

28   A longstanding cause of complaint from women has been the enforcement and policing of the 'cohabitation rule', which has been (and continues to be) intrusive into women's personal lives. See Pascall (1986, pp.215–18).

29   See para. 7 of *Cohabitation*, Supplementary Benefits Commission, 1971.

30   The exception to this now is that, under the Child Support Act 1991, an element of the child support paid by an absent parent, normally a father, will be for the support of the carer parent. This applies to absent parents whether or not they were married to the child's other parent.

31   See Morris (1987), Millar (1988), Dilnot and Kell (1989), Millar *et al.* (1989) and McLaughlin *et al.* (1989).

32   See the study conducted in Hartlepool by Morris (1987).

33   Persons could not normally claim ICA after reaching pensionable age of 60 for women and 65 for men unless they were entitled immediately before attaining that age. A ruling by the European Court of Justice (ECJ) in March 1993 means that women will be able to claim ICA until the age of 65, see Chapter 4.

34   The earnings 'disregard' was increased from £12 to £20 in April 1990, and has recently been increased to £50. In calculating the £50 earnings there are certain allowable

expenses, such as childminding costs, fares to work and National Insurance contributions.

35   The Child Poverty Action Group (CPAG) has been trying, over a number of years, to challenge the childcare costs rule. Its second test case on the issue, *Meyers*, has just overcome the first hurdle. The ECJ has recently found that family credit is covered by Directive 76/207/EEC (see Chapters 4 and 7). The next hurdle is whether or not a national court will agree that the effect of the rule indirectly discriminates against women.

36   This was the outcome of the first set of CPAG test cases (see note 35 above) in the *Jackson and Cresswell* cases.

37   I am grateful to both Rikki Holtmaat and Mary Daly for suggesting this line of analysis to me.

38   Benefit rates given are for weekly payments between April 1995 and April 1996.

39   Benefits from the UK social insurance system have consistently offered low replacement of earnings, poor coverage of risks and relatively tough eligibility conditions (Ginsburg, 1992, p.144). This in part explains the widespread claiming of means-tested benefits.

40   This rule has already been the subject of an unsuccessful legal challenge in the ECJ under Directive 79/7/EEC on the grounds of its indirectly discriminatory effects on women, but has recently been successfully challenged under Directive 76/207/EEC (see Chapters 4 and 7).

41   To the extent that maintenance comes from an (ex)-male partner, and is income which is mediated through a man, it is difficult to conceive of it as an independent income (*contra* Duncan *et al.*, 1994).

42   See para. 114, emphasis added.

43   Para. 107, emphasis added.

44   Quoted in Lewis (1983, p.19).

45   An exception has been the extra conditions having to be met by married women when claiming a dependant's addition for their spouses with their basic state pensions. See Chapters 4 and 7.

46   Linda Luckhaus has challenged me on the issue of how far it can be taken as 'read' that benefit rules actually encourage particular behaviour or choices. I agree that it cannot be assumed that people have enough information at their disposal as to the complex workings of the benefit system to enable them to make exact calculations about their various options. I also accept that people may not make calculations as to the choices they will make from the primary point of view of maximizing the amount of benefits and without regard as to cultural factors, such as a man's perceived role as the 'breadwinner' and thus benefit claimant. However, I maintain that a particular structure of benefits, at the very least, helps to shape a societal environment in which certain choices are made more likely. Certain choices, from a financial point of view, are hardly viable; so that men's relatively higher earnings to women, combined with poor benefit provision for carers, substantially decreases the likelihood of a man undertaking this work in preference to a lower-paid female partner.

47   There is an abundant literature describing and analysing the changes to the social security system in the UK since the late 1970s. See Smart (1987), Dominelli (1988), Alcock (1989), Dilnot and Webb (1989), Deacon (1991), Lister (1991; 1992, pp.30–60) and Clarke and Langan (1993b).

48   Policy is also tending towards using means-tested benefits to supplement low pay from employment (in-work benefits). Family credit, the principal in-work benefit, gives a £10 bonus to those claimants, with children, working more than 30 hours per week. A

pilot scheme is currently being run for an 'earnings top-up' benefit, which would supplement the low pay of workers by means-tested benefits, and this would cover single persons and persons who are not disabled. See DSS (1995).

49   Conventional measures may underestimate the extent of poverty among women. Research often assumes an equal sharing of resources between members of a family/household unit, and further that living standards are mainly determined by income and other material resources, rather than by the way resources are generated or managed, most notably by time expenditure (see Glendinning and Millar, 1991, p.26; Daly, 1992, pp.7–10).

3 Equality in Law: A Feminist Critique

Equality is traditionally the demand of disadvantaged groups, and the demand for equality has had an intimate connection with the whole history of feminism as a conscious social and political movement (Mitchell, 1987, p.26). The legal concept of equality is the springboard for legislation enacted to challenge inequalities in the gendered social reality. The principle of equality of treatment is to be found at the core of Directive 79/7/EEC, of which Article 4(1) provides that 'there shall be no discrimination whatsoever on grounds of sex either directly, or indirectly by reference in particular to marital or family status'.

There are three principal models of equality:

1 formal equality (allowing no distinctions on the grounds of sex);
2 equality of opportunity (the proverbial 'level playing field');
3 equality of outcomes (also called substantive equality).

These three models will provide the basis for the evaluation of the implementation of Directive 79/7/EEC in the four countries (see Chapters 6 and 7).

In this chapter I focus on two particular models of equality: first, the sameness–difference model of equality in Directive 79/7/EEC and, second, a model of substantive equality. The broader question underlying the discussion is the strategic issue of which model is best placed to promote the goal of greater financial independence for women.

In the preceding chapter I have examined the gendered social reality, in relation to women's access to independent income from the social security system and the labour market, and women's income dependence on men in households. In the following two chapters I cast a critical eye on Directive 79/7/EEC on equality of treatment between men and women in statutory social security schemes. Before turning to a detailed analysis of the Direc-

tive and the interpretation of its provisions by the ECJ, it is worth considering some strands of a feminist critique of the concept of equality, both as a
moral value and as a legal principle, in order to enrich the discussion. The
feminist literature used in this chapter is drawn partly from North America,
and partly from Western Europe (Italy, France and the UK). The body of law
drawn upon are cases interpreting EC equality law.

This chapter will briefly consider feminist engagement with equality,
then look at the sameness–difference model of the Directive, before turning
to substantive equality.

FEMINIST ENGAGEMENT WITH EQUALITY

The concept of equality has an important place within feminism and cam-
paigns on behalf of women. Equality has been 'called upon' by feminists to
provide a principle of freedom, a measure of justice, an expression of
respect for personhood and a political or legal strategy (Gibson, 1989,
p.435). Mary Jo Frug (1992, p.666) described the relationship between
feminism and equality in law in the following way:

> ... the issue of what constitutes equality for women and how they can achieve it
> is at the heart of the feminist legal project.

Feminist engagement with the concept of equality concerns equality both
as an end in itself (that is, as a moral value) and as a strategic concept (a
means to an end). Engagement with equality as a moral value has created
conflicts between women as to whether women are the 'same' as men, with
different sex-role socialization, or whether women are 'different' from men
in terms of qualities and aspirations and whether they want these differences
to be recognized. The meanings of 'equality' and 'difference' as moral
values continue to be debated and discussed at a conceptual level both in
Europe and in the USA and beyond (see Bock and James, 1992, p.1–13).
Feminists have, for instance, disagreed over whether or not 'independence'
for women should be achieved by conforming to male patterns and taking
up full-time paid work,[1] or whether they want their social role adequately
valued, or protected so that they are no longer penalized for their 'labours of
love'.[2]

In a more strategic understanding of equality, feminists have long debated
over what model of equality can most effectively be presented and pursued
in the courts (Majury, 1987, p.169). In recent times, the most intense
feminist engagement with equality in this strategic sense has emerged
from across the Atlantic and has been dominated by debates over whether

granting statutory leaves in the workplace specifically for pregnant workers constitutes 'equal treatment' or 'special treatment', and which of these two strategies is the best one to adopt (see Bacchi, 1990, pp.108–33; Bacchi, 1991b). Advocates of an equal treatment approach argued that sex-neutral laws, such as parental leave, should be introduced instead of maternity leave (see Williams, 1982; 1985). On the other hand, special treatment advocates have countered that, unless women's unique position as childbearer is taken into account, their interests could not be protected and they would continue to be disadvantaged in the labour market (More, 1993, p.50).[3]

THE SAMENESS–DIFFERENCE MODEL OF THE DIRECTIVE

To relate the above discussion more closely to the issues which are at the core of this book, the tension between equality and difference as both moral values and as strategic issues is clearly visible in the text of Directive 79/7/ EEC. The model of equality in the Directive can, I contend, be characterized as a 'sameness–difference' model, in which women are to have the same treatment when they are the same as men (women as paid workers), and different treatment when they are different from men (women as dependants and carers).[4]

The Directive excludes from the scope of the equality principle a number of benefits and risks that could be characterized as 'feminine', in the sense that they are related to maternity and to women's social role as carers and dependants (Article 3(1)). Outside the scope of the equality principle are also family benefits, survivor's benefits, and provisions relating to women on the grounds of maternity (respectively, Articles 3(2) and 4(2)). Further, the Directive allows Member States to maintain a number of advantages for, or on behalf of, women as dependent spouses and carers (Article 7(1)), including a different pension age (a lower pension age for women compensating them for shorter paid-work careers), or advantages in old age pensions for persons who have brought up children, or indeed the granting of old age or invalidity benefit entitlements by virtue of the derived entitlements of a wife.

The equal treatment principle applies, with one exception, to masculine risks – that is, employment-related income-loss risks – provided through statutory schemes or social assistance intended to supplement or replace statutory schemes; in relation to these there shall be no direct or indirect discrimination between men and women. The only exception to this was provided by a decision of the ECJ in the *Drake* case.[5]

On the one hand the Directive has the aim of eliminating all differences in treatment regarding employment-related risks, so that rules apply to both sexes; on the other hand, benefits which relate to women's role as carers (and dependants) are to be untouched. Implicit within these two aims may be an expectation that women will be able to acquire the same entitlements to social security as men if rules which discriminate against them are removed and, conversely, a belief that women-only benefits *do* provide a recognition of women's unpaid care work and therefore should not be interfered with by a formal equality principle.

The tension between equality meaning sameness (equal rights) and difference (special rights) can also be seen in Directive 76/207/EEC on equality between men and women in access to employment, training and working conditions. Women and men are to be treated in the same way, except in relation to maternity, or where sex is a determining factor. Further, Article 2(4) provides that this Directive shall be without prejudice to measures to promote equality of opportunity, in particular by removing existing inequalities.

In the next section I consider the question of whether the adoption of a sameness–difference model can promote the goal of greater financial independence for women. This discussion will draw mainly on the area of equality in social security, but I also refer to other areas of EC equality law, such as provisions for maternity, the prohibition on nightwork for women and measures in employment to ease women's double burden.

THE SAMENESS–DIFFERENCE MODEL CRITICALLY APPRAISED

The sameness–difference model of the Directive is an expression of the Aristotelian principle of equalitywhich holds that persons in similar situations should be treated in similar ways, while persons in dissimilar situations should be treated in dissimilar ways. Directive 79/7/EEC treats women as being in a similar situation to men when they are workers, and as being in a dissimilar situation when they are involved in activities related to women's social role, such as (unpaid) caring work.

This section is divided into three parts. In the first, I discuss the problems associated with a sameness approach in altering women's lack of access to independent income in social security. In the second part I consider the difference approach from the same perspective, and in the third part I look at how the sameness–difference model operates as a united entity in the light of the above goal.

A sameness approach

Under a sameness approach, persons in similar situations are to be treated in similar ways. This may necessitate the removal of rules which treat persons in similar situations in a different way. This has a particular resonance in the social security sphere, where married women, and at times women cohabitees, in all the four countries have been denied a range of benefits given to men and single women because they were deemed to be supported by their male partners (see, further, Chapters 6 and 7). Eliminating differences in treatment for similarly situated persons can therefore mean that women are given, for the first time, the opportunity to claim certain benefits on the same terms as men. There are, however, a number of significant limitations, in terms of altering the current gendered social reality, associated with the elimination of differences in treatment between similarly situated persons. I consider these problems in turn below.

First, treating people as if they are the same does not produce equal results where rules of entitlement to benefits interact with a deeply unequal society. In other words, applying the same rules to both men and women will have very different effects on both sexes because of the pre-existing gendered social reality. In Chapter 2 I showed that women's position in the social security system is structurally different from men's. This includes not only women's different position from men in relation to a social insurance system geared to a 'standard employment relationship', but also in qualitatively and quantitatively inferior provision for feminine risks, such as caring, compared with provision related to masculine risks. In the UK, for instance, some 2.25 million working women fall outside the contributory benefits system because of the earnings threshold – the lower earnings limit (Lister, 1992, p.27). It will also be recalled that women comprise between only 20–30 per cent of claimants of contributory benefits for the risks of unemployment, sickness and invalidity (Chapter 2).

There will, however, be women – described by Rubenstein (1990, p.89) as 'exceptional' women – who can benefit from a sameness approach. These are women who, for instance, are working in a 'standard employment relationship' over significant periods of their lives. Patterns of labour market participation affect access to contributory benefits, and there are bound to be clear differences in the entitlements to benefits of women who work full-time and women who either work part-time or have interrupted careers.

Second, in more abstract terms, the sameness approach essentially reinforces the status quo – that is, the existing gendered social reality. Suzie Gibson (1989, p.439) captured this problem thus:

... 'equal rights' can be no more than a demand for access to the structure. If it is the structure which is the problem, equal rights to it are not an exciting prospect.

A sameness approach does little to profoundly alter a particular social reality in terms of its practices, institutions and structures. In the area of social security, although women who can build up the necessary entitlements may be able to claim and receive contributory benefits for the first time, the desirability of the contribution principle cannot itself be challenged under a sameness approach. That is, the question, 'Should social insurance be linked to stable, relatively uninterrupted, and full-time employment?' is never posed. In Chapter 2 I argued that the inequalities facing women in gaining a personal income from social security go beyond discrimination – that is, applying different rules to women. They are related, in part, to the fact that unpaid care work cannot be counted as a contribution towards social insurance, and that thresholds may be so high as to exclude many part-time and other atypical workers. In order for there to be a change to women's lack of personal entitlements to contributory benefits, there would at least need to be a rethinking of some of the structures by which these entitlements are built up.

Third, the sameness approach may lead to either levelling up or levelling down – that is, the same treatment can be negative or positive. A sameness approach may, for instance, lead to protection or to rights being taken away from women because men do not have them. In the words of Jeanne Gregory (1987, p.28), same treatment 'is perfectly compatible with a process of "levelling down", which merely ensures an equal measure of misery for all vulnerable groups'.[6]

This is perhaps best illustrated by the prohibition on nightwork for women. Catasta (1993, p.15) argues that the *Stoeckel*[7] judgement, discussed below, does not specify a solution to the problem of nightwork. Rather, it merely says that the rules must be the same for men and women. From this may flow either the abolition of protection for all workers or protections for both sexes (Catasta, 1993, p.15). This will be seen in the following discussion of two ECJ decisions regarding the compatibility of prohibitions on nightwork with Directive 76/207/EEC.

In *Criminal Procedure against Alfred Stoeckel*, an employer was to be fined for employing women to work at night, following a reorganization of his factory. Article L-213-1 of the French Code du Travail (Labour Code) places a prohibition on certain forms of nightwork for women, although a number of exceptions are permitted. Mr Stoeckel claimed that this provision contravened Directive 76/207/EEC. The ECJ agreed with him, finding that there were no reasons which justified this difference in treatment between men and women.[8] In a subsequent case, *Ministère Public et Direction du*

Travail et de l'Emploi v. *Lévy*,[9] the European Commission sought to introduce arguments relating equal treatment as meaning adequate treatment for all workers. The Commission referred the ECJ to ILO Convention No. 171 and ILO Recommendation No. 178, both of 26 June 1990, which both tend towards the idea that the same rules should apply to men and women in this area and that all workers should be entitled to the same protection in as much as nightwork is dangerous for their health. The ECJ, however, merely stated that, although the prohibition on nightwork is contrary to Directive 76/207/EEC, this Directive does not outlaw national provisions which seek to bring conformity with ILO Convention No. 89, in which women's nightwork is prohibited. The ECJ omitted all mention of the later ILO texts and thus refused to give any guidance or encouragement towards a solution that could have improved the material working conditions of many workers.

Two further contemporary examples of processes of equalization by levelling down can be given (and more are to be found in Chapters 6 and 7). First, the vogue in several European countries (the UK, Austria[10], Greece) is to equalize the pensionable ages of men and women by raising the qualifying age for women. The UK government announced in November 1993 that the pensionable age for women would be raised from 60 to 65 between 2010 and 2020. This change means that women will have to wait five years longer for a basic state pension (whether on their husband's insurance record or on their own), as well as adding five years on to the number of contributory years needed for a full basic state pension. Some women will probably find it harder to build up the requisite number of contributory years for a pension in their own right. In Belgium, although the pensionable age for women is not being raised, it is intended that, by the year 2006, the number of years over which earnings are calculated for the pension will be raised from 40 years to 45 years in line with the number of years applying to men (see Chapter 6). However, currently women have on average, substantially fewer years in employment than this.[11]

Second, the response of some British employers to the ECJ's ruling in *Barber*,[12] regarding the application of the equal pay principle under Article 119 of the Treaty to payments made under occupational pension schemes (that is, men and women must be paid pensions at the same age), has been to increase the age at which women may claim pensions from the scheme. This means that, if women employees want to retire earlier, they may lose up to 20 per cent of their pension. The ECJ ruled in September 1994 that, once equalization has occurred in schemes, Article 119 requires merely that the same rules as applied to men and women, with no regard to the standard of that protection, and that there may be no transitional provisions to cushion women's pensions.[13]

Summary

A sameness approach is at its most positive when it extends to women a range of benefits, or rights, for the first time. Yet a sameness approach also fundamentally ignores gender differences in structures such as the labour market, the household and the social security system (the 'gendered social reality'). In terms of social security, more specifically, a sameness approach allows women the same access to claiming benefits, or to building up entitlements to benefits (or 'equality of access' in the sense used in Chapters 6 and 7). But, in fact, the women most likely to gain from this are those women who already fit most closely to the typical male employment pattern around which the social insurance system is structured. As will be recalled from Chapter 2, this only scratches the surface of the difficulties faced by women in gaining an independent income.

A difference approach

A difference approach is the other side of the Aristotelian principle, holding that persons in dissimilar situations should be treated in a dissimilar way. In social security terms, this means that women should have different rights or benefits when their social roles are different. Described thus, a difference approach could mean either different-and-worse treatment, or different-but-favourable treatment. In many cases, however, it is simply a matter of (political) opinion whether rules which treat women and men differently are to be seen as different-and-worse treatment or different-but-favourable treatment. A topical example of this tension is the prohibition on nightwork.[14]

Different-and-worse treatment was found in the UK social security system in the pre-1975 married women's option (see Chapter 2). As will be recalled, under the Beveridge Plan, married women were seen as being in a dissimilar situation from men and single women because they had 'other duties'. In terms of structures in social security, different-and-worse treatment includes a situation in which caring, or feminine risks, results in quantitatively inferior provision and qualititatively lesser provision because it leads to few personal entitlements to social security benefits. Also from the point of view of women gaining personal entitlements to benefits, several of the derogations to the principle of equality, contained in Article 7(1) of the Directive, which seem to advantage women may not in fact do so as they perpetuate a system in which feminine risks attract derived rights and benefits as dependants.

A different-but-favourable approach, I would argue, situates itself within a recognition of an unequal gendered social reality. In terms of social security, this could involve crediting women with contributions for social insurance benefits for years which they have spent out of the labour market or exempting certain categories of women, such as married women, from requirements to pay contributions or, indeed, paying women for domestic work (such as a 'home carer's wage'). A contemporary example of this approach relates to pensionable ages. A lower pensionable age for women is often justified by the fact that women have shorter (paid) working lives because of the years they have spent in unpaid caring work (which is a positive action type of formulation). In Belgium, for instance, the government is explicit both about its recognition that women build up far less contributory years than men and about their desire to give women a chance to acquire an adequate pension. In relation to debates about equalizing pensionable age, there is a desire not to make women 'pay the price' for equality. In the employment sphere, a different-but-favourable approach could mean child-related benefits for women, or indeed the prohibition on women's nightwork, to ease women's double burden of paid work and caring.

In the discussion of the different-but-favourable approach, it is helpful to distinguish between its two possible aspects. The first aspect refers to situations where only women are given particular rights (which I call 'women-specific') and the second to situations where rules are phrased in a sex-neutral way but mainly benefit women (these are referred to as 'gender-sensitive' rights – see below). In this section I first examine the difference approach in EC legislation, then in the ECJ case law and, finally, consider how far a difference approach could promote women's greater financial independence.

EC legislation

A difference approach can be seen in a number of EC equality laws. In Directive 76/207/EEC, for instance, it is clear that the sameness approach alone cannot remove all the inequalities of the workplace. Article 2(4) of this Directive allows some possibilities for positive action to remedy existing inequalities. In Directive 79/7/EEC, Article 7(1) contains a number of exemptions in areas where women's social role is considered to be different from men's. Both these Directives further contain provisions stating that the principle of equal treatment is without prejudice to the protection of women on grounds of maternity and pregnancy (Article 4(2) Directive 79/7/EEC and Article 2(3) Directive 76/207/EEC).

More recently, a clause in the Social Policy Agreement, annexed to the Maastricht Treaty and inserted at the insistence of the French and German governments, refers to allowing Member States to maintain and adopt 'specific advantages to make it easier for women to pursue a vocational activity or to prevent or compensate for disadvantages in their professional careers'. It appears that the German government intended this chiefly to apply to the issue of the differential pensionable age, which it wishes to retain as a lower age for women.[15] It is still unclear, however, as to what effect, if any, this clause will have. Its wording does suggest provisions which are strongly reminiscent of the type of advantages that, as will be seen below, were held to be contrary to EC law in the case of *Commission* v. *France* (Ballestrero, 1992b, p.775).

ECJ Case Law

The ECJ requires that derogations from a sameness approach are strictly interpreted, and has in fact limited a difference approach to women's child-bearing and maternal role, as opposed to the social role of carer. I now consider three cases relating to a 'difference' approach in Directive 76/207/ EEC: the *Hofmann* case,[16] then *Johnston*[17] and, finally, *Commission* v. *France*.[18] The judgements of the ECJ will be described, with a critical analysis of the cases, in the following section. Of relevance to this discussion is also the above-mentioned *Stoeckel* case regarding the prohibition on nightwork.

The *Hofmann* case related to maternity leave. Under German law women were entitled to a compulsory period of convalescence of eight weeks after childbirth in which they received their net remuneration, paid either by a sickness fund or by their employer. At the expiry of this eight-week period, they had the option of taking maternity leave until the child reached the age of six months, in which case they received a daily allowance of DM 25. Mr Hofmann's partner had a child and returned to work at the end of the eight-week period. He obtained unpaid leave from his employer and cared for the child until it was six months of age. The case arose because Mr Hofmann claimed, and was denied, the daily allowance for the maternity leave period.

Mr Hofmann contended that this was outside of the scope of Article 2(3) of Directive 76/207/EEC which provides that the 'directive shall be without prejudice to provisions concerning the protection of women, particularly as regards pregnancy and maternity'. He argued that the true purpose of the payment was not to afford protection to women on biological grounds but rather to reduce the multiple burdens arising from employment and bringing up a child, and that therefore it should also be given to men. The sickness fund and the German government both contended that the primary purpose of maternity leave was related to considerations of protecting mothers' health.

The ECJ began by considering the purpose of the Directive – equality in access to employment, promotion and working conditions – and made the now famous statement that the '[d]irective is not designed to settle questions concerned with the organisation of the family, or to alter the division of responsibility between parents'.[19] It went on to say that Article 2(3) of the Directive recognizes the legitimacy, in terms of the principle of equality, of protecting women's needs in two respects.[20] First, it is legitimate to ensure the protection of women's biological condition during pregnancy and until such time as her physiological and mental functions have returned to normal. Second, it is legitimate to protect the 'special relationship between a woman and her child' over the period following pregnancy and childbirth by preventing that relationship from being disturbed by the multiple burdens resulting from simultaneous employment. The Court thus concluded that this leave was legitimately reserved to women in view of the fact that only mothers may find themselves subject to undesirable pressures to return to work prematurely.[21]

In *Johnston* v. *Royal Ulster Constabulary*, Mrs Johnston's contract as a police officer was not renewed because she would have been assigned to duties involving the use of firearms. It had been RUC policy that male officers were to be given firearms for their normal duties, but that female officers should be unarmed. Mrs Johnston complained that the non-renewal of her contract was contrary to Directive 76/207/EEC. The ECJ held that, although the derogation to the principle of equality where sex constitutes a determining factor, must be interpreted strictly, the possibility cannot be excluded that in a situation characterized by internal disturbances the carrying of firearms by policewomen might create additional risks of their being assassinated and might therefore be contrary to the requirements of public safety. In such circumstances therefore the sex of a police officer could constitute a determining factor within the meaning of the Directive.[22]

In the third case, the European Commission brought infringement proceedings against France because it allowed a number of women-only advantages in collective agreements to stand (*Commission* v. *France*). These advantages included extended maternity leave, a reduction in the working hours of women aged 59 and above, an earlier retirement age, time off to care for sick children, extra days' holidays each year per child, a day off on the first day of the school term, some hours off on Mother's Day, daily breaks for women working on computer equipment or as typists or switchboard operators, the grant of bonuses from the birth of the second child for pension calculation, and the payment of allowances to mothers who have to pay costs of a nursery or childminder.

Article 2(4) of Directive 76/207/EEC provides that 'this directive shall be without prejudice to measures to promote equal opportunity for men and women, in particular by removing existing inequalities which affect women's opportunities' in access to employment, including promotion, and to vocational training and working conditions. Early versions of the draft of this Directive had contained definitions of equal treatment that allowed for positive action (More, 1993, p.57). This more outcomes-oriented definition of equal treatment was, however, gradually narrowed and finally removed as the draft passed through the various discussion stages. As a compromise it was agreed that positive action would number among the permitted derogations to the principle of equal treatment (More, 1993, p.57).

Part of the French government's argument against the Commission's infringement proceedings was that Article 2(4) of the Directive permits the retention of measures to promote equal opportunity by removing existing inequalities and that, as part of such a process, particular rights for women can be retained. It tried to demonstrate that family responsibilities do affect women's opportunities in the workplace and that it is impossible to restrict the concept of 'existing inequalities' to the workplace alone.[23] The French government appeared to think that the blanket sex-neutral approach was naive, since women first required special treatment in order to remedy the *de facto* inequalities they face in the household.

Advocate General Slynn stated in his Opinion that, following the ECJ's decisions in *Hofmann* and *Johnston*, most of the women-only rights could not be justified under Article 2(3).[24] He argued that it could not be said that men would never need such advantages, and in modern social conditions fathers may be just as responsible for child care.[25] AG Slynn also stated that the women-only rights could not be justified under Article 2(4) – first, because they had never been given to men, so that there existed no inequalities in favour of men affecting women's opportunities in the employment field[26] and, second, because it is not permissible to argue that any provisions favouring women in the employment field are valid *per se* as part of the levelling process between men and women.[27] On the French government's final argument – that to withdraw these advantages would be a socially retrograde step – the Advocate General agreed with the Commission that equality could be achieved just as effectively by a levelling-up process applying the same benefits to men. He also rejected the government's argument that levelling up would be too expensive.

The judgement of the ECJ was rather terse: it simply restated the law, referring to *Hofmann*, concluding that the advantages at issue went beyond those allowed under EC law.[28] Some advantages benefited women in their capacity as older workers or as parents, and male workers, the Court said, could equally be in this position.[29] Article 2(4), said the ECJ, has the narrow and limited object of authorizing measures, which, though discriminatory, aim to eliminate or reduce *de facto* inequalities only in working life.[30]

To summarize, in these three cases, as well as in *Stoeckel*, it can be seen that the ECJ will limit derogations from the sameness approach only to situations in which women need to be protected on account of their role in childbearing and in the earliest stages of childrearing. Beyond this, it appears that rules and rights must be sex-neutral. Two observations may be made. First, an aim here appears to be that rules should, as far as possible, be sex-neutral in order to open the possibility of role-sharing, although this is role-sharing of a permissive nature – that is, it is allowed but not positively encouraged. Second, in relation to the nightwork ban, Ballestrero (1992b, p.774) has argued that *Stoeckel* shows that the ECJ condemns the traditional way of protecting women at work, consisting of negative measures which have actually excluded them from a number of sectors and types of employment. In the terms used in this discussion, the ECJ rejects the different-and-worse approach, where prohibitions on nightwork in practice protect women from certain types of work and working structures. The lesson which Ballestrero draws from the *Stoeckel* decision is that, although this is not necessarily followed in EC law, equal opportunity policies must be achieved by positive measures of equalization (*eguagliamento*) (1992a, p.586).

Critical analysis

It is now necessary to pose some critical questions regarding the difference approach. How far does it encourage women to become trapped in their gender roles? How far does a difference approach itself construct differences between men and women? It is arguably helpful here to draw a clear distinction between women-specific rights on the one hand and sex-neutral rights (which I call 'gender-sensitive' rights) which in fact mainly benefit women on the other.

A women-specific approach, although situated within a recognition of an unequal gendered social reality, could nevertheless trap women in their gender roles. This may happen where these rights entrench an association between women and particular social roles, such as caring. Reinforcing this link may mean, in part, that it is only economically viable for women to engage in unpaid caring activities. There is indeed a fine line between allowing women to better negotiate their double burden, in recognition of current realities, and merely making it realistic for women to undertake these activities. In terms of social security there is also a fine line between compensating women for their unpaid care work by giving married women derived entitlements to benefits and maintaining the link of dependence between breadwinner and dependent by means of these benefits. Where the latter happens, arguably, there is a freezing of the current division of care and family roles (Ballestrero, 1992b, p.775; Treu, 1986, p.132). This tension was at the heart of the *Commission* v. *France* case, as well as *Hofmann*.

Further, if a goal is the sharing of family responsibilities between parents, then child or care related women-only advantages will constitute an impediment to this.

Underpinning the discussion so far is the fear that women's social role becomes held up as being 'natural' which would, it is submitted, limit women's choices even if caring work were adequately valued (which at present it is not). The association of certain activities with a woman's so-called 'natural' role is, it is contended, always politically dangerous for women, even if this is disguised as 'protection'. Arguments that certain qualities or 'differences' inhere in women do not fundamentally challenge the idea of differences as being 'natural', as opposed to socially and culturally constructed. If these rest on women's biology, there is a great difficulty in trying to rescue biology from its bad reputation in supporting and colluding in a concept of women as inferior to men and reinvesting it with moral value (Kingdom 1991 p.124).

Part of a process of rendering women's social role into a 'natural' phenomenon, which then justifies different (and possibly worse) treatment, can also be seen in decisions of the ECJ, such as *Hofmann* and *Johnston*.[31] The ECJ's approach in *Hofmann* suggests that giving women different rights, or special 'derogations' from equal rights, can be used to reinforce stereotypical notions of womanhood (More, 1993, p.60). In these cases the ECJ did not appear to appreciate that 'differences' relate to gender roles, which are culturally and socially determined. In *Johnston* the ECJ took a culturally constructed stereotype and treated it as an immutable difference, which then precludes equal treatment with men (More, 1993, p.53). Not to challenge the prescription of certain roles to women and the way this translates in terms of power, choice and economic security is, I would argue, fundamentally limited.

A final criticism of the principle that persons in dissimilar situations may be treated in a dissimilar way is that the status quo remains the defining standard. That is, treating women differently from men allows men to be standard of comparison (Majury, 1987; MacKinnon, 1989; Rhode, 1989; Holtmaat, 1989; More, 1993). This leads, as much as the sameness approach, to a freezing of the status quo or the current gendered social reality. Although this approach appears to be a different conceptualization of 'equality', it may in fact it may be the reverse image of the sameness approach (More, 1993, p.58). What is not challenged by treating women differently from men is that life patterns which differ from the typical man's remain outside the privileged arena of access to resources, such as personal rights in social security. But why should personal entitlements to social insurance benefits be linked to paid work? Why should the price of caring work be qualitatively and quantitatively inferior social security provision and lesser access to independent income?

The real issue here, it is argued, is not whether women are more or less different from men, it is the fact that unequal treatment flows from a finding of difference. As MacKinnon has argued (1979, p.140) men are as different from women as women are different from men:

> ... [h]owever, while men are equally different from women, men are not equally inferior to women in social terms. There is nothing in a difference that dictates inferiority; there is only society that makes the content of those differences into inferiorities.

To summarize, a number of dangers may flow from an approach to equality in which women are treated differently when they are in a different situation from men. Where women are treated in a different-but-worse fashion, their dependency and disadvantage is increased. A women-specific approach may also lead to women being trapped in certain gender roles. A gender-sensitive approach, whereby rights are sex-neutral but are in fact aimed at benefiting women, could be seen as a kind of 'positive action' approach, in the sense that the aim is to produce substantive changes for women.

The sameness–difference model of equality critically appraised

In this section I examine the sameness–difference model of equality as a united entity, in order to be able to draw conclusions about the sameness–difference model in Directive 79/7/EEC and its contribution to the promotion of women's financial independence. First, I consider the issue of when women should be treated as the same or different and, second, I examine the market/family dichotomy contained in the Directive.

When are women the same and when are they different?

A general criticism of a sameness–difference model of equality is that it fails to provide clear guidance as to when women are to be considered 'the same' as men and when they are to be considered 'different'. Unless criteria exist for determining where women and men are similar or different, it becomes the responsibility of the person applying the rule to apply their own standards (More, 1993, p.64). Perhaps the most classic example of this problem has been the interpretation of unequal treatment on the grounds of pregnancy. In some cases courts have found that, since pregnancy is unique to women, there are no relevant men for them to be compared with, and that different (and worse) treatment is justified.[32] This was mitigated to some extent where sex-neutral categories in relation to which the sexes could be compared, such as a comparison between pregnant women and men with a temporary disability (see Lacey, 1987, p.417; Curtin, 1989, p.216), could be referred to. The latter 'solution' creates its own absurdities, however, by masking the disadvantage that only women can face because of pregnancy, such as loss of their job. In 1990 the ECJ seemed effectively to have dealt with this issue in *Dekker*, by finding that a refusal to take on an employee on the grounds of pregnancy was contrary to Directive 76/207/EEC since 'only women can be refused employment on grounds of pregnancy ... such a refusal therefore constitutes direct discrimination on grounds of sex'.[33]

This lack of guidance, it has been argued, shows the fundamental emptiness of the principle of equality. Westen (1982, pp.543–52) contended that the proposition that equality means that 'likes should be treated alike' has no meaning unless it incorporates external values that determine which persons and what treatment are alike. Treatment can therefore only be alike in reference to a moral rule. Hence '[e]quality is entirely circular. ... Equality is an empty vessel with no substantive moral content of its own' (Westen, 1982, p.547). To say therefore that two people are 'equal' and are entitled to be treated 'equally' is to say that both fully satisfy the criteria of a governing rule, but says nothing at all about the content or wisdom of the governing rule. This argument could equally be made of the proposition that persons in 'different' situations should be treated in 'different ways'. The problem of the lack of criteria for assessing sameness and difference is also that of not knowing the desired end goals. Neither the sameness approach nor the difference approach provides goals with which to assess equality, such as a requirement that equality may not mean levelling down, or that different treatment should mean different but not worse. Without such end goals, however, a sameness approach can function essentially as a rule of procedure: as long as rules which apply to men and women look the same the equality test is satisfied.

Criteria perpetuating a paid/unpaid work dichotomy

However, a further problem may be that criteria are (implicitly) provided, but that these criteria are not conducive to promoting women's access to independent income. In social security terms, and in relation to the Directive, the problem of when women are the 'same' or 'different' appears to turn on whether or not they are in the labour market. But is the dichotomy between paid and unpaid work, or between the market/family, to be accepted? What effect does this dichotomy have in practice?

On the one hand, the sameness–difference model allows women in certain forms of employment access to benefits for the first time, but it may also play a part in confirming women's lack of access to independent income and their unequal financial position in the 'private' sphere of the family. Feminists have long challenged the dichotomy between the market and the family – between the public and the private – or, as I prefer to call it, the dichotomy between paid and unpaid work. Feminist literature has argued that there is in fact no clear division between these spheres.[34] In terms of women's access to social security, the disadvantage facing women simply cannot be understood unless one considers the interaction between women's (and men's) activities in both spheres. Taking one example from Chapter 2, it will be recalled how far women's poor pension entitlements reflect the years in which they have been in unpaid care work. Moreover, accepting the current division between paid and unpaid work, in which paid work is seen as more valuable, could mean that derived benefits are seen as a 'good thing' for women. Where paid work is seen as the proper means of gaining benefits, then derived benefits – giving women benefits for being dependants – can be seen as women getting 'something for nothing' (that is, for no paid contributions). However, derived benefits create a strong tension between what is positive for women in the short term (that is, a social security benefit) and in the long term (no personal entitlements).[35]

Nor does accepting the distinction between paid and unpaid work in the Directive challenge the gendered social reality which, as was seen in Chapter 2, accords better access to independent income and personal entitlements through the employment-related social insurance system. Why should better provision be accorded to employment-related rather than caring-related risks? Why is the choice structured in this way? It is all too easy to become caught up in the either/or choice, without standing back to question how the choice itself is limiting.[36] Feminists have argued that equality – whether women are treated the same as men or differently from men according to the Aristotelian principle – remains the standard of comparison. Concealed in the equality principle, argues MacKinnon (1989, pp. 220–1), is the substantive way in which

> ... man has become the measure of all things. Under the sameness rubric, women are measured according to their correspondence with man ... [u]nder the difference rubric, women are measured according to their lack of correspondence from man.

Accepting that women should be treated the same as men when they are paid workers, or differently when they are not paid workers, allows no challenge to structures which best fit male patterns, or indeed the qualitatively and quantitatively better provision for masculine risks in social security systems. In relation to EC equality law in the employment sphere, the 'subtle interplay between ideas of sameness and difference' highlights the realization that if the workplace were structured differently, by becoming more accommodating to the realities of care responsibilities, then a different standard would be applied in which women's needs would not appear 'different' (More, 1993, p.63). Applying this to social security, the interplay between sameness and difference obscures the realization that social insurance could be structured differently. The system could be designed in such a way that women's social role is no longer constructed as being 'outside' the normal bounds of an insurance system, thereby giving women better access to independent income.

May we therefore conclude that even where criteria are offered for assessing when women are to be treated the same as men or differently from men, this may still not be conducive to promoting substantive equality? In the context of the Directive, do the implicit criteria mean that, as long as women are not workers, it is legitimate to discriminate against them? This could have the effect that the principle of equal treatment need only first of all 'establish that women are not in fact the breadwinner/paid worker before they proceed to discriminate against them' (Hoskyns and Luckhaus, 1989, p.334).

Summary

I have shown a number of limitations of a sameness approach, in terms of ignoring the gendered social reality and not sufficiently challenging the gendered status quo. I have also demonstrated that a difference approach may trap women further into their gender roles, and consequently into dependency and disadvantage. Further, this approach may not sufficiently challenge the existing gendered social reality. A sameness–difference model of equality itself poses the problem that it is not immediately clear in what circumstances women and men are to be considered the same or different and, even where there are criteria to assess this, these may simply perpetuate a dichotomy between paid and unpaid work, in which the former continues to be privileged in terms of qualitative and quantitative aspects of social security provision.

In the following section I shift focus to possible ways of producing outcomes and results, in terms of increasing women's access to independent income.

SUBSTANTIVE EQUALITY: AN EMPHASIS ON PRODUCING GIVEN OUTCOMES

Substantive equality, or equality of outcomes, is a model of equality which is focused on the achievement of a given set of outcomes for a particular group or category. Equality of outcomes as an end result, in the sense used in this book, would aim at changing the current gendered social reality and in particular improving women's access to independent income through the social security system. Phrased in this way, it becomes clear that a focus on specific outcomes to be achieved builds upon a conception of inequality, in this case women's lack of independent income, which is to be tackled. Equality of outcomes therefore puts the issue of inequality (or 'disadvantage') to the forefront. Ballestrero (1992b, p.778) has aptly described substantive equality as a principle of inequality.

In this section, I consider first some of the end goals of a concept of substantive equality, then two models of an inequality approach, followed by a discussion of substantive equality in EC law. I end by proposing the idea of 'gender-sensitive' rights.

End goals

First, how is one to define more explicitly what would be substantive equality in the longest-term view? Two writers, Carol Bacchi and Letitia Gianformaggio, have, arguably, summarized the end goal very well. Bacchi calls the long-term goal 'inclusion', arguing that what is needed is a model 'which includes rather than excludes the particular needs of women ... and of men who do not match the male prototype' (1991a, p.2). By this she means campaigning for far-reaching social changes in the institutions where currently the burden of difference is assigned to those who depart from the norm (1991a, p.2). Inclusion does not mean adding women to existing standards, but reformulating standards with women as active participants in the process (Bacchi, 1990, p.132).

The latter point is also expressed in a useful way by Gianformaggio (1992, p.198), who argues that equality can be understood as difference since mere assimilation to the prevailing norms is to be rejected as a goal. What is demanded is not to be accepted at the game table once the game has begun, but rather to participate in the setting of the rules of the game.[37]

In terms of social security, the inclusion model would require that, for instance, the social insurance system would no longer be structured around a full-time lifetime earner. Women's gendered life patterns should be explicitly recognized in this reform, and caring work should be given greater economic recognition. An inclusion model would also challenge the situation whereby female risks receive qualitatively and quantitatively inferior provision. If the social security system were reformed along these 'inclusionary' lines, a significant step would be taken along the road towards promoting women's financial independence.

Models

Having set out some of the goals in this area, how can these be achieved within the legal arena? In this section I consider the frameworks proposed by two US feminist legal scholars, Catharine MacKinnon (1979, 1989) and Deborah Rhode (1989, 1990, 1992) who have argued that, instead of a sameness–difference model, what is needed is a standpoint of inequality (MacKinnon) and gender disadvantage (Rhode). Having discussed the frameworks proposed by MacKinnon and Rhode, I examine a possible model of substantive equality in EC law: the prohibition on indirect discrimination.

Catharine MacKinnon

In her work on sexual harassment MacKinnon (1979) identified two underlying rationales that the US courts have used in sex discrimination cases. The first, as will be recalled, is the sameness–difference model, while the second is the 'inequalities approach'. The inequalities approach implicitly conceives of the social situation of the sexes as unequal, rather than basically different. Implicitly, MacKinnon argues, this approach assumes that the social meaning given to the gender difference has little or no biological foundation, nor is biology itself particularly relevant.

This perspective also goes beyond the problem of the 'stereotype'. MacKinnon argues that US sex discrimination law attacks instances where individual women are discriminated against because of the 'stereotypes' which pertain to all women. An inequalities approach would recognize that stereotypes may be true – in that, for instance, women are primary carers – but then looks deeper into the reasons behind the stereotype, such as the existence of cumulative disadvantage. Although, MacKinnon argues, no legal doctrine fully adopts the inequality approach, several are conducive to it, including the concept of 'disparate impact'.

Under an inequality approach, detrimental differentiations based on sex are discriminatory whether accurate or not. A rule or practice is discriminatory if it participates in the systemic social deprivation of one sex because of sex. The only question for litigation, then, is whether the policy or practice in question integrally contributes to the maintenance of an underclass or a deprived position because of sexual status – that is:

> ... being deprived because of being a woman or man, a deprivation given meaning in the social context of the dominance or preference of one sex over the other. (MacKinnon, 1979, p.117)

Courts could have particular difficulty with MacKinnon's inequality approach. She argues, it will be recalled, that courts should ask whether a policy or practice contributes to the maintenance of a deprived position on account of sex in the context of the domination of one sex over the other. Arguably, this way of putting the issues involved rests more easily with cases of sexual harassment than inequality in social security, since in the latter disadvantage is not obviously linked to 'domination' in the form of violent or conflictual personal contacts.

Deborah Rhode

Rhode (1989, pp.3–4; 1992, pp.155–7) argues that analysis of whether the sexes are similarly situated should turn on whether legal recognition of sex-based differences is more likely to decrease or reinforce sex-based disparities in political power, social status and economic security. The disadvantage framework would require policy-makers to look at the ends and means of government policies, demanding that they include a substantial commitment to gender equality. This framework also seems to ask courts to engage in the overt political balancing of interests.

In the employment sphere, for instance, the disadvantage framework would involve assessing whether the workplace can be restructured to make gender less relevant. What sort of public and private initiatives are necessary to avoid penalizing parenthood? What changes to working schedules, in hiring and promotion criteria, leave policies and childcare options are necessary to reconcile home and family responsibilities? A number of questions would need to be answered to sort out the competing concerns inherent in gender preference provisions. This strategy, argues Rhode, requires a deeper understanding of the harms of sex-based classifications and the complexity of strategies designed to deal with them. She contends that the disadvantage framework focuses on the right question: how best to achieve a society in which sexual identity does not correlate with social inequalities.

There are, of course, a number of problems with an approach to equality which is explicitly related to inequality and disadvantage. First, in terms of bringing lawsuits, these frameworks encounter the problem that outcomes would depend on how sympathetic the judges hearing the case would be, not only in accepting that particular gendered effects are in fact instances of 'disadvantage', but also in terms of their willingness to apply a conception of equality as disadvantage or inequality (Law, 1984, p.1005). There is always the possibility that courts would find justifications for the inequalities (O'Donovan and Szyszczak, 1988, p.9). In terms of social security, courts could easily contend that women 'choose' caring roles (and the financial consequences of this) without actually recognizing any of the factors which structure particular choices.[38]

Summary

Although an inequality or disadvantage approach may be too 'political' to be accepted by a judiciary who view themselves as neutral and non-interventionist (Williams, 1987, p.122), these frameworks do emphasize the right issue: explicitly tackling women's structural inequality.

Indirect discrimination in EC equality law

The ECJ does not refer to 'substantive equality' in its judgements,[39] but the prohibition on indirect discrimination in EC equality law has been seen as a potential vehicle to bring it about. The prohibition on indirect discrimination, or 'disparate impact' as it is called in US law, is sensitive to structural inequality in the sense that this concept allows us to ascertain whether there is discrimination, or unequal treatment, by reference to the impacts of rules or conditions on particular groups. In EC equality law, this concept has been particularly well developed in relation to challenging rules which disadvantage part-time workers (see *Bilka-Kaufhaus*[40] and *Rinner-Kühn*[41]).

Although indirect discrimination is sensitive to the impacts of rules, it may be wondered how far it can achieve or produce equality of outcomes, in the sense of modifying rules or structures which impede women's access to personal income. In Chapter 6 I examine how the prohibition on indirect discrimination in Directive 79/7/EEC has been applied. In this section I consider the relationship, if any, between a prohibition on indirect discrimination and the achievement of substantive equality.

Ballestero (1992a) has described the notion of indirect discrimination as the horizontal application of the notion of the process of *eguagliamento* – that is, equalization or the bringing about of equality of opportunity between men and women. Ballestrero (1992b, pp.779–80) argues that the concept of indirect discrimination strikes at the unjustified disparity which exists between the opportunities available for different social groups. The principle of equalization (*eguagliamento*), she continues, throws into relief the disparities in society experienced by particular social groups. Further, the concept of discrimination is enriched by being extended to include rules that are formally neutral, but from which unequal and prejudicial consequences flow.

Ballestrero praises the concept of indirect discrimination for being able to 'see' the negative impact of formally neutral rules on members of particular groups. She cites the example of the *Nimz* case,[42] in which a collective bargaining agreement treated part-time workers less favourably, in terms of building up seniority and promotion, than full-time workers. Ballestrero contends that, in this situation, the discrimination consisted in the refusal of the equal opportunity for promotion. Further, she argues that, in finding that this was discriminatory, the decision of the ECJ that the members of the disadvantaged group were entitled to be treated in the same way as the advantaged group (see Chapter 5) can only be seen as a positive form of equalization or the bringing about equality of opportunity (*eguagliamento*). But to what extent is indirect discrimination really an application of the principle of equality of opportunity? Ballestrero's enthusiasm for the potentially radical effect of the prohibition on indirect discrimination might be explained by the relative novelty of this concept in the Italian legal culture.[43]

From another perspective entirely, the prohibition on indirect discrimination is seen as primarily a way of ensuring a fair procedure or, in other words, a minimalist equality of opportunity.[44] In this sense the characteristics of a group are taken into account only in so far as necessary in order to allow the individual to compete unhampered by restrictions which effectively keep individuals within groups or which are irrelevant or detrimental to rational decision-making on merit (McCrudden, 1982). This idea of indirect discrimination does not necessarily assume that one particular pattern of the distribution of goods will result from these fair procedures (ibid.).

Returning to EC equality law, where it is found that a particular rule is indirectly discriminatory, what is the effect of this finding? It may mean that part-timers need to be treated on a *pro rata* basis similar to full-time workers, or it may mean that part-time workers must have the same rules applied to them as full-time workers in the calculation of social security benefits.[45] Yet the effects of a finding of indirect discrimination are limited to requiring 'sameness' for the previously disadvantaged group. While this can, of course, have a significant impact on outcomes for this group of workers, in the sense of increasing their access to personal benefits, a sameness approach still represents access to a pre-existing structure, whereas more fundamental changes are needed to bring about substantive equality. This is particularly true of the social security sphere, in view of the different qualitative and quantitative provision given to feminine risks, and the fact that caring does not normally earn entitlements to social insurance benefits.

This is illustrated nicely by the ECJ's decision in the case of *Bilka-Kaufhaus*. This case concerned rules excluding part-time workers from an occupational pension scheme, which the ECJ found were indirectly discriminatory on the grounds of sex. The referring court also asked the ECJ whether Article 119 obliges an employer to organize its occupational pension scheme so that it takes into account the fact that family responsibilities prevent women workers from fulfilling the requirements for such a pension. The applicant argued that the disadvantages suffered by women because of the exclusion of part-time workers from the occupational pension scheme must at least be mitigated by requiring the employer to regard periods during which women workers have had to meet family responsibilities as periods of full-time work.

The ECJ observed that Article 119 is limited to the issue of pay discrimination between men and women workers, and that problems related to other conditions of employment are covered by Articles 117 and 118 of the Treaty of Rome.[46] The imposition therefore of an obligation, such as that argued for by the applicant, goes beyond the scope of Article 119 and has no other basis in Community law as it stands.[47] Therefore Article 119 does not have the effect of requiring an employer to organize its occupational pension scheme so that meeting the conditions of entitlement to such a pension[48] takes into account the particular difficulties faced by persons with family responsibilities.

Clearly, the ECJ stopped well short of producing an 'inclusionary' effect for part-time workers.[49] This aspect of *Bilka-Kaufhaus*, argues Fredman (1992, p.126), shows that the prohibition on indirect discrimination has a limited redistributive effect. Although this decision achieves *pro rata* equality for part-time workers, it does not demand a resolution of the underlying structural problems which disadvantage women in the workplace, such as why women congregate in part-time work, nor does it demand different childcare responsibilities or better nursery provision (Fredman, 1992, p.126). Although Fredman's argument reveals a rather exaggerated perception of the potential of the law, she does accurately point out that indirect discrimination does not represent a 'positive action' type of measure aiming to equalize starting points between men and women. In social security terms, indirect discrimination does not equalize the possibilities of building up entitlements to personal benefits by allowing caring to become a contribution towards social insurance benefits.

In Chapter 1, I described briefly the arguments of Nancy Dowd (1989) as to the limitations of a discrimination analysis. She argues that even the 'disparate impact' analysis, which is similar to the concept of indirect discrimination in EC law, has a limited reach towards remedying structural discrimination. Dowd describes this thus: 'it is a bit like trying to stuff a brilliant, multi-colored, ungainly figure into a tidy, angular, small box' (1989, p.137). Essentially, the argument is that discrimination analysis cannot ask the 'big questions' about why structures are designed in particular ways. A major weakness, Dowd argues, is that inequalities do not arise from barriers in the structure but rather from inadequacies within that structure. In Dowd's words: 'the problem is not so much what is there as what is not there' (1989, p.139). There are, of course, barriers to part-timer workers' access into the social insurance system and, as we have seen, these may be attacked by the concept of indirect discrimination, but its efficacy stops short of countering the qualitative inferiority of provision for caring.

Another important factor which undermines indirect discrimination as an instrument for potentially radical change is the objective justification which, interestingly, is not even mentioned by Ballestrero in her discussion of the concept (1992a, 1992b). The author of the discriminatory rule may objectively justify the rule, and where this is done there is no illegality. But allowing the possibility of an objective justification means that other goals may take priority over the application of the principle of equality, even though this principle is held to be part of the fundamental principles of EC law.[50] The overriding of equality by other factors, such as the costs of implementing equal treatment, is particularly prevalent in relation to Directive 79/7/EEC (see Chapter 5).

Although the concept is sensitive to structural inequality, gendered factors may themselves constitute the objective justification. This necessarily limits the ability to change the gendered social reality. An example of this is instances where social security benefits are structured so that higher benefits are given to primary earners with dependants (that is, to men), and where this policy can be objectively justified on the grounds that a legitimate social policy consists of giving greater resources to persons with greater family responsibilites (that is, male breadwinners). This of course can be minimized by having a strict standard of review of the objective justification – an important legal battle in itself – but it still does not detract from the original argument that the objective justification limits the scope of change in the indirect discrimination concept.

To summarize, the prohibition on indirect discrimination principally enlarges the scope of what is considered to be unequal treatment by looking at the effects of sex-neutral rules and not just at sex-specific rules. It has been argued that this is, however, limited in its capacity to produce substantive social change, due to the objective justification – the fact that indirect discrimination does not require 'positive action' to equalize starting points – as well as the employment bias of EC equality law. Although the prohibition on indirect discrimination may allow challenges to rules which disadvantage women part-time workers in terms of access to social insurance benefits, wider issues, such as the qualitatively inferior provision given to feminine risks, cannot be tackled (see, further, Chapter 5). In the words of Sacha Prechal:

> ... the prohibition of indirect discrimination should be ... considered as a remedy to treat some of the symptoms [rather than] as an instrument getting to the root of the problem (Prechal, 1993, p.97).

Gender-sensitive rights

A substantive equality model has already been hinted at in this chapter – that of 'gender-sensitive' rights, which have been defined as sex-neutral rights which are not 'gender-blind'. Gender-sensitive rights would involve policies that are aimed at men and women but which favour a redistribution of resources towards women in order to ensure a greater equality in outcomes. An example would be the crediting of contributions to benefits for periods in care work. Such rights also aim to reduce the coupling of certain activities from their sexual reference. In the words of Joan Williams (1989b, p.802) gender-neutrality

> ... does not preclude helping women disadvantaged by their adherence to gender roles since such women can be protected in a sex-neutral fashion by protecting all people (regardless of biology) who are victimized by gender.

These policies must go hand-in-hand with an ends-oriented understanding of equality; otherwise, measures favouring women's gender role could be struck down as indirectly discriminating against men.

In this way, gender-sensitive rights have a number of important features. First, they are sex-neutral and so would not trap women into particular roles to the extent that women-specific benefits or advantages may do. Second, they are situated within an understanding of the current gendered social reality, and thus of inequality. There would always be the risk, however, that gender-sensitive rights could, in some instances, reinforce particular gender roles for women as a result of giving greater economic recognition to the work women currently do. Nevertheless, gender-sensitive rights combine the lessons to be learned from the failings of the sameness–difference model of equality and, while counteracting the inequalities facing women, they could also offer benefits to men in feminine social roles.

Although gender-sensitive rights are part of a substantive equality model, there remains at least one tension between the two. This centres around the question of changing gender roles. A model of substantive equality in the longest-term view would, I argue, aim to modify existing gender roles, so that men would take a greater role in caring. There are ways in which the social security system could encourage this, such as by means of sex-neutral rules which give clear incentives for men to carry out such work.[51] One method has been proposed by Ina Sjerps[52] who argues that the social insurance system should be redesigned so that a person may not gain full entitlements unless they have spent both periods in paid work and periods in caring work. In principle this proposal offers a number of positive characteristics from an equality of outcomes standpoint:

1 It profoundly challenges the status quo.
2 It includes women's gender roles within the structure of the social insurance system on a par with men's gender role.
3 It would enable many women to gain personal entitlements through the social insurance system.

However, given the context of the contemporary political world, the proposal does have a strongly Utopian aspect.[53]

On the other hand, the proposal of gender-sensitive rights takes as its priority the adequacy of benefits for women, in their existing social roles, with the aim that women should nevertheless not be trapped in these roles. This may or may not encourage some men into taking up caring work, but this would be a lesser priority than that of tackling the existing inequalities faced by many women. In this book, the choice has been made to concentrate on the latter goal, while recognizing that substantive equality could go much further.

CONCLUDING REMARKS

The discussion in this chapter has raised a number of important questions. First, can substantive equality be achieved by a sameness–difference model? I have shown that both a sameness and a difference approach have significant limitations. A sameness approach ignores the deeply unequal gendered social reality, and a difference approach may trap women further into their gender roles, without attacking the reasons for that disadvantage. A sameness–difference model, operating as a united entity, is also limited in that it does not challenge the existing gendered social reality, it merely replicates the status quo. In social security terms, what is not challenged is that (personal) entitlements to social security are linked to paid work. But why should caring penalize a person in terms of a lack of personal entitlements to benefits or in terms of qualitatively inferior provision?

Second, what goals would comprise substantive equality? It has been argued that the longest-term goal would be an 'inclusionary' model, which would involve redesigning social security systems so that women would no longer be denied qualitatively and quantitatively adequate social security provision because of their caring work. In the interim, however, substantive equality could be achieved by gender-sensitive rights, which are sex-neutral but constructed so as to advantage women. It has been argued that the advantages of these rights is that they do not trap women in their gender roles to the extent that women-specific rights might do. Further, gender-sensitive rights are grounded in a perspective encompassing the existing inequality and are explicitly aimed at having a significant impact on changing outcomes for women. At the policy level, there are a number of forms which gender-sensitive rights might take, such as credits for social insurance benefits for carers.

In the following two chapters I consider in detail Directive 79/7/EEC, picking up the themes of the sameness–difference model of the Directive, as well as the discussion on whether the prohibition on indirect discrimination has been a means of achieving substantive equality.

NOTES

1   This debate is particularly strong in the Netherlands.
2   See, in relation to the debates over equality and difference, and different feminist goals, as well as over equality rights: in the UK, Coyle (1980), Lacey (1987), Jarman (1991), Lewis and Davies (1991); in France, Savy (1990), Kaufmann (1991), Collin (1991), Baudoux and Zaidman (1992); in Italy, Ballestrero (1979, 1989, 1992a, 1992b), Gaeta and Zoppoli (1992), Gianformaggio (1992), Guastini (1992), Scarponi (1992); and in the Netherlands, Bussemaker (1991, 1993, 1994), Loenen (1992), Holtmaat (1993a).
3   In relation to 'special rights' see Krieger and Cooney (1983), Wolgast's (1980) 'bivalent' view, and Scales' (1980) 'incorporationist' model. For a critique of Wolgast and Scales, see Kingdom (1989, pp.31–3).
4   This draws on, and adapts, Catharine MacKinnon's insights into discrimination law.
5   *Drake* v. *Chief Adjudication Officer*, Case 150/85 [1986] ECR 1995. This case is discussed in greater detail in Chapter 4.
6   Majury (1987 p.180) is more pragmatic, arguing that it is inevitable 'in an unequal society, [that] equality will always be a double-edged instrument'. If indeed formal equality is the only form of equality to which one has recourse this is certainly likely to be the case.
7   Case C-345/89 [1991] ECR I-4047.
8   At para. 15 of the judgement.
9   Case C-158/91 [1993] ECR I-4287.
10 Austria has, however, softened the blow by introducing measures to improve women's position in employment and to ease the reconciliation of paid work and family responsibilities, see *European Industrial Relations Review*, (239), December 1993, pp.25–7.

11   Intervention by a representative of the Belgian Ministère de la Prévoyance Sociale at the conference 'Equality of Treatment between Women and Men in Social Security', Lincoln College, Oxford, 4–6 January 1994. The representative, Mme Clotuche, said that only 14 per cent of women have a full pensions record as opposed to 60 per cent of men, and that on average women have 16 years of paid contributions over their working lives.

12   *Barber* v. *Guardian Royal Exchange*, Case C-262/88 [1990] ECR I-1889.

13   *Smith and others* v. *Avdel Systems*, Joined Cases C-420/93 and C-28/93 [1994] ECR I-367 (see, in greater detail, Chapter 5).

14   A number of cases have been referred to the ECJ relating to this issue in the recent past, and on 7 March 1994 the European Commission announced that it is bringing infringement proceedings against France, Italy, Belgium, Greece and Portugal regarding their legislation.

15   This statement was made by a representative of the German government at the conference 'Equality of Treatment between Women and Men in Social Security', Lincoln College, Oxford, 4–6 January 1994.

16   *Hofmann* v. *Barmer Ersatzkasse*, Case 184/83 [1984] ECR 3047.

17   Case 224/84 [1986] ECR 1651.

18   Case 312/86 [1988] ECR 6315. See also *Integrity* in which a man challenged a rule which allowed married women with very low earnings from self-employment to be exempted from social insurance contributions (see, further, Chapter 5).

19   At para. 24 of the judgement.

20   At para. 25 of the judgement.

21   At para. 26 of the judgement. In an earlier and similar case (*Commission* v. *Italy*, Case 163/82 [1983] ECR 3278), regarding maternal leave on the arrival in a family of an adopted child, the ECJ held that it was not contrary to EC law that this leave was not also given to adoptive fathers. In Germany, after the *Hofmann* decision, the (maternal) leave payment was made available to men (Docksey, 1991, p.272). In December 1991, a *pretore* (judge at first instance) in Turin, Italy decided that a clause in a collective agreement which compensated only women workers for certain child-related expenses, such as costs of nursery care, should be extended to men (see Ballestrero, 1992b, p.775, note 5).

22   At para. 37 of the judgement.

23   Report of the Hearing [1988] ECR 6315, at p.6322.

24   [1988] ECR 6315, at p.6328. Article 2(3) provides that Directive 76/207/EEC shall be without prejudice to provisions concerning the protection of women, particularly as regards pregnancy and maternity.

25   Similar arguments as to the necessity of allowing role reversal were used by Advocate General Jacobs in *Integrity*, (Case C-373/89 [1991] ECR I-4243) (see Chapter 5).

26   [1988] ECR 6315, at pp.6328–9.

27   [1988] ECR 6315, at pp.6329.

28   At para. 14 of the judgement.

29   At para. 14 of the judgement.

30   At para. 15 of the judgement.

31   The ECJ would not, however, accept the arguments for protecting women against nightwork, in part because of women's greater risk of assault at night (see *Stoeckel*). Nor would the Court allow specific advantages for women in employment which were not strictly related to women's biological role of childbearing or related to protecting the 'special relationship' between a woman and her child (see *Commission* v. *France*).

32   The UK case of *Turley* v. *Allders Department Stores Ltd*, ([1980] ICR 66), is an

excellent example of this. The Employment Appeal Tribunal stated that 'you must compare like with like, and you cannot. When she is pregnant a woman is no longer just a woman, she is a woman ... with child, and there is no masculine equivalent'.

33   Case C-177/88 [1990] ECR I-3941, at para. 12 of the judgement. But see also the case of Mrs Hertz, *Handels-og Kontorfunktionaerenes Forbund i Danmark* v. *Dansk Arbejdsgiverforeniging* (Case C-179/88 [1990] ECR I-3979).

34   For a critique of the market–family dichotomy in both EC equality law and EC law relating to discrimination on the grounds of nationality, see Scheiwe (1994).

35   I believe this tension is particularly well illustrated by the *Integrity* case (see Chapter 5).

36   This has been a key insight of a number of feminists in relation to the so-called equal treatment versus special treatment debate. See, in particular, Bacchi (1990; 1991a) and Scott (1988).

37   In the original:

> ... significa chiedere non solo di essere accettati alla tavola da gioca quando il gioco – vale a dire le sue regole – già esiste, cioè quando ... i giochi sono già fatti ... ma significa chiedere sopratutto (ed in casi estremi soltanto) di essere ammessi alla tavola delle trattative per la fissazione delle regole del gioco. (Gianformaggio, 1992, p.198)

38   The remarks by the ECJ in *Bird Eye Walls* v. *Roberts* (Case C-132/92, [1993] ECR I-5579) in this regard were worrying. In relation to married women's poorer access to pensions in their own right, as a result of exercising the married women's option (see Chapter 2), the ECJ said that the option of paying lesser contributions for their state pension comes within the free choice of married women, who gained a certain financial advantage from it (at para. 27 of the judgement).

39   Unusually, in the case of *Habermann-Beltermann* v. *Arbeitwohlfahrt, Bezirsverband Ndb./Opf e. V.* (Case C-421/92), Advocate General Tesauro argued that, in relation to differences in treatment based on pregnancy, 'substantive equality between men and women in employment requires that an event which, by definition, only occurs to women should not be taken into consideration even as regards the moment of entry into employment' (at para. 11 of the Opinion).

40   *Bilka-Kaufhaus* v. *Weber von Hartz*, Case 170/84 [1986] ECR 1607.

41   *Rinner-Kühn* v. *FWW Spezial Gebaüdereinigung*, Case 171/88 [1989] ECR 2743.

42   *Nimz* v. *Freie und Hansestadt Hamburg*, Case C-184/89 [1991] ECR I-297.

43   I am grateful to Claire Kilpatrick for this point. Although this concept was included in the equal treatment law of the late 1970s, it was never invoked (legge no. 903/77). In a recent law on positive action (legge no. 125/91), indirect discrimination has been given greater prominence.

44   McCrudden (1982) argues that this conception underpinned the new concept of indirect discrimination in the Race Relations Act 1976.

45   As in the case of *Ruzius-Wilbrink* v. *Bestuur van de Bedrijsvereniging voor Overheidsdiensten* (Case C-102/88 [1989] ECR I-4311) – see Chapter 5.

46   At para. 41 of the judgement.

47   At para. 42 of the judgement.

48   At para. 43 of the judgement.

49   This refers back to Carol Bacchi's inclusion model above.

50   See *Defrenne (No 3)* v. *SABENA*, Case 149/77, [1978] ECR 1365.

51   This idea is drawn from Kaufmann's discussion of the different types of parental leave

(1991, pp.124–5). She has identified three types; first, the individualist type of parental leave, where the mother is given protection and the couple decides what the father's co-responsibility will be, although he is unable to receive any help from the state. The second type, the liberal type, gives fathers the opportunity to take leave and be given benefits if they do, but it is up to the parents how they share the leave or whether one parent takes it all. Thirdly, the radical type encourages real changes in behaviour, by specifying that parental leave must be shared between the parents for them to benefit fully from it, so that if one parent chooses not to use their leave it is lost.

52   Intervention during the conference 'Equality of Treatment between Women and Men in Social Security', Lincoln College, Oxford, 4–6 January 1994.

53   A social insurance system such as the one proposed by Ina Sjerps would disadvantage persons who do not have children or other dependants to care for. It may be speculated that many such persons – certainly two-earner couples without children – would nevertheless have access to other forms of income security, such as occupational provision.

4   Directive 79/7/EEC: Risks and Benefits

Can Directive 79/7/EEC make a significant impact on the structural inequality facing women in their access to independent income? When the Directive was passed at the end of the 1970s, the construction of the 'problem' to be dealt with was of the reality of the greater numbers of (married) women entering the labour market, who were still subject to grave forms of discrimination in terms of access to social security benefits. The rationale of the Directive was that women were not to be discriminated against if they were workers. The challenge of modifying the structural inequalities of the 1990s, of which I have traced a modern map in Chapter 2, is rather different from the challenges of 20 years ago. Many rules in social security are now sex-neutral in terms of their wording. Moreover, the contemporary 'problem', in my opinion, is inequality in access to independent income. Is the Directive able to tackle these problems? How does the Directive react to the climate of the 1990s?

The key issues to be considered in this chapter are the Directive's personal and material scope, and the implications of the Directive's narrow coverage on altering women's lack of access to independent income. I also consider the issue of remedies in addition to that of invoking the Directive. In Chapter 5 I analyse the principle of direct and indirect discrimination contained in the Directive. The discussion in this chapter begins with a brief history of the passing of the Directive.

OUTLINE OF THE PROVISIONS OF DIRECTIVE 79/7/EEC

Article 4(1) of Directive 79/7/EEC provides that there shall be no 'discrimination on the grounds of sex either directly or indirectly by reference in particular to marital or family status'.

The Directive applies to persons in the working population (including self-employed persons) whose work is interrupted by illness, accident or involuntary unemployment, as well as to persons seeking employment and to retired persons (Article 2).

The material scope of the Directive is set out in Article 3. Article 3(1)(a) provides that the Directive covers:

> ... statutory schemes that provide protection against sickness, invalidity, old age, accidents at work and occupational diseases, and unemployment.

In addition, Article 3(1)(b) states that the Directive covers 'social assistance in so far as it is intended to supplement or replace the schemes referred to in (a)' above.

Article 3(2) of the Directive specifies that the equality principle does not apply to survivor's benefits or family benefits, unless family benefits are given to supplement benefits accorded for risks in Article 3(1).

There are a number of exemptions to, or derogations from, the principle of equal treatment. These are contained in Article 7(1), and, in brief, cover the fixing of pensionable ages, certain derived rights and additions for dependent spouses with certain long-term benefits.

HISTORY OF THE DIRECTIVE

The European Community's equality of opportunity policies for women can be likened to a rare bird in a zoo largely populated with economic creatures. Economic policies have undoubtedly predominated over social policies in the EC. Many of the EC's social policies have a definite economic tinge – that is, the perceived need for social policy has largely stemmed from the smooth running of economic objectives. The policies on equality of opportunity have, in some measure, been the exception, and the ECJ has undoubtedly played a key role in developing not only an impressive body of sex equality law, but in elevating this area of law to one of the more influential parts of EC law generally.

In the early years of the Community there was little or no action on the issue of equality. Active EC intervention in the field of equality between men and women can be traced back to the 1970s.[1] The early part of this decade witnessed the first of the path-breaking *Defrenne* cases. In *Defrenne (No 2)*[2] the ECJ held that the social objectives of Article 119 are as important as the economic, and that the right to equal pay could be invoked by individuals in national courts. In 1974 a Social Action Programme was drawn up, which included the objective of bringing about equality between women and men in the labour market. Many of the Social Action Programme's proposals were in fact set aside in the wake of the first oil crisis in

1973, but a number of important Directives were adopted: Directive 75/117/ EEC on equal pay,[3] Directive 76/207/EEC on working conditions and access to employment;[4] and Directive 79/7/EEC on equal treatment in state social security schemes.[5]

These equal treatment Directives are undoubtedly rooted within an economic framework (O'Donovan and Szyszczak, 1988, p.196). As a body they relate to inequalities in the public sphere of the workplace, or arising from work-related social security risks, and do not extend into the private sphere of the household and unpaid caring work. Despite this, the Directives have certainly had not only an important symbolic value, but have also been a valuable lever pressing for change in the legal systems of the Member States.

A memorandum which accompanied the draft Directive argued that 'socio-economic realities' no longer justified social security systems being oriented exclusively towards the man as the breadwinner and head of household (Hoskyns and Luckhaus, 1989, p.322). These 'realities' were the greater numbers of married women who were entering the labour market and suffering from many forms of overt discrimination (ibid.). Moreover, there was a belief that married women should be treated on a par with married men in relation to social rights (see Laurent, 1979, p.245).

In preparing the draft for a Social Security Directive, the principle of the individualization of benefits was immediately rejected as being too expensive (ibid., p.323). The equal treatment principle in the Directive was made to cover employment-related social security risks and workers. A number of areas of social security, in which women gained derived rights because of their unpaid caring and domestic work, were kept outside the scope of the equality principle. It was presumably felt that requiring equality of treatment here might lead to hardship for many women if benefits were taken away (see Watson, 1980, p.48). In any case, this Directive was seen as only the first step in a process of 'progressive implementation', and benefits such as survivor's benefits were intended to be included in subsequent legislation (Hoskyns and Luckhaus, 1989, p.323).

In its final form the Directive has been aptly described as 'an ambiguous instrument, full of important exceptions' (Prechal and Burrows, 1990, p.166). In fact, by the time the Directive was passed, albeit in a delayed and watered-down form, much of the willingness in the Council of Ministers to pass social policy legislation had faded. Directive 79/7/EEC in fact represents the last of the 'strong' Directives, adopted when there was still some push behind the early 1970s idea of the Community extending its competence into the social field (Hoskyns and Luckhaus, 1989, p.321).

ARTICLE 2: ONLY WORKERS CAN CLAIM EQUAL TREATMENT

The personal scope of the Directive is defined as:

> ... the working population – including self-employed persons, workers and self-employed persons whose activity is interrupted by illness, accident or involuntary unemployment and persons seeking employment – and to retired or invalided workers and self-employed persons.

The narrowing of the personal scope in the equality Directives to those persons in paid work stemmed from the belief that EC competence did not extend beyond the employment sphere (More, 1993, p.56). The exclusive focus on paid workers means, however, that caring work remains outside the privileged arena of access to the equality principle. As will be recalled, women's position in the social security system is profoundly affected by the lack of value accorded to their unpaid caring work, and manifests itself partly in fewer personal rights to social insurance benefits. Extending the principle of equal treatment only to workers misses out this crucial dimension of women's unequal relationship to the benefit system. In so far as it does this, the Directive reinforces the already existing privileged dichotomy between worker and non-worker, paid and unpaid work, in which the former has greater access to personal social security rights and independent income.

ECJ case law has narrowed the scope of Article 2 even further. In *Drake*[6] the Court had to decide whether Mrs Drake, who had given up her employment to care for her disabled mother, should be entitled to the invalid care allowance (ICA). The ICA, given to carers, specifically excluded married and cohabiting women from receipt of the benefit. With regard to the question of who is a worker, Mrs Drake proposed, in argument before the ECJ, a very wide definition of the 'working population'. This would include any individual who has worked, who wishes to return to work, who is of working age, or a person who is temporarily unable to work because of some particular risk covered by the social security system.

The ECJ did not adopt this definition and, in considering the meaning of 'working population', it applied Article 2 in conjunction with Article 3(1) and stated that:

> ... a person whose work has been interrupted by one of the risks referred to in Article 3 belongs to the working population.[7]

In deciding that the invalid care allowance formed part of the statutory scheme for the risk of invalidity, the ECJ found that Mrs Drake's employment was interrupted by a risk in Article 3(1). Arguably, the wording of Article 2 does not require a 'worker' to be tied in to exit from the labour market by reason of one of the risks mentioned in Article 3(1). The ECJ's decision has therefore contributed to the further narrowing of the Directive's personal scope.

The limiting of the personal scope to exit from paid work because of the 'classic' masculine risks covered by the social insurance system has significant implications for women. A reason for labour market exit not mentioned in Article 3(1), which affects considerably more women than men, is exit from paid work in order to care for children. The Directive therefore is structurally unable to offer equality of treatment to persons, mainly women, whose entry into, and exit from, the labour market is affected by a range of childcare commitments.

This further narrowing of the personal scope was confirmed by the ECJ in *Achterberg*.[8] In this case the ECJ unequivocally stated that the Directive does not apply to persons who have never been available for employment or who have ceased to be available for a reason other than the materialization of one of the risks in Article 3(1).[9] The ECJ went further and found that the Directive only covers persons who are working at the time when they become entitled to claim an old age pension or whose employment was previously interrupted by one of the risks in Article 3(1).[10]

This interpretation of Article 2, according to the Court, is in conformity with the objectives of EC law, as seen in Article 119 and the other equal treatment Directives. The Court concluded that these legal instruments implement equal treatment between men and women only in their capacity as workers rather than in a general sense.[11] This echoes a statement in *Hofmann*,[12] in which the ECJ observed that Directive 76/207/EEC is not designed to alter the division of responsibility between parents. This reasoning introduces a market–family dichotomy (or paid work–unpaid work dichotomy), which we have already criticized for ignoring the role played by the interrelationship between these two spheres in structuring women's relationship to the social security system. The Court's reasoning is, however, consistent with the original aim of the Directive, which was concerned with only according married women in employment the same social security treatment as men (Hoskyns and Luckhaus, 1989, p.333).

In *Johnson (No 1)* the ECJ brought into prominence a small part of Article 2, taking an opportunity to deliver a less restrictive ruling on this article than its decision in *Achterberg*. In this case the applicant had left her job to care for her daughter and was prevented from re-entering the labour market by a physical incapacity. The ECJ stated that, although a person who has given up work in order to attend to the upbringing of her or his children does not fall within Article 2, this person may still be regarded as falling within the scope of the Directive as a person seeking employment whose search is made impossible by the materialization of one of the risks specified in Article 3(1).[13] In such circumstances it is for the national court to determine if the person was seeking employment, taking account of a number of factors, such as whether she or he was registered with an organization dealing with offers of employment or helping people to find work, whether she or he has sent job applications to employers and whether certificates were available from firms stating that the person concerned had attended interviews.[14]

Although the *Johnson (No 1)* decision does represent some slackening of the tight reins of *Achterberg*, as noted in Chapter 2, tests of availability for work are not necessarily themselves gender-neutral. Many women with children find it harder to satisfy these tests because they, and not men in a similar situation, are subjected to questions as to their childcare arrangements, or they are made to sign declarations relating to childcare (Scheiwe, 1994, p.259).[15] Moreover, national rules as to proof of seeking employment may require that claimants are available for full-time employment, and this may not correspond to many women's circumstances or realistic options.

There are a number of ways in which the notion of who comes within the 'working population' could be expanded by a more generous interpretation of Article 2 (accepting that, to some degree, there will be a dichotomy between paid and unpaid work in the Directive). Until now the ECJ has shown no inclination to expand its interpretation of the personal scope, and therefore Article 2 continues to represent a major hurdle to invoking the Directive – one which is manifestly higher for women to clear. I now consider, in turn, three possible avenues for a more expansive interpretation of Article 2, each of which would represent at least a partial improvement for women.

First, the ECJ could adopt the wide definition of 'working population' offered by Mrs Drake. Women's employment, and employment expectations, in most Member States have changed markedly in the last 50 years. It is now more common, especially among younger women, to work after leaving school and to expect to be in paid employment for significant periods over a lifetime. A definition of 'working population' which encompassed any individual who has worked, who wished to work, or who is of working age, would fit closely with the current sociological reality in a number of EC countries. If this were accepted, most women could be deemed to be in the working population. This notion of 'worker' would also uncouple the link between being in paid work and leaving a job by reason of one of the risks in Article 3(1).

A second option would be for the ECJ to find that employment interruptions for childcare should not be considered, within certain limits, to constitute a 'dropping out' of the working population. National laws – for instance, in Germany – provide that the employment relationship does not cease during periods of parental leave, which can last up to three years. Scheiwe (1994, p.260) suggests therefore that, during a period until at least three years after the birth of the youngest child, a female employee who leaves paid work for reasons of childcare should still be considered a part of the working population in terms of Article 2 of the Directive.

The third, and perhaps most radical, argument that could be put to the ECJ, is that where a woman has to interrupt employment for reasons of care, this may be considered 'involuntary unemployment' within Article 2 (ibid.). This is because, argues Scheiwe (1994, p.260), the time organization of employment, combined with the lack of childcare facilities, infrastructures and public assistance to bring up children, effectively limit parents' choices and may force mothers to temporarily give up work.

Adopting one or more of these options would bring significantly greater numbers of women within the personal scope of the Directive. This would go, it is argued, at least some way towards softening the blow inflicted on persons seeking to invoke the Directive by the link between equality and paid work.

ARTICLES 3 AND 7: RISKS AND BENEFITS

The material scope of the Directive is one of the more substantial (and political) aspects of the Directive, and has been very much under the spotlight during the last few years. The provisions of the Directive defining the material scope (as well as many of the ECJ's decisions) raise important questions, such as the extent to which there is a sameness–difference model of equality in the Directive, as well as whether women can use the Directive to challenge rules in benefit schemes which offer them qualitatively inferior provision. The ECJ's interpretation in recent cases raises questions as to this Court's commitment to equality in substance as opposed to equality in form. For instance, a key theme underpinning many of the decisions is the imperative not to upset the financial equilibrium of social security systems.[16]

In this section, I will first consider the question of which risks are within the scope of the equality principle, before looking at the type of social security schemes which are covered by the Directive. An issue of general interest, which is not discussed in this book, is that of the meaning of 'statutory social security scheme' within the Directive.[17] In the final part of this section, I consider the scope of the derogations in Article 7(1) of the Directive.

Equality and feminine and masculine risks

The risks covered by Article 3(1)(a) of the Directive are those which are traditionally associated with work in the labour market; thus, in this sphere, women can claim equality of treatment with men. The need for income maintenance in situations which relate to women's social role as carers is not included within the risks covered by the Directive. Maternity is specifically excluded from the principle of equal treatment (Article 4(2)), as indeed are family benefits and survivor's benefits (Article 3(2)). The Directive therefore only offers equality of treatment in relation to the classic 'masculine' social security risks, linked to the 'standard employment relationship'. Feminine risks, such as childcare or the care of the elderly and sick, remain outside its scope.[18] The derogations in Article 7(1) represent a sort of half-way position: they are exempted from the equal treatment principle with the caveat that Member States review the derogations (see Article 7(2)). Why was this sameness–difference model adopted? What implications does this choice of equality model have for producing equality of outcomes?

There are a number of reasons which could explain why benefits for women's social role (or feminine risks) were not included within the equality principle or, to put it another way, why women may be treated differently in situations in which they are deemed to be dissimilar to men. I will mention a number of the possible reasons below.

The Commission memorandum to the original proposal for the Directive explained that survivor's benefits, maternity protection and family benefits were not to be covered by the Directive because the first two are specific to women and because family benefits are related more to family policy than to working conditions (Hoskyns and Luckhaus, 1989 p.323). The intention may have been to remove differences in treatment which harmed women, but not those which were seen as advantaging women (such as a lower pensionable age than men). Atkins and Luckhaus (1987, p.106) have suggested that the derogations in Article 7(1), such as the differences in pensionable age, can be seen as a partial recognition of the value and importance of the unpaid domestic work generally performed by women. Another reason may have been that the drafters of the Directive were worried that extending the equality principle to benefits or advantages for feminine risks (such as where derived benefits are paid) would lead to their withdrawal and therefore a penalization of many women (Watson, 1980, p.48).

This leads to the second question posed – that of the implications of this choice of equality model on producing equality of outcomes. To recap, the sameness–difference model allows women to have the same benefits as men when they are the same situation as men (that is, in paid work), while allowing women to be treated differently from men in relation to benefits given to carers and dependants.

Opening access to masculine risks is beneficial for women with particular employment patterns who are already suffering labour-market related risks – or as Rubenstein (1990, p.89) calls them, 'exceptional women'. Most women are not, however, similarly situated to men in relation to employment, and nor therefore in relation to social insurance.[19] Allowing different treatment between men and women to remain in benefits relating to women's social role may reinforce traditional gender roles where benefits for that social role are qualitatively inferior. Where negative financial consequences accrue – where, for instance, women are unable to claim dependant's additions for their husbands, or where men are unable to gain access to derived rights or advantages given in recognition of unpaid work, such as bringing up children – it is unlikely that the traditional gender division of labour will change and that women will be able to secure more equal access to independent income. Yet the derogations in Article 7(1) also provide women with compensation for the unpaid caring work they do, in the form of benefits or less onerous entitlement conditions (such as the lower pensionable age). However, overall, I would observe that allowing different treatment between men and women in these areas does little to challenge those elements of the social security system which reflect and reinforce women's role as dependants.

The sameness–difference model of equality cannot therefore contribute to imaginative recastings of the (gendered) social reality in ways which would substantially modify outcomes for women. It allows the model of personal entitlements and social insurance rights for paid workers to remain the standard of reference, and cannot tackle a situation in which benefits for women's social role are qualitatively inferior.

Benefit schemes: direct and effective links to risks

Broadly speaking, women find it much more difficult than men to establish personal entitlements to social insurance and are underrepresented as claimants of benefits providing against the risks listed in Article 3(1)(a). Yet, given that the Directive includes the 'classic' social insurance risks within its scope, women workers have not encountered difficulties in successfully challenging rules in social insurance benefits providing against paid work-related risks. Successful actions have been brought against rules in unemployment benefits,[20] invalidity benefits,[21] and old age pensions.[22] Claimants have also, it should be noted, successfully challenged discriminatory rules contained in non-contributory benefits for carers,[23] and non-contributory benefits for invalidity.[24] The latter was possible, as will be seen below, because the ECJ adopted a broad and purposive approach in determining the construction of protection for a given risk within the UK social security system in one early case.

In relation to social assistance schemes, the Directive provides in Article 3(1)(b) that these will be covered by the equality principle where these schemes are intended to replace or supplement statutory schemes in protecting against the employment-related risks in Article 3(1)(a). In a number of countries, such as the UK, the principal social assistance schemes are designed as general schemes which provide benefits to persons with no other income, regardless of the cause of their poverty. The ECJ has decided that such general schemes cannot come within the material scope of the Directive. Before considering the Court's reasoning, it is worth commenting on the significance of these decisions for women's access to independent income.

First, women are more likely than men to be forced to claim general social assistance (or means-tested) benefits as they often will not have satisfied the earnings-related conditions to enter the social insurance system (although the UK may increasingly be an exception to this rule, especially in relation to the unemployed, in that contributory benefits have been, and continue to be, significantly eroded).

Second, women encounter a number of rules in social assistance benefits that lessen their chances of, or deprive them of the chance of, gaining income not mediated through a male partner. This may be due to joint assessment of resources (the aggregation rule), or because rules of entitlement and receipt restrict the labour market participation of either a claimant or of his or her partner. Under the ECJ's present jurisprudence none of these rules could be challenged using the Directive.

Third, the means-tested net is spreading in a number of Member States. Not only has there been an increase in the absolute numbers of persons dependent on these benefits, but there has also been an emergence of new 'client groups' who have exhausted, or never built up, entitlements to contributory benefits (see Room *et al.*, 1989; Oorschot and Schell, 1991). In the UK, for instance, official policy is to 'target' social security to the most needy, by means of extending means-tested benefits and eroding the contributory benefit system. The net result is that greater numbers of persons suffering employment-related social security risks are also having to look to social assistance benefits to provide them with social protection. For women this can mean that, even having paid their contributions, they have few chances of gaining personal entitlements to benefits as provision becomes extensively means-tested. I now turn to the ECJ's interpretation of the material scope of the Directive in relation to means-tested benefits.

A 'broad' approach to the construction of Article 3(1): the Drake *case*

In the initial drafts of the proposal for Directive 79/7/EEC, the Commission apparently intended to give Article 3(1) the widest possible coverage of schemes. The memorandum to the original draft of the Directive explained that a broad coverage was necessary because of the very different ways in which the same contingencies were covered across the Member States: by contributory, non-contributory or means-tested provision, or indeed by a combination of these (Hoskyns and Luckhaus, 1989, p.323).

In the *Drake* case the ECJ showed that it clearly understood the necessity for such a broad approach. As will be recalled, Mrs Drake gave up her employment to look after her severely disabled mother, and sought to claim invalid care allowance (ICA) which, at the time, was denied to married or cohabiting women. Severely disabled persons in the UK could be given an attendance allowance (AA) payable directly to them and, under certain conditions, persons 'regularly and substantially involved in caring' for them could receive the ICA. Mrs Drake had given up employment because of one of the risks in Article 3(1), but the Adjudication Officer argued that this had to be a risk which directly affected her. The Court ignored the Adjudication Officer's submissions that the two benefits, AA and ICA, were separate and that ICA was a benefit for caring and therefore not linked to the scheme for invalidity (Luckhaus, 1986b, pp.531–2).

In its judgement the Court observed that Member States provide protection against the consequences of invalidity in various ways. In order to ensure the progressive implementation of Article 4(1) in a 'harmonious manner' throughout the Community, it stated that:

> Article 3(1) must be interpreted as including any benefit which *in a broad sense* forms part of one of the statutory schemes referred to or a social assistance provision intended to supplement or replace such a scheme. (emphasis added)[25]

The Court went on to add that the fact that the benefit is paid to a third party does not place it outside the scope of the Directive, otherwise 'it would be possible by making formal changes to existing benefits covered by the Directive, to remove them from its scope'.[26] This decision therefore allowed some expansion of Article 3(1), since it meant that a person could be covered by the Directive even for a risk that does not affect them directly. However, the basis of that expansion was the rather tenuous one of a judicial willingness to construe the purpose of benefits and social security schemes in a broad way. The dangers inherent in relying on this have become apparent in two important cases decided in 1992.

Are general social assistance benefits covered by the Directive?

The approach to construing Article 3(1) in *Drake* was rejected in two decisions of 1992: *Smithson*[27] and *Jackson and Cresswell.*[28] The ECJ gave a very narrow interpretation of Article 3(1), preferring to look to the form of benefit provision over the substance of risk protection. In so doing, the Court has opened the way for Member States to make formal changes to limit the scope of Directive 79/7/EEC in their national systems (Luckhaus, 1992b, p.322; Hervey, 1992, p.465).

In the first case, Mrs Smithson challenged her denial of a 'higher pensioner premium' in the calculation of her housing benefit (HB), a means-tested benefit given to help those on low income with their housing costs. The ECJ had to consider whether housing benefit could fall within Article 3(1). It was argued for the applicant that HB, or at least the premium, came within Article 3(1) since, in practice, this provides protection against the risks listed in that Article.

Advocate General Tesauro essentially agreed with Mrs Smithson. Drawing on the approach taken by the ECJ in *Drake*, he argued that any other approach would enable Member States to avoid the application of Directive 79/7/EEC to a benefit which covered one of the risks in that Article simply by including it within a scheme of general scope.[29] He concluded, therefore, that a benefit such as the premium was a form of social assistance under Article 3(1)(b).[30]

The ECJ, in a short judgement, came to the opposite conclusion. It quoted *Drake* to the extent of saying that while the mode of payment of a benefit is not decisive, a benefit must be directly and effectively linked to the protection of one of the risks specified in Article 3(1).[31] It stated quite tersely that Article 3(1)(a) does not refer to statutory schemes which are intended to guarantee a social security benefit to any person whose real income is below a notional amount.[32] As to the premium, it observed that age and invalidity are only two criteria taken into consideration and, because they are not decisive as to eligibility, they are not sufficient to come within Article 3(1)(a).[33] Nor could the premium, the Court continued, be characterized as separate from the benefit and thus as an autonomous scheme.[34]

The ECJ chose to ignore the role that housing benefit plays in practice in providing for persons suffering the risks set out in Article 3(1)(a). Further, the Court unaccountably failed to consider whether housing benefit or the premium could fall within Article 3(1)(b), even though this point was explicitly referred to by Advocate General Tesauro. It is certainly arguable that housing benefit could be described as a supplement to statutory schemes. Hervey (1992, p.465) has described this decision as placing a 'question mark' over the ECJ's commitment to equality in this area.

This question mark can only have been reinforced by *Jackson and Cresswell*, decided in July 1992. Here the benefits, supplementary benefit (SB) and its successor income support (IS), are both means-tested. The applicants were essentially challenging rules creating disincentives to work for lone parents on means-tested benefits or training allowances. The rules did not allow them to deduct childcare costs from their earnings before these earnings were taken into account to reduce the level of their benefits. The applicants argued that these rules were indirectly discriminatory against women. Before turning to this issue, however, the ECJ had to decide whether or not SB and IS fell within Article 3(1).

The applicants also invoked the 'broad' approach used by the ECJ in *Drake*, arguing that SB and IS do in fact play a significant role in providing against the risks set out in Article 3(1), especially the risk of unemployment. This meant, they argued, that maintaining a rigid distinction between contributory and means-tested benefits is increasingly artificial. The European Commission argued that, for the Directive to apply, it is sufficient that the benefit schemes do, as a matter of fact, cover one of the risks listed in Article 3(1). The UK government, on the contrary, contended that even if SB and IS had to be regarded as social assistance schemes, they nevertheless fell outside the scope of the Directive because they were not intended to replace or supplement any of the schemes in Article 3(1)(a).

Advocate General Van Gerven identified the main issue as being whether:

> ... in order to fall within Directive 79/7/EEC, a scheme must be intended by the legislature to constitute protection against risks listed in Article 3(1)(a) or whether it is sufficient that it does in fact afford protection against such risks.[35]

He argued that it was appropriate not only to have regard to the explicit or implicit intentions of the legislature, but also to consider the effect of the scheme and the actual protection provided in the context of the Member State's social protection as a whole.[36] This would not depend on the actual situation of the applicants, who here were lone parents, but on the relevant national scheme. An exclusive link between benefits and a scheme would not be required by EC law, he observed, although it would be an important factor.[37] The Advocate General gave short shrift to the UK's submission that SB and IS were intended to provide against poverty and not against the risks listed in Article 3(1). AG Van Gerven simply, but effectively, noted that:

> ... protection against the risks specified ... ultimately boils down to protection against loss of income or poverty resulting from the occurrence of one of those risks.[38]

Again, the ECJ chose to ignore the realities of benefit provision. Referring to *Drake* and *Smithson* the Court briefly stated that, to come within Article 3(1), a benefit must constitute the whole or part of a statutory scheme providing protection against one of the specified risks.[39] It went on to say that, although the mode of payment is not decisive, nevertheless the benefit must be directly and effectively linked to the protection provided against one of the risks in that Article.[40] The Court repeated that Article 3(1)(a) does not refer to a statutory scheme which, under certain conditions, provides a person whose resources are below a legally defined limit with a benefit to enable them to meet their needs.[41] This finding was not affected, it continued, by the fact that the recipient of the benefit was actually in one of the situations covered by the Directive.[42] Indeed, the fact that some of the risks listed in Article 3(1) were taken into account in order to grant a higher benefit (a premium) was not sufficient to bring it within the scope of the Directive.[43]

In consequence, the Court said, exclusion from Directive 79/7/EEC is justified *a fortiori* where, as in this case, the law sets the amount of the theoretical needs of the persons concerned, which is used to determine the benefit in question, independently of any consideration relating to the existence of any of the risks listed in Article 3(1).[44] Moreover, because in certain situations, as in the case of lone parents, SB or IS exempts claimants from the obligation to be available for work, this 'shows that the benefits in question cannot be regarded as being directly and effectively linked to protection against the risk of unemployment'.[45]

To summarize, the main basis of the judgement was that because IS and SB were intended to provide against poverty, as opposed to one of the risks covered by the Directive, these benefits could not come within the material scope of the Directive. Yet, as Luckhaus (1992b, p.322) has succinctly noted:

> Sonia Jackson and Pat Cresswell, of course, were claiming benefit precisely because they were in poverty. The irony of their being deprived of that benefit solely because it was intended to protect them from it would probably not have escaped them.

If this reading of the decision is correct, then Member States could, by a little redesigning, bring benefits out of the scope of Directive 79/7/EEC. This is precisely what the Advocate Generals in *Smithson* and in this case, as well as the ECJ in *Drake*, had warned against. As Luckhaus has argued, as a result of these two decisions '[D]irective-proof measures could well become the order of the day' (1992b, p.322).

Luckhaus has also argued that 'pivotal' to the decision in *Jackson and Cresswell* was the 'idea of purposeful, aim-driven state activity in the sphere

of social policy' (1992b, pp.321–2). This explains, she contends, the importance in the ECJ's reasoning of the answer to the question of what was
intended in the supplementary benefit and income support schemes. There
are a number of ways, according to Luckhaus, of analysing intentions in the
social policy and social security sphere. The claimants in this case proposed
looking at intentions as a matter of practice and design, which exposed the
essential role played by social assistance benefits, such as SB and IS, in
providing an income for the unemployed, pensioners, the sick and disabled,
as well as lone parents. One can also look at intentions in terms of design,
and in particular at the content of rules and how they interact with each
other, but any particular set of design items can be represented in different
ways. Intentions may also be probed through history, which would have
revealed that the UK government in the late 1970s and early 1980s believed
that SB was covered by the Directive. Finally, intentions may be probed
through the witness box, by allowing the present-day guardians of social
policy to speak for themselves (ibid., p.322). The final method of ascertaining intentions was, of course, the method ultimately preferred by the ECJ in
this case.

As an aside, it is revealing to compare the ECJ's approach in *Jackson and
Cresswell* to its approach in a case decided on the same day. The *Hughes*[46]
case related to migrant workers and Regulation 1408/71, and involved a
refusal to grant family credit, a means-tested benefit, to an Irish resident,
whose husband worked in the UK, on the ground that she was not resident
in the UK. The ECJ was asked to decide whether family credit constitutes a
social security benefit within Regulation 1408/71 and thus whether it is
'exportable' to another Member State. On this occasion the ECJ gave short
shrift to the manner in which the benefit was classified by the government
and concluded that family credit is a social security benefit within Regulation 1408/71.

Scheiwe (1994, pp.248–54) has shown the wide discrepancy between the
ECJ's approach to cases of unequal treatment between men and women in
social security, and the exacting tests applied where obstacles are placed in
the way of the freedom of movement of migrant workers. In cases where an
absence of rights or benefits for a family could function as an impediment to
a (male) worker's mobility, the Court has consistently held that this is
contrary to the attainment of the EC's objectives. In this situation, the ECJ
has given a wide interpretation to 'social security benefits' in Regulation
1408/71 and has even extended its competence into new fields, such as
education. The ECJ's stance in these cases contrasts sharply with many of
its decisions under Directive 79/7/EEC (Scheiwe, 1994, p.250).

The *Smithson* and *Jackson and Cresswell* decisions have meant that rules
which disadvantage women in general social assistance schemes cannot be

challenged under Directive 79/7/EEC, which is all the more regrettable given the widening net of these benefits. In the words of Advocate General Van Gerven, the *Jackson and Cresswell* decision amounts to a 'significant narrowing' of the scope of the Directive (Van Gerven, 1994, p.34).

One glimmer of hope for women in the situation of Pat Cresswell and Sonia Jackson, who are claimants of family credit, was provided by the ECJ in the *Meyers* case.[47] At issue was precisely the same rule as in *Cresswell and Jackson*, but this time it was challenged as being an obstacle to employment and thus prohibited under Directive 76/207/EEC on equality in treatment between men and women with regard to access to employment and vocational training. In this case the ECJ found that family credit does come within the scope of Directive 76/207/EEC, vindicating the argument made by Scheiwe (1994) which I discussed above. The *Meyers* ruling is, however, only the first step in challenging the childcare costs rule, since the Court was not asked whether this rule could be considered as indirectly discriminatory against women. The question of indirect discrimination will be decided by a national court.

Interpreting the derogations: Article 7(1) and preserving financial equilibria

The derogations (or exemptions) to the principle of equal treatment in Article 7(1) define the circumstances in which differences in treatment between men and women are allowed. The derogations are not, however, unlimited, since the differences are to be periodically examined in light of social developments to ascertain whether they are still justified (Article 7(2)).

Article 7(1) allows Member States to maintain differences between women and men in a number of areas, including:

- the fixing of pensionable age for the purposes of granting old age and retirement pensions and the possible consequences thereof for other benefits;
- advantages in respect of old age pension schemes granted to persons who have brought up children and the acquisition of benefit entitlements following periods of interruption of employment due to the bringing up of children;
- the granting of old age or invalidity benefit entitlements by virtue of derived entitlements of a wife;
- the granting of increases of long-term invalidity, old age, accidents at work and occupational disease benefits for a dependent wife (Article 7(1)(d)).

In earlier sections of this chapter, I described the derogations as relating to areas in which women's social role of carer and dependant is considered to be different from men's social role, thereby justifying different treatment. However, the derogations allowed in Article 7(1) are not all of the same type; the difference in pensionable age may, for instance, be seen as a positive recognition of the years which women have spent in caring work leading to shorter paid work careers. Other derogations may be aimed at preserving derived entitlements to benefits, and thus a benefit structure in which persons in caring work are treated as dependants (receiving income mediated through another person) with no personal rights to social insurance benefits.

There has been litigation at the EC level in relation to the consequences of the difference in pensionable age on other benefits (Article 7(1)(a)), and more recently in relation to the granting of additions with long-term benefits for dependent wives (Article 7(1)(d)). No clear line of reasoning emerges from the ECJ in these cases, although the theme of preserving the financial equilibrium runs, implicitly or explicitly, through them. A number of other tensions emerge, such as the extent of Member States' discretion to interpret the derogations, as well as the question of whether unequal treatment consists of applying stereotypes of women as a group to the disadvantage of individual women.

Differences between women and men in contributory years for pensions:
EOC *and* Van Cant

In the *EOC* case,[48] the Equal Opportunities Commission (EOC) challenged the difference in pensionable ages in the UK,[49] arguing that men are discriminated against by having to pay contributions for five years longer than women to gain the same basic pension. Further, where men work between the ages of 60 and 65 they continue paying contributions, whereas women in the same situation are no longer obliged to pay them. The EOC argued that Article 7(1)(a) should be construed narrowly, so that it only covers the age at which pensions become payable, and not the extent of the obligation to pay contributions in respect of those benefits. Article 7(1)(a), as will be recalled, provides that Member States may maintain a different pensionable age between men and women and the possible consequences thereof on other benefits.

Advocate General Van Gerven found that the words 'possible consequences' of the difference in pensionable age also refer to the financial consequences which flow from fixing of the pensionable age for the old age and retirement pension. He concluded that a Member State may still derogate under Article 7(1)(a), as the UK has done, but with the qualification:

... unless such unequal treatment of men can be eliminated by the national court without unduly jeopardising the coherence or financial equilibrium of the national social security system concerned.[50]

The ECJ decided, on a narrower ground than this, that the discrimination in contributions was necessarily linked to the fixing of pensionable age and thus within the scope of the derogation.[51] The Court deduced from the nature of the derogations in Article 7(1) that it had been intended that Member States should be able to temporarily maintain the advantages accorded to women in relation to pensionable age in order to enable states to progressively adapt their pension systems without disrupting their complex financial equilibrium.[52] Any interpretation of Article 7(1)(a) whose effect would be to restrict the scope of the derogation and to exclude discrimination in contributions would lead to financial disequilibrium, concluded the Court.[53]

This decision can scarcely have been a surprise but, given that the derogations are not intended to be unlimited, as can be seen by Article 7(2), it may be wondered why the ECJ did not accept AG Van Gerven's proviso. The outcome of the ruling would have been the same, but the control over Member States' discretion would not have been so diminished. Interestingly, the ECJ's attitude to this derogation was much stricter in the later case of *Van Cant*.[54]

In Belgium, pensionable age was 65 years of age for men and 60 years for women until 1990. Pensions were calculated on the basis of a number of contributory years, which were different for men and women, multiplied by a percentage of past remuneration. A law in 1990 provided for a flexible age of retirement and permitted men to retire at 60 for the first time. However, the numbers of contributory years for men and women were not altered. When Mr Van Cant reached the age of 65 he was given a pension calculated over his 45 best earning years. He argued that, had his pension been calculated over his best 40 years, as it would have been if he were a woman, his pension would have been higher, and so he challenged the 1990 law as discriminating against him.

Essentially the question before the ECJ was whether Article 7(1)(a) would permit a Member State to have the same pensionable age for men and women, while retaining a different way of calculating the pension. The ECJ replied unequivocally that once a Member State has eliminated the difference in pensionable ages between men and women, and is therefore outside the scope of the derogation, then it may not be permitted to maintain a different mode of calculation of that pension, where the calculation was linked to that prior difference in pensionable age.[55]

It appears 'remarkable' according to Advocate General Van Gerven (1994) that, in this case, the ECJ did not take account of the financial equilibrium of the retirement pensions system. Indeed, the ECJ 'remained deaf' to the Belgian government's 'incantations' about the financial equilibrium of the pensions scheme (De Vos, 1994, p.179). Yet as De Vos (ibid.) observes, the ECJ did not say a word as to the inevitable imbalance which would result from the alignment of the 'less favoured' group (men) with the 'more favoured' group (women). This very imbalance, as De Vos points out, was the reason why the mode of calculation had remained different when the pensionable age was made equal. The effect, so long as the legislation remains unchanged, is that men will be entitled to the mode of calculation applicable to women, and as a result the expenses of the scheme will grow, to the advantage of those persons who already enjoy higher pensions (ibid., p.180).

It appears therefore that, once a Member State has decided to equalize a difference in treatment allowed under a derogation, then it will be required to implement equality in every respect. This may, given the complexity of the financing of social security schemes, encourage equalization by levelling down (albeit that, in this case, the Belgian government was reluctant to level down provision for women – see Chapter 5).

The 'possible consequences for other benefits': Thomas

The *Thomas*[56] case raised the issue of how far the difference in treatment in pension ages could justify differences in treatment between men and women in other social security benefits. In the UK, being under pensionable age is a condition of entitlement to a number of benefits, such as unemployment benefit, incapacity benefit, severe disablement allowance and the invalid care allowance. This means that many women who claim the above benefits between the ages of 60 and 65 may be denied any contributory benefits, because they cannot claim, for instance, unemployment benefit, but nor do they qualify for a state pension because of insufficient paid or credited contributions.

The *Thomas* case related to two of the above benefits: severe disablement allowance and invalid care allowance. These benefits were not given to persons over pensionable age, unless claimants had been entitled to them immediately before pensionable age was attained. The five women claimants argued that they had suffered direct discrimination contrary to Article 4(1) because a man in their situation (that is, aged between 60 and 65) would have been entitled to claim SDA or ICA. The UK government sought to invoke the Article 7(1)(a) exemption, arguing that SDA and ICA as income-replacement benefits are linked to pensionable age in an appropriate and necessary manner. The government maintained that, to retain their character as income-replacement benefits, SDA and ICA had to have a cut-off point related to when persons stop working. The cut-off point adopted, the government argued, is pensionable age, because this is when most people do in fact stop working, and because most women do in fact retire at the age of 60.

The Court stated that exceptions to the prohibition of discrimination on grounds of sex must be interpreted strictly.[57] It continued, following the *EOC* case, forms of discrimination provided for in benefit schemes other than old age or retirement pension schemes can be justified as being the consequence of determining a different pensionable age

> ... only if such discrimination is *objectively necessary* in order to avoid disrupting the complex financial equilibrium of the social security scheme or to ensure consistency between retirement pension schemes and other benefit schemes. (emphasis added)[58]

The Court found that the granting of non-contributory benefits, such as SDA and ICA, has no direct effect on the financial equilibrium of contributory pension schemes.[59] Further, that since provisions on overlapping benefits prevent the payment of both a contributory pension and SDA or ICA to a woman over 60, discrimination between men and women under SDA and ICA is unnecessary to preserve the financial equilibrium of the whole social security system.[60] On the issue of ensuring consistency, the Court was equally dismissive of the government's argument that, since SDA and ICA are income-replacement benefits they must cease upon retirement, and that the age of 60 for women was appropriate since most women do in fact retire at that age. The Court observed that in *Marshall (No 1)* it was held that women may go on working after pensionable age at least until the age at which a man is supposed to retire.[61] Thus, the Court stated, where women have continued to work beyond pensionable age, or do not yet receive an old age pension, they are entitled to receive benefits such as SDA and ICA.[62] The Court also observed that

> ... an *individual* right ... cannot be denied them on the ground that, statistically, their situation is *exceptional* by comparison with *most women*. (emphasis added)[63]

The ECJ therefore concluded that, where a Member State prescribes different pensionable ages for men and women, the scope of the derogation in Article 7(1)(a), insofar as it concerns other benefits, is limited to forms of discrimination which are necessarily and objectively linked to the difference in retirement age.

Two interesting points emerge from this decision. The first is that, unlike in the *EOC* case, the ECJ displayed scepticism as to arguments regarding disruption of a pension scheme's financial equilibrium. Moreover, the Court retained a larger degree of control over the interpretation of the scope of the derogation than it has left itself in the *EOC* case. In fact, the UK government had tried to argue that a Member State, in interpreting the scope of the derogation, is free to choose from the various possibilities that it considers appropriate and apt to achieve the objectives which its social security system seeks to achieve.[64] The ECJ, in putting forward the 'objectively necessary' test, I would argue, implicitly rejected that argument.

Second, this case raised the issue of whether 'unequal treatment' is to be understood as consisting primarily of applying stereotypes about women as a broad group to the disadvantage of individual women. Although, arguably, women as a group, were disadvantaged by the linking of the two benefits to pensionable age, because of their poor entitlements to a state pension in their own right, the ECJ focused on the fact that the UK had based the link between the benefits on the assumption that all women will retire at the age of 60, when in fact 80 per cent retire at this age. In the judgement the Court expressly referred to the fact that the claimants in this case had worked beyond pensionable age, and that women may legally carry on working at least as long as men can. It was clear in both the judgement and AG Tesauro's Opinion that individual women are to not be penalized by assumptions made based on the behaviour of women as a whole.

This understanding of unequal treatment is worth further scrutiny. It fits with the rationale for Directive 79/7/EEC, which was originally that the 'socio-economic reality' of the increasing numbers of married women in the working population no longer justified the broadly applied assumption that married women as a group were the full dependants of their husbands. However, if equality here means a rejection of an analysis of group disadvantage, then it should be noted that, when women follow the path of their 'stereotyped' role, they encounter financial dependence along the way. Where unequal treatment is only conceived of as the unfair application of group stereotypes to 'exceptional' individuals, then the broader issues of the financial dependence which is associated with certain activities are pushed out of the picture. These are, however, the very issues which, I would argue, should be placed sharply into focus.

Article 7(1)(a): Graham[65]

The *Graham* case was another referral from the UK, relating to invalidity benefit (which has now been replaced by incapacity benefit). In brief, on reaching pensionable age, invalidity benefit payments are revised according to the level of the retirement pension that a claimant would receive. In Mrs Graham's case the revision was made at the age of 60 years, and it caused a substantial reduction in her benefit payment because of her insufficient contributions for a retirement pension due to her absence from the labour market to perform caring work. The effect of this rule would be less serious for men because of their fuller contribution records. Mrs Graham argued that, had she been a man, the revision would have taken place at the age of 65 years (and thus she would have enjoyed five further years of the invalidity benefit). It was her contention that this was contrary to Directive 79/7/EEC since she was not treated in the same way as a man would be in her situation.

The ECJ found that where, pursuant to Article 7(1)(a), a Member State has set the pensionable age for women at 60 years and that for men at 65 years, then this derogation allows that Member State to provide that the rate of invalidity benefit paid before having attained pensionable age is to be limited to the actual rate of retirement pension from the age of 60 for women and from 65 years for men.

Article 7(1)(d): Bramhill[66]

After equal treatment reforms in 1984, married women became entitled to claim additions with contributory unemployment, sickness and invalidity benefits on the same terms as married men. To prevent the sharp drop in income for women already receiving additions to unemployment, sickness and invalidity benefits for their husbands, on attaining pensionable age and switching to the basic state pension, married women were also allowed to claim additions to the basic state pension, provided that they had been receiving an addition to another contributory benefit prior to the age of 60. No such rule applied to married men.

Mrs Bramhill argued that the rule applying to married women came within the principle of equal treatment which includes the 'calculation of benefits including increases due in respect of a spouse' (see Article 4(1)). The UK government argued that, on the contrary, this rule fell within the derogation in Article 7(1)(d) in relation to additions for a dependent wife.

The ECJ defined the essential question as being whether the Directive precludes a Member State from providing that additions to long-term benefits for a dependent spouse can only be paid to men, and from then abolishing that discrimination solely in regard to women who fulfil certain conditions.[67] The Court accepted the UK government's argument that, prior to 1984, the additions for married men were within the derogation. It went on to say that the Directive is intended to bring about progressive implementation of the equality principle,[68] and therefore to bring a Member State outside the derogation where it has taken measures to reduce the extent of unequal treatment that would be incompatible with the Directive and likely to jeopardize the implementation of the principle of equal treatment.[69]

It is not clear in this case why the ECJ should have adopted this approach. One might have thought that, along the lines of the *Thomas* decision, given that Mrs Bramhill was a worker, the rule in question was precisely the type at which the Directive aimed to abolish. Unusually, the ECJ did not adopt the line that 'role reversal' between partners in a household is an important aim of equal treatment law in this field. Moreover, this decision is also difficult to square with the approach taken in *Van Cant*. It may be that underpinning this decision was a reluctance to impose further costs on the UK government, especially in an area in which having a derogation encouraged the belief that the same treatment was not required. In this ruling, however, the ECJ neglected to take an opportunity to enhance the role reversal possibilities in the UK contributory benefits system (albeit that such a decision would not have challenged a payment structure in which social security for a dependent partner is 'mediated' through a claimant partner).

Summary

It is difficult to disentangle the legal issues from those relating to women's lack of independent income in the cases interpreting the derogations. The ECJ is rather ambivalent in its concern, and then disregard, for the implications of decisions on the financial equilibrium of pension systems.

INVOKING THE DIRECTIVE

When the implementation period of Directive 79/7/EEC had expired, on 23 December 1984, there were still several Member States which had not complied with the Directive – most notably Belgium, the Netherlands and Ireland. In fact the Commission had received complaints about Belgium in 1981 and the Netherlands in 1983 relating to the enactment of laws which continued to discriminate against women (see Chapter 6).[70]

Failures to implement on time were the subject of several of the early references to the ECJ on Directive 79/7/EEC, and the Court laid down a number of important principles. First, the Directive is sufficiently clear and precise to be directly effective, and thus to be relied upon in national proceedings where a Member State has maintained rules that discriminate between men and women beyond 23 December 1984 (*State of Netherlands v. FNV*). Until such time as a Member State adopts the necessary implementing measures to conform with the Directive, women are entitled to be treated in the same manner as men in the same situation, since in these circumstances the Directive is the only valid reference point. The fact that directives leave national authorities the choice of form and methods of achieving obligations under Community law cannot constitute a ground for denying all effect to those provisions (*Cotter and McDermott (No. 1)* v. *Minister for Social Welfare*).[71]

Second, a Member State may not maintain discrimination beyond 23 December 1984 which, contrary to the Directive, stem from transitional regulations which carry over past discrimination beyond this date (*Clarke* v. *Chief Adjudication Officer*). In *Dik* v *College en Wethouders*,[72] the ECJ added that, where implementation is effected by belated measures having retrospective effect, these must also fully respect the rights the Directive has conferred on individuals. That is, they may not reduce the substance of the directly effective rights in the period between actual and required implementation.

Third, in *Cotter and McDermott (No. 2)* v. *Chief Adjudication Officer*[73] the ECJ held that a national court may not apply rules of national law to restrict or refuse compensation in circumstances where allowing such compensation would offend against national principles.[74] This is the case, stated the Court, even if the application of the equal treatment principle would cause double payments of benefit because permitting reliance on the prohibition of unjust enrichment would enable national authorities to use their own unlawful conduct as a ground for depriving the Directive of its full effect.[75]

Finally, in 1991 in *Verholen and others* the ECJ confirmed that the equality principle does not provide for any derogation from which a Member State could authorize prolonging the discriminatory effect of any national provision, regardless of whether the benefit in question was contributory or not.[76] It appeared from this decision that any person who was excluded from social insurance prior to 1984 on discriminatory grounds will now have to be treated as though she or he was insured (Cousins, 1992a, p.62).[77] The potential effect of this decision was therefore enormous. However, this interpretation seems to have been undermined by a recent ECJ decision in *Roks*,[78] in which it was held that Article 4(1) of the Directive does not preclude a Member State from making the continuance of a social insurance benefit subject to a condition which has the effect of withdrawing from women in the future rights which they derive from the direct effect of the Directive.[79]

More recently, a number of references have related to the effect of national procedural rules on limiting the direct effectiveness of the Directive. This raises the important issue of the extent to which victims of past discrimination can claim redress, or whether claims for redress are repeatedly given a lesser priority than current budgetary constraints. A very wide principle was laid down by the ECJ in the *Emmott* case[80] but, regrettably, the Court has since substantially retreated from this position.

Turning to *Emmott* first, the ECJ held that Member States must ensure the full application of Directives and that, where a Directive has not been correctly transposed, individuals are unable to ascertain the full extent of their rights, even if there is an ECJ judgement declaring that Directive's direct effect.[81] Only proper transposition would halt this state of uncertainty and so, until a Directive has been correctly transposed, a defaulting Member State may not rely on an individual's delay in initiating proceedings in order to protect rights conferred by a Directive.[82] Therefore time periods laid down by national law within which proceedings must be initiated cannot begin to run until proper transposition.[83]

The *Emmott* principle seemed clear and easy to apply to a range of situations and had already been hailed as an important advance in ensuring the rights of individuals under Directives (see Curtin, 1992a, pp.46–8; Szyszczak 1992b, pp.611–13). However, in the field of social security, the progress of this principle on behalf of victims of discrimination was brought to an abrupt halt in *Steenhorst-Neerings*,[84] most recently confirmed in *Johnson (No. 2)*.[85]

In *Steenhorst-Neerings*, the applicant, as a result of a court decision, became entitled to an invalidity benefit from the date on which she first became disabled. However, because of a rule in the AAW scheme which limits backpayment of benefit to one year before the claim, the claimant could not receive all the backpayment due to her. In its decision, the ECJ first distinguished this case from *Emmott*, and then outlined administrative and cost reasons to justify the finding that *Emmott* should not be applied here. First, the ECJ considered that *Steenhorst-Neerings* could be distinguished from *Emmott* because the latter case concerned the right of a woman to have the same rules applied to her as a man in access to an invalidity benefit scheme.[86] In *Steenhorst-Neerings*, on the other hand, the provision at issue did not prejudice the applicant's right to invoke the Directive before a national court, but rather it sought to limit benefit claims in time. This, according to the Court, corresponds to the necessity of avoiding doubts as to the legality of administrative claims stretching out indefinitely.[87] In *Emmott* the Court decided that this necessity could not be invoked as long as a Member State had not correctly transposed its obligations under Community law. In *Steenhorst-Neerings*, observed the Court, the rule at issue has a completely different aim – namely that it answers the requirements of good administration, which includes the possibility of checking whether an individual has complied with all benefit entitlement conditions.[88] The rule the Court judged, also pursues a necessary objective of preserving the financial equilibrium of the social security system which pays out benefits in any one year on the basis of the contributions paid in that same year.[89]

It is debatable whether the distinction offered by the ECJ is convincing. Mrs Steenhorst-Neerings was certainly able to invoke Directive 79/7/EEC to gain the AAW benefit for a 12-month period. But why should partial enjoyment of a right be seen as a lesser denial of a person's rights under a Directive? In offering this distinction the ECJ was silent as to why, in principle, partial enjoyment of a right should cancel out the *Emmott* principle. Indeed, the distinction seems to depart from the ECJ's own consistent line of case law that, where the Directive has not been properly implemented, a Member State may not prolong the discriminatory effects of any previous national provisions beyond December 1984 (most recently, see the decision in *Verholen*). Arguably, this distinction overlooks (or ignores) that Mrs Emmott's own judicial review was about the past and that, in effect, there may be little difference between a denial of rights by means of judicial review or by a rule as to time-limits in benefit claims and receipt.

The underlying reason for the distinction would appear to rest in the second reason advanced – that of the requirements of efficient administration and the necessity of preserving the financial equilibrium of the Dutch invalidity benefit system. But to place these considerations over a recognition of remedying past discrimination is inevitably to undermine equality as one of the fundamental principles of EC law.[90] In a more recent decision on a broadly similar issue in *Roks and others*[91] the ECJ avoided all reference to *Steenhorst-Neerings*. At first it was unclear whether this should be interpreted as a distancing from the *Steenhorst-Neerings* decision or as a reflection of other, more important issues at stake in *Roks*. Cause for optimism has, however, now been squashed by the ruling in *Johnson (No. 2)*[92] in relation to a non-contributory benefit. In this case the ECJ simply confirmed the decision of *Steenhorst-Neerings*.

In the next chapter we concentrate on the principle of equal treatment in the Directive.

NOTES

1   There is an abundant literature on the EC's policies in the field of equality of opportunity between men and women. See Warner (1984); Hoskyns (1985, 1986, 1992); Mazey (1988); Rutherford (1989); Meehan (1990) and O'Donovan and Szyszczak (1988, pp.194–6).

2   *Defrenne (No. 2)* v. *SABENA*, Case 43/76 [1976] ECR 455.

3   OJ L 45/19, 19 February 1975.

4   OJ L 39/40, 14 February 1976.

5   OJ L 6/24, 10 January 1979.

6 *Drake* v. *Chief Adjudication Officer*, Case 150/85 [1986] ECR 1995.
7 At para. 22 of the judgement.
8 *Achterberg te-Riele and others* v. *Sociale Verzekeringsbank Amsterdam*, Joined Cases C-48/88 C-106/88, C-107/88 [1989] ECR I-1963.
9 At para. 11 of the judgement.
10 At para. 10 of the judgement.
11 At para. 12 of the judgement.
12 *Hofmann* v. *Barmer Ersatzkasse*, Case 184/83 [1984] ECR 3047.
13 At para. 20 of the judgement.
14 At para. 22 of the judgement.
15 In so far as women with children are denied the status of 'seeking employment' on grounds that are not applied to men, an argument could be made that this constitutes indirect discrimination under the Directive (see Scheiwe, 1994, p.259). It would normally, however, be rather difficult to prove that in any given factual situation it was the factor of caring for children which determined a particular decision.
16 The extent to which the equality principle in the Directive is overriden by other factors, including costs and budgetary considerations, is discussed in Chapter 5.
17 There are two different, albeit interrelated, strands which could be pursued here. The first is the extent of overlap between 'statutory social security schemes' in Article 3(1) of the Directive and the occupational schemes covered by Article 119. In a number of social security systems it is unclear whether particular benefits are occupational or statutory, and therefore under which legal instrument they would fall: see, generally, Van Gerven (1994) and the Opinion of Advocate General Jacobs in *Algemeen Burgerlijk Pensioenfonds* v. *Beune*, Case C-7/93, Opinion of 27 April 1994. Second, in a number of social security systems there is, arguably, a blurring of the 'frontiers between employment and welfare', to borrow Fitzpatrick's (1991) phrase. That is, benefits which were traditionally provided by statutory schemes are being transferred to occupational provision. This also leads to uncertainty over which legal instrument applies to them.
18 The *Drake* case, however, brought benefits for the care of a sick person within the Directive.
19 Taking the UK system as an example, it will be recalled that women comprise only between 20–30 per cent of the claimants of the contributory benefits for the risks of unemployment, invalidity and industrial injury. See Chapter 2.
20 See, for instance, *Cotter and McDermott (No. 1)* v. *Minister for Social Welfare and Attorney-General*, Case 286/85 [1987] ECR 1453; *Cotter and McDermott (No. 2)* v. *Minister for Social Welfare and Attorney-General*, Case C-377/89 [1991] ECR I-1155; *State of the Netherlands* v. *Federatie Ö derlandse Vakbeweging*, Case 71/85 [1986] ECR 3855.
21 See, for instance, *Ruzius-Wilbrink* v. *Bestuur van de Bedrijfsvereniging voor Overheidsdiensten*, Case C-102/88 [1989] ECR I-4311; *Clarke* v. *Chief Adjudication Officer*, Case 384/85 [1987] ECR 2865.
22 See, for instance, *Verholen and others* v. *Sociale Verzekeringsbank Amsterdam*, Joined Cases C-87/90, C-88/90 and C-89/90 [1991] ECR I-3757.
23 See, for instance, *Drake* v. *Chief Adjudication Officer*, Case 150/85 [1986] ECR 1995; *Secretary of State for Social Security* v. *Thomas and others*, Case C-328/91 [1993] ECR I-1247.
24 See also *Secretary of State for Social Security* v. *Thomas and others*, Case C-328/91 [1993] ECR I-1247.
25 At para. 23 of the judgement.

26   At para. 25 of the judgement.
27   *The Queen* v. *Secretary of State for Social Security, ex p. Smithson*, Case C-243/90 [1992] ECR I-467.
28   *Jackson and Cresswell* v. *Chief Adjudication Officer*, Joined Cases C-63/91 and C-64/91 [1992] ECR I-4737.
29   At para. 5 of the Opinion.
30   At para. 6 of the Opinion.
31   At para. 14 of the judgement.
32   At para. 18 of the judgement.
33   At para. 16 of the judgement.
34   At para. 17 of the judgement.
35   At para. 10 of the Opinion.
36   At para. 16 of the Opinion.
37   Ibid.
38   Ibid.
39   At para. 15 of the judgement.
40   At para. 16 of the judgement.
41   At para. 17 of the judgement.
42   At para. 18 of the judgement.
43   At para. 19 of the judgement.
44   At para. 20 of the judgement.
45   At para. 21 of the judgement.
46   *Hughes* v. *Chief Adjudication Officer*, Case C-78/91 [1992] ECR I-4839. This case is discussed in detail by Cousins (1992b).
47   *Meyers* v. *Adjudication Officer*, Case C-116/94, Judgement of 13 July 1995, not yet reported.
48   *The Queen* v. *Secretary of State for Social Security, ex p. Equal Opportunities Commission*, Case C-9/91 [1992] ECR I-4297.
49   For women it is 60 and for men 65, although pensionable age is to be equalized at 65 between 2010 and 2020.
50   At para. 14 of the Opinion.
51   At para. 19 of the judgf~ènt.
52   At para. 15 of the judgement.
53   At para. 17 of the judgement.
54   *Van Cant* v. *Rijksdienst voor Pensionen*, Case C-154/91 [1993] ECR I-3811.
55   At para. 13 of the judgement.
56   *Secretary of State for Social Security* v. *Thomas and others*, Case C-328/91 [1993] ECR I-1247.
57   See *Marshall (No. 1)* v. *Southampton and South West Hampshire Area Health Authority*, Case 152/84 [1986] ECR 723.
58   At para. 12 of the judgement.
59   At para. 15 of the judgement.
60   Ibid.
61   At para. 17 of the judgement.
62   At para. 18 of the judgement.
63   At para. 19 of the judgement.
64   This aspect of the judgement is analysed in greater depth in Sohrab (1993b, pp.361–2).
65   *Graham* v. *Chief Adjudication Officer*, Case C-92/94, Judgement of 11 August 1995, not yet reported.
66   *Bramhill* v. *Chief Adjudication Officer*, Case C-420/92, [1994] ECR I-1086.

67   At para. 15 of the judgement.
68   At para. 20 of the judgement.
69   At para. 21 of the judgement.
70   The complaint against Belgium was settled at the administrative stage and, while the Commission did not take action against the Netherlands, the basis of this complaint was dealt with by the ECJ in the *Teuling* case (see Chapter 5).
71   In *Francovich and Bonifaci* v. *Italian Republic*, Joined Cases C-6/90 and C-9/90 [1991] ECR I-5357 (see below) the ECJ confirmed explicitly that, even where substantive discretion has been left to Member States under the terms of a Directive, provisions can still be directly effective (Curtin, 1992b, p.76). The Court relied for this on its decisions in *Cotter and McDermott (No. 1)* and the *FNV* case.
72   *Dik and Others* v. *College van Burgemeester en Wethouders Arnhem and Winterswijk*, Case 80/87 [1988] ECR 1601.
73   Case C-377/89 [1991] ECR I-1155.
74   At para. 21 of the judgement.
75   Ibid.
76   At para. 28–29 of the judgement.
77   Advocate General Darmon was more elaborate on this point: at para. 46 he said that retrospective effect

   ... could deprive the Directive of a substantial part of its effectiveness if one was (sic) forced to take the view that the Directive should only be applied fully in respect of persons who did not begin to make contributions until after December 1984.

78   *Roks and Others* v. *Bestuur van de Bedrijfsvereniging voor Gezondheid, Geestelijke en Maatschappenlijke Belgangen and others*, Case C-343/92 [1994] ECR I-571.
79   At para. 30 of the judgement.
80   *Emmott* v. *Minister for Social Welfare and Attorney-General*, Case C-208/90 [1991] ECR I-4269.
81   At para. 21 of the judgement.
82   At para. 22 of the judgement.
83   At para. 23 of the judgement.
84   *Steenhorst-Neerings* v. *Bestuur van de Bedrijfsvereniging voor Detailhandel, Ambachten en Huisvrouwen*, Case C-388/91 [1993] ECR I-5475.
85   *Johnson (No. 2)* v. *Chief Adjudication Officer*, Case C-410/92 [1994] ECR I-1675.
86   At para. 21 of the judgement.
87   At paras 22–23 of the judgement.
88   At para. 23 of the judgement.
89   Ibid.
90   *Defrenne (No. 3)* v. *SABENA*, Case 149/77 [1978] ECR 1365.
91   *Roks and Others* v. *Bestuur van de Bedrijfsvereniging voor Gezondheid, Geestelijke en Maatschappenlijke Belgangen and others*, Case C-343/92 [1994] ECR I-571.
92   *Johnson (No. 2)* v. *Chief Adjudication Officer*, Case C-410/92 [1994] ECR I-1675.

5 The Principle of Equal Treatment

Article 4(1) of Directive 79/7/EEC provides that:

> ... the principle of equal treatment means that there shall be no discrimination whatsoever on grounds of sex either directly, or indirectly by reference in particular to marital or family status.

The principle of equal treatment applies to three aspects of social security systems in particular:

1 the scope of schemes and the conditions of access thereto;
2 the obligation to contribute and the calculation of contributions;
3 the calculation of benefits including additions in respect of a spouse and for dependants and the conditions governing the duration and retention of entitlement to benefits.

Article 4(1) can be seen as the core of the Directive, and the conception of equality that it embodies has the potential of being either a strong motor driving forward substantive change for women or, conversely, a weak and shaky carriage with little or no potential for change.

This chapter examines the interpretation given to both the concepts of direct and indirect discrimination contained in the Directive, drawing, where relevant, upon the wider field of EC sex equality law.[1] It is hoped that this discussion will contribute to the understanding of the impact of the Directive in the four countries considered in the following chapter. The discussion here is not intended as a comprehensive doctrinal exposition,[2] but rather aims to highlight a number of critical issues in relation to the interpretation of the concept of discrimination, such as decisions negating special (or 'different') treatment for women and the question of how far the prohibition on indirect discrimination can contribute to substantive equality, as well as the extent to which the principle of equality is overriden by other factors.

I begin the chapter with a discussion of the interpretation of direct discrimination, then turn to an analysis of the interpretation of indirect discrimination in both social security and employment sex equality law. I then consider whether or not equality is to be understood as levelling up, and then I examine the factors which regularly override the equality principle.

DIRECT DISCRIMINATION

Direct discrimination occurs where persons in similar situations are treated in a different way. It is worth quoting the formulation that the ECJ has used to describe this in two cases. In the *Drake* case, the ECJ found that:

> ... [direct] discrimination on grounds of sex contrary to Article 4(1) of Directive 79/7 arises where legislation provides that a benefit which forms part of one of the statutory schemes referred to in Article 3(1) of that directive is not payable to a married woman who lives with or is maintained by her husband, although it is paid in *corresponding circumstances* to a married man. (emphasis added)[3]

In the *FNV* case, the ECJ stated that:

> ... women are entitled to be treated in the same manner, and to have the same rules applied to them, as men who are in the *same situation*. ... (emphasis added)[4]

In social security systems it has been common for both married women and women cohabitees to be treated differently from men in a similar situation. These groups of women have been prevented from claiming particular benefits, or have only been able to claim certain benefits if they could show they were the breadwinners in their households, or have been subject to different rules than men and single women (see Chapter 6). The basis for these differences in treatment was (at least in part) the assumption, subsequently given prescriptive force, that married and cohabiting women would be supported by the earned income (or social security benefits) of someone else, and that therefore they did not need their own benefits and entitlements.

The Directive itself, by its simple requirement to remove all direct discrimination within its material scope, has been the motor driving a number of profound changes. This has been backed up by legal actions in instances where national governments have been reluctant to implement the Directive by removing directly discriminatory provisions which have excluded whole classes of women from benefits, or from the same payments as men have been receiving. The Directive had an important impact in allowing whole classes of women to claim benefits for the first time (or for the first time on the same terms as men), such as in the cases of *Drake, FNV, Clarke*[5] and *Cotter and McDermott (No. 1)*.[6] The ECJ has dealt with these cases in a way that cuts through the complexities of different social security provisions and economic constraints (O'Donovan and Szyszczak, 1988, p.205). The Court has required that, in cases of direct discrimination, the disadvantaged party is entitled to have the same rules applied to them as the previously advantaged group (in other words, 'levelling up'). In this way, the prohibition on direct discrimination in the Directive has had an impact on women's financial independence, by forcing the removal of rules which have denied women the possibilities of claiming benefits, thereby reinforcing women's financial dependence on men.

A more controversial issue arises when the demand to remove differences in treatment relates to provisions which have accorded benefits solely to women, or which appear to be to the advantage of women. As will be recalled, a sameness approach to equality may be a double-edged sword for disadvantaged groups, where equality leads to levelling down. Two interesting cases from Belgium have emerged which, superficially at least, raise questions of whether the sameness approach of the Directive to employment-related risks should be allowed to abolish women-only benefits, or whether women should be treated differently from men. The *Integrity* case relates to an exemption for certain categories of low-earning self-employed persons, including married women, from paying contributions for a number of social insurance benefits. The *Van Cant* case, already referred to in Chapter 4, related to differences between men and women in the number of contributory years for pension. In this section we will first discuss *Integrity*, then *Van Cant*, and then offer a critical commentary on the two decisions.

Integrity[7]

Integrity is the case under Directive 79/7/EEC most similar to the *Commission* v. *France* action under Directive 76/206/EEC, in which the ECJ found that a number of women-only benefits in collective agreements were in breach of the principle of equality of treatment (see Chapter 3). There are two main similarities between these cases: first, in the arguments put forward by the governments to justify the differences in treatment and, secondly in the ECJ's reasoning in both cases.

Integrity concerned the Belgian social security scheme for the self-employed, governing family benefits, retirement pensions, survivor's benefits, sickness and invalidity benefits.[8] Contributions for these benefits are paid on the insured person's income. Article 12(2) of this scheme allows certain persons to be relieved of the requirement to pay contributions if, in addition to their self-employed work, they are habitually engaged in another main occupation and their income from self-employed work does not exceed a certain limit. The scope of the exemption from the requirement to pay contributions was extended by Article 37 of the Royal Decree of 19 December 1967 to include married women, widows and students. Persons covered by the exemption, if they choose to exercise it, are unable to gain benefits in their own right, although many of the persons using the exemption would in fact have access to derived rights – that is, benefits paid for by the contributions of husbands or by parents in the case of students.

The plaintiff, a self-employed architect, was taken to court by a social security body who were claiming unpaid contributions from him. He argued that, since he had a low income, he should have been able to avail himself of Article 37, and the fact that he could not meant that the rule of equality between men and women had been infringed.

The Belgian government offered a number of arguments to justify the exemptions in Article 37, which are described in turn. First, the government argued that its aim was to exempt certain categories of workers from contributions liability, such as housewives and students, whose self-employed activities were subsidiary and whose main activity did not constitute 'work' for the purposes of labour law. Any self-employed activity carried on by these persons, it went on, would be carried out for short periods and the earnings would necessarily be modest.

Second, the exemption did not depend on sex, but rather on socio-economic criteria, since male students could also request the exemption from contributions liability, and since married women and widows are more likely to carry on self-employment on a subsidiary basis.

Third, to extend these provisions to married men and widowers, or to repeal them, would create indirect discrimination. Repealing the exemption would result in more women than men being required to pay contributions, because there are more married women than married men who, on top of their domestic responsibilities, work to a limited extent on a self-employed basis to help make ends meet. If, on the other hand, Article 37 were extended to married men, it would be necessary, argued the government, to ensure that both spouses in one household did not seek to rely on it, otherwise a situation might arise where neither member of the couple would be entitled to a benefit.

Fourth, since many married women only engage in paid work for a fraction of their potential working lives, the benefits payable would, in some circumstances, be less generous where the husband invoked Article 37 than where the wife did so, given the differences in men's and women's employment careers.

The ECJ did not enter into the merits of these different arguments, limiting itself to stating that Article 4(1) of the Directive must be interpreted as precluding national legislation which reserves to married women, widows and students the possibility of being exempt from paying contributions when this is not granted to married men and widowers.[9]

The Court's decision can hardly have been a surprise, given that the legislation at issue did not fall within any of the derogations to the principle of equality. It is more interesting to consider Advocate General Jacob's Opinion, which is explicit in its vision of the underlying philosophy of the Directive. On the issue of whether rules which apparently advantage women can be allowed under the Directive, the Advocate General stated that:

> Directive 79/7/EEC makes no distinction between positive discrimination in favour of the members of a particular sex and negative discrimination. Within its field of application, it requires all discrimination on grounds of sex to be abolished.[10]

With regard to the Belgian government's arguments that persons invoking the exemption from contributions liability would have access to derived rights, the Advocate General made a number of interesting observations. AG Jacobs pointed out that implicit in the Belgian system is the assumption that, in all marriages, the husband will be the principal breadwinner and the wife's paid work would be ancillary.[11] He argued that these assumptions are themselves discriminatory, because

> ... [t]hey make no allowance for couples who wish to organise their lives on alternative lines. It was for the benefit of such people, among others, that Directive 79/7/EEC (and the Community's other legislation on equal treatment for men and women) was adopted.[12]

He continued that each of the problems alluded to by the Belgian government could have been resolved in a non-discriminatory manner, so that a person's right to invoke Article 37 would depend not on an 'arbitrary characteristic' such as sex, but rather on objective factors such as income and extent of participation in paid work.[13] The Advocate General was categoric:

> ... [i]f a choice has to be made as to which spouse in a family is entitled to the benefit of a provision such as Article 37, Member States are not entitled to prevent the husband from doing so on the assumption that it will always be more advantageous to the family for the wife to do so.[14]

In this Opinion we find clear echoes of two underlying themes in EC sex equality law. The first is the importance of creating the conditions, in terms of applying the same rules to men and women, which would allow couples to reverse (or modify) their social roles if they so wish. The second theme is the importance accorded to the notion that social security rules should not assume that married women are outside the labour market and financially dependent on their husbands, without ascertaining whether these women are in fact dependent on their husbands.[15] In a sense, the criteria of income and extent of participation in the labour market are no more 'objective factors' than sex, contrary to the view expressed by the Advocate General. If, within certain age bands, income and paid work do correlate very closely to sex, then an equality law must be able to recognize the sexual subtext behind factors – such as income and extent of labour market participation. This is the function of indirect discrimination, to which I turn later in the chapter.

Van Cant[16]

In Belgium, prior to 1990, the pensionable age was 65 years for men and 60 years for women. Pensions were calculated as a percentage of average lifetime earnings (75 per cent for persons with dependent spouses and 60 per cent for single persons), divided by 45 years for men and 40 for women. In 1990 a law was passed on flexible retirement, with the aim of allowing persons to retire at any time between the ages of 60 and 65. The 1990 law did not, however, alter the number of contributory years (years over which average earnings were calculated), so that pensions were still calculated over a higher number of years for men. This could mean that they would receive a lower pension than a woman if they retired at the age of 60 years. To give an example: an unmarried man retiring at the age of 60 with 40 years' service would receive a pension of 40/45 of 60 per cent of covered earnings, whereas an unmarried woman retiring at the age of 60 after 40 years' service would receive a pension of 40/40 of 60 per cent of covered earnings (that is, a pension of 60 per cent as opposed to the 53.33 per cent received by the man in this example).[17]

It will be recalled that the ECJ found that, once a Member State has eliminated a difference in treatment allowed by Article 7(1) of Directive 79/7/EEC, the derogation can no longer be invoked to allow a difference in the method of calculating a pension which was related to the (different) pension age.

In finding that the rule regarding contributory years was outside the scope of the derogation, the ECJ was in fact forcing the Belgian government to apply the same treatment to men and women (but omitting to say whether provision had to be levelled up or down). It appears, however, that part of the reason for which the Belgian government did not alter the numbers of contributory years was not to make women – whose average working lives are far shorter than men's – 'pay the price' for equality, but to allow them to preserve their acquired rights.[18]

A critique of the cases

The *Integrity* case is very interesting because it is a 'hard case' which demands close analysis of the complex equality issues involved. The decision can be read at its most transparent level – that is, debating the merits of equal rights versus special rights (or a 'sameness' approach over a 'difference' approach) – or it can also be read at another level – that is, as raising issues of derived rights and of the individualization of entitlements to benefits. The latter reading, it is argued, points more clearly to a resolution of this case than an equal rights versus special rights analysis. This is also in keeping with a 'bottom-up' approach which, as I argued in Chapter 1, is preferable to a 'top-down' approach. In other words, the latter reading enables us more effectively to see how different options or choices 'pan out' in practice, and it embraces a sounder understanding of what is at stake. An equal versus special rights reading of *Integrity* is unsatisfactory because it involves taking an *a priori* position on what is best for women. I argue that it is preferable to adopt a context-specific, as well as case-specific, approach to the resolution of the kinds of difficult question posed by the *Integrity* case.

Before considering the two alternative readings of *Integrity*, it is worth pausing to take issue with Fredman's assessment of what this case shows about EC equality law in general. Fredman (1992, pp.128–30) has argued that the *Integrity* decision shows that EC law applies equality law neutrally between men and women, and that this makes a false assumption about symmetry. That is, the law wrongly assumes that men and women are similarly situated, which presumably, according to Fredman, means that rules would have similar effects whether applied to men or women.

This assessment of EC equality law is, I would argue, mistaken because it betrays too exclusive a focus on an abstract sense of equality. In my opinion it is more useful to focus on the purpose of particular Directives and to challenge the vision of equality which they contain. In this way it can be argued that EC equality law, or certainly Directive 79/7/EEC, had the purpose of removing the more obvious forms of discrimination against married women. The removal of direct discrimination allows, for instance, a sharing of roles between spouses (as seemed to be the thrust of the ECJ's decision in *Commission* v. *France*), but does little else to encourage changes in gender roles. The law can therefore be described as 'permissive', and it is this which can be criticized for being too limited to produce substantive modifications to the gendered social reality. To return to Fredman, EC equality law does not assume symmetry between men and women, rather it allows women (or some women in particular) to compete more freely in the workplace, or to be paid more, or to have the same opportunities, formally at least, to gain social insurance benefits. It is this aspect which needs to be attacked for failing to address many of the issues of structural inequality facing women.

Turning to the first possible reading of *Integrity*, the ECJ's decision that the same rules should apply to both men and women, and in particular the reasoning of the Advocate General, seem to confirm all our prejudices about a sameness approach to equality ignoring the unequal gendered social reality. Interpreting equality of treatment to mean essentially the removal of differences in treatment has been strongly criticized by a number of feminist commentators, such as Fredman (1992, p.128) and More (1993 p.64). Sandra Fredman (1992, p.128) has argued that the ECJ's decision in *Integrity* shows that equality in EC law is treated as an end in itself rather than as a mechanism for correcting disadvantage. Gillian More (1993, p.61) notes that Directive 79/7/EEC contains no derogation along the lines of that contained in Directive 76/207/EEC which allows for positive action-type measures to remedy inequalities against women. Fredman (1992, p.130) goes on to argue that, in the interests of combating gender disadvantage, 'special' treatment or women-only provisions should be allowed, given a balancing of a number of factors.

Reading the *Integrity* case in the above way leads to a re-run of equal rights versus special rights arguments: should women have the same rights as men or, in view of the unequal gendered social reality, should they have different ones? In this case, the ECJ took up the equality as sameness position, with feminist commentators countering that inequalities need to be taken account of by applying different rules to women in some instances. It is helpful for us to examine more closely what consequences could flow from either an equal rights or special rights decision, to enable us to judge whether this analysis of *Integrity* is, in fact, of any use in finding a solution to this factual situation.

Two results could flow from a sameness approach. First, a 'levelling-up' solution could be adopted, which would extend the contributions exemption to married men and widowers. This would allow low-earning men to be exempted from paying contributions. The net result of this could be an extension of a system of derived rights, if low-earning men could gain benefits through their wives' contributions. Alternatively, levelling-up could mean that low-earning men would be left without social insurance benefits entitlements and be forced on to social assistance. A second result of a sameness approach could be 'levelling-down', in the sense of a withdrawal of the exemption for all persons, and thus a liability for paying contributions on even small amounts of income. Although this appears to be a negative consequence, it could in fact bring more people within the social insurance system, and thus within reach of personal benefits.

What would be the outcome of a difference approach? In order to challenge 'gender disadvantage' would it be necessary here, as suggested by Fredman, to allow women to retain advantages based on their unequal social position? If the ECJ had found that the rules did not have to treat men and women in the same way, as the Belgian government contended, then the rules exempting certain categories of married women and widows would have been left untouched. What effect would this have for women or for challenging gender disadvantage? In fact, it allows a situation to continue in which women pay no contributions to social insurance, therefore receive no personal benefits from this system and are forced to depend on derived benefits. Yet, are special rights to no personal entitlements to social insurance worth 'reserving' for women? Derived benefits, such as widows' pensions, are normally withdrawn on remarriage or cohabitation, on the assumption that the new partner will provide financial support. Personal rights to social insurance benefits are not normally withdrawn depending on sexual vicissitudes.[19] Derived benefits maintain the conceptual links of women's financial dependence on men and can be argued to mask the caring services which women provide in the home. This argument, which is developed further in Chapter 8, states, in brief, that derived benefits are normally given for 'dependants' who have been unable to build up personal rights to benefits. In my view, giving rights to 'dependents' creates the misleading impression of non-activity, whereas in fact many of the women who would fall in this category are likely to have invested a considerable number of years in unpaid caring work.

Arguably, neither the sameness nor the difference approaches offer a satisfactory outcome. A more fruitful way to consider the thorny issues raised by *Integrity* is to focus on the tension between derived rights versus personal entitlements (or the individualization of benefits). What decision is most likely to lead to greater personal entitlements, and therefore potentially greater access to personal income? On the above analysis it appears that a sameness approach could have this impact, since it is the only option which could have lead to the withdrawal of the exemption. A difference approach would only reinforce the system of derived benefits.

The question remains – and this is a matter of political choice – whether a withdrawal of the exemption or reliance on derived benefits, at least in the short term, is 'better' for women. A withdrawal of the exemption could lead to the individualization of benefits in a way in which special treatment could not do. While there are important reservations to individualizing entitlements, it could be an important element in a strategy of promoting women's financial independence. I emphasize, however, that I have taken a context-specific and case-specific approach to the analysis of this case, and that the conclusions I have reached may not apply to other factual situations.

If the questions at issue in *Integrity* are viewed only in equal treatment-special treatment terms, then a very different answer is obtained. Special treatment – in this case, the retention of the exemption from social insurance – may have a more immediate appeal since it takes explicit account of the gendered social reality. However, this either/or choice can oversimplify complex issues; each of the choices needs to be investigated further in relation to other criteria and, where concepts such as 'disadvantage' are used, these need to be fleshed out and defined – for instance, as an absence of personal entitlements to social security benefits or a qualitatively inferior provision for feminine risks.

A different set of issues is raised by *Van Cant*. The lower number of years over which pensions are calculated can be described as a 'difference-specific' approach. The ECJ's decision in *Van Cant*, which requires 'same treatment', has posed a dilemma for the Belgian government over how to equalize rules in the interim period until the year 2006 when pensions will be calculated over 45 years for both men and women. The dilemma is between implementing same treatment by either disrupting the financial equilibrium of the pension system through reducing the number of contributory years for men, or by penalizing women through increasing the number of years of earnings over which the pensions are calculated when women as a broad group have far fewer earning years.[20] Using the arguments that I employed in relation to the *Integrity* case, the ECJ should have left the derogation alone. If they had done so, the government would have been free to allow the difference in treatment to continue until 2006, thereby permitting a more gradual process of equalization. But, if the number of years for women were to be increased, this would decrease women's access to their old age pensions.

The situations in these cases can be distinguished. In *Van Cant* women's unpaid caring work is recognized in a positive way.[21] Women need fewer years in the labour market to receive a full pension (even if this means that women with a full-pension career gain a higher pension at 60 than a man of the same age). As Atkins and Luckhaus (1987, p.106) have argued, certain of the derogations in Article 7(1), including that with regard to the difference in pensionable ages, could be seen as a partial recognition of care work and of the importance of unpaid domestic work. These derogations enable Member States to retain these provisions, but do not prevent them from extending these to men. In *Integrity*, however, the exemption from the social insurance system and the forced dependence on derived rights is arguably to women's detriment in the long term.

Summary

As will also be seen in the following chapters, the prohibition on direct discrimination prompted the elimination of differences in treatment and has allowed many women to claim benefits for the first time. The 'hard cases' arise where the prohibition on direct discrimination means that women-only advantages should be eliminated. It has been argued that, in *Integrity*, the decision reached was, on balance, the one most likely to promote individual entitlements to benefits (although certainly it was not on these grounds that the case was decided). Conversely, it has been suggested that, in *Van Cant*, the ECJ should have left the contributory years rule outside the scope of the equality principle in order not to prejudice women's access to the contributory pension benefit. The fact that the Court failed to this is all the more surprising given the ECJ's statements in the *EOC* case as to the importance of not disturbing the financial equilibrium of social security systems.

In fact, a compromise may have been found, which does not seem to disadvantage women. The Belgian government proposed to make a technical change to the pension law,[22] which would push the pensionable age for men back up to 65 years, although men will still be able to retire at 60 if they either accept a lower pension or satisfy the requirement of having had a career of at least 15 years (including years as an employee, as a self-employed worker or as a civil servant in Belgium or abroad). It is expected that most men will still be able to retire at 60 with a pension if they wish, since, on average, they have 43 years of contributions. By reinstating the difference in pensionable age (and again invoking the derogation in the Directive) it is hoped that the higher pensions for women can be maintained, in view of the fact that women suffer handicaps due to the years they spend in bringing up children, to which men are not subject.

INDIRECT DISCRIMINATION

In this section, I will touch upon a number of topics related to indirect discrimination: first, a brief definition of the scope of the concept and the social context in which the legal definition operates, followed by a consideration of the way in which the ECJ has interpreted this concept, both in cases related to the employment sphere and in relation to social security and, finally, a few observations about implementation and the strength of this concept in attacking indirectly discriminatory rules and structures in national systems.

Indirect discrimination: legal definition and social context

Indirect discrimination, in this sphere, occurs where the effect of sex-neutral rules is, in practice, disadvantageous to one sex group. In the words of the ECJ in *Roks*,[23] the most recent judgement on indirect discrimination under the Directive:

> Article 4(1) of Directive 79/7 precludes the appplication of a national measure which, although formulated in neutral terms, works to the disadvantage of far more women than men, unless that measure is based on objectively justified factors unrelated to any discrimination on grounds of sex.[24]

By focusing attention on the effects of neutral rules, the concept of indirect discrimination can capture within its parameters a greater range of inequalities facing women than simply direct discrimination. Where a rule or provision is found to have a *prima facie* indirectly discriminatory effect, however, the author (an employer or a Member State) has an opportunity to show that it is nevertheless objectively justified. If a rule or provision is found to be objectively justified then there is no illegality. This involves courts engaging in a delicate balancing of interests in assessing whether rules which treat men and women differently in practice can in fact be objectively justified (Prechal, 1993, p.87). The focus on the disadvantaging effects of rules, and the potential there is for remedying this, is what makes the concept of indirect discrimination so exciting.

In the social security field there are a number of rules which disadvantage more women than men, a number of which will have already become apparent from the discussion of the first layer of structural inequality in Chapter 2. For the purposes of this present discussion, I set out a number of the indirectly discriminatory aspects of social security systems identified by an EC Network of Equality Law Experts (see Bieback, 1993a, pp.7–8):

1   cut-backs affecting more women than men;
2   rules relating to access to schemes (earnings thresholds, requirements for a certain period of contributions), which affect part-time workers or persons working in family businesses or self-employed homeworkers;
3   rules impeding access to schemes following interruption of employment after periods of caring and childrearing;
4   calculations of benefits, including additions for a spouse and dependants, in which either higher benefits are given to the head of household, or the calculation of benefits is based on joint resources or the aggregation of needs and/or income;

5   administrative rules, such as the requirement of availability in unemployment benefit
     schemes.

A glance at the case law

In this section, I first consider the way in which the prohibition on indirect discrimination has been interpreted by the ECJ, by looking at cases concerning part-time workers, and then in relation to additions for dependent spouses. Generally, the ECJ seems prepared to take a more interventionist approach in national social policy with regard to issues affecting part-time workers than in cases where additions for dependent spouses are at issue. This is probably due to the fact that, where women are in part-time work, they are in a similar role to men – that is, in paid work – but additions for dependent spouses relate to an area of state policy in which the social role of caring is to the fore and traditional family policy may be at stake (Bieback, 1993a, p.6). The Directive is in fact firmly embedded in a worker-related ethos, as has been seen from the discussion of its personal and material scope in Chapter 4.

Part-time workers

So far there has only been one ECJ ruling concerning indirect discrimination against part-time workers in the social security sphere.[25] There have, however, been many important cases relating to part-timers and the equal pay principle in Article 119, such as *Bilka-Kaufhaus, Kowalska, Nimz, Bötel*,[26] and *Kirsammer-Hack*,[27] which are briefly discussed after considering the ECJ's decision in the social security sphere.

In relation to Directive 79/7/EEC, the *Ruzius-Wilbrink* case[28] concerned payments for incapacity for work under the Dutch national social insurance scheme for invalidity benefits (AAW). This scheme grants to all insured persons – with the exception of those working part-time – entitlement to a benefit unrelated to previous income, which corresponds to the level of the minimum subsistence income. Certain categories of workers who have no, or only very little, income in the year before the incapacity arose are also entitled to that minimum subsistence income. Only the benefit granted to part-time workers is calculated by reference to the insured person's income, and the benefit is therefore necessarily lower than the minimum subsistence income.

In the Netherlands there are considerably fewer male than female part-time workers, and so this method of calculation disadvantages more women than men. The applicant was granted an invalidity benefit on the basis of her average daily earnings in the year prior to the onset of her incapacity, during which she had, on average, worked 18 hours per week. She challenged this decision on the grounds that it was indirectly discriminatory against women.

The ECJ found that this method of calculation constituted indirect discrimination contrary to Article 4(1) of the Directive, unless it could be objectively justified.[29] The test used for objective justification was the *Rinner-Kühn* test,[30] in which case the ECJ laid down that, in order to be objectively justified on grounds of sex, national legislation must respond to legitimate objectives of social policy, and the means used must be both appropriate and necessary to reach this objective. The only justification that the Dutch government offered for the difference in the treatment of part-time workers was the need to ensure they did not receive a benefit that was higher than their previous income. The ECJ brushed this argument aside, observing that, in a substantial number of other cases, the level of the invalidity benefit was in fact higher than a claimants' previous income.[31] Therefore, the Court found that Article 4(1) precluded the benefit being calculated in this way.[32] The ECJ went on to find that, by analogy to the *FNV* case, members of the group placed at a disadvantage were entitled to have the same rules applied to them as are applied to the other beneficiaries of the benefit.[33]

In a number of cases concerning indirectly discriminatory provisions against part-time workers in the employment sphere, the ECJ has given a wide scope to the principle of pay under Article 119, and has set a strict standard of objective justification. I consider these decisions in brief, focusing on the test of objective justification and the consequences of a finding of indirect discrimination.[34]

The prohibition on indirect discrimination was clearly defined by the ECJ in the leading case of *Bilka-Kaufhaus*. This related to the denial of a pension from an occupational scheme to a woman who had not completed the required number of years in full-time work for the employer, because she had moved into part-time work. In this case, the ECJ held that it is for the national courts to determine whether, and to what extent, the grounds put forward by an employer to explain the adoption of a pay practice which applies independently of a worker's sex but in fact affects more women than men may be regarded as objectively justified on economic grounds.[35] If the national courts find the measures chosen by Bilka correspond to a real need on the part of the undertaking, are appropriate with a view to achieving the objectives pursued and are necessary to that end, the fact that measures affect a greater number of women than men is not sufficient to show that they constitute an infringement of Article 119.[36] This test continues to be used; in relation to state social policy, the test applied is that from the *Rinner-Kühn* case.[37]

What is the obligation under EC law once a provision or rule is found to be indirectly discriminatory against women?[38] In *Kowalska* and *Nimz* the ECJ, drawing upon its decision in *Ruzius-Wilbrink*, stated that, on a finding of indirect discrimination, Article 119 remains the only valid reference point and that the class of persons placed at a disadvantage by reason of that discrimination must be treated in the same way and made subject to the same scheme.[39] In *Kowalska* this finding meant that part-time workers had to be subject to the same severance pay scheme as full-time workers, in proportion to the numbers of hours worked. In *Nimz* the ECJ held that, on a finding of indirect discrimination, a national court is required to set aside a provision, in which it took much longer for part-time workers to move up the work hierarchy, without requesting or awaiting its prior removal by collective bargaining or any other procedure, and to apply to the members of the group disadvantaged by the discrimination the same arrangements as are applied to other employees.[40]

In the employment sphere, Article 119 has dealt a number of fatal blows to rules which disadvantage part-time workers. However, as *Bilka* demonstrates, Article 119 does not force the economic recognition of unpaid work-related activities within an employment-related scheme, even though these activities contribute to shaping women's employment patterns. If Article 119 were to do this, this would be a step towards an inclusion model, or substantive equality. The equal pay principle in fact accords women the same treatment as men in the workplace, whether that different treatment flows from sex-specific or sex-neutral criteria.

In *Bilka-Kaufhaus* one of the questions asked by the national court was whether Article 119 obliges an employer to organize its occupational pension scheme so as to take into account the fact that family responsibilities prevent women workers from fulfilling the requirements for such a pension. The applicant argued that the disadvantages suffered by women because of the exclusion of part-time workers from the occupational pension scheme must at least be mitigated by requiring the employer to treat periods during which women workers have had to meet family responsibilities as periods of full-time work.

The ECJ observed that Article 119 is limited to the issue of pay discrimination between men and women workers, and that problems related to other conditions of employment are covered by Articles 117 and 118 of the Treaty of Rome.[41] The imposition, therefore, of an obligation, such as that argued for by the applicant, goes beyond the scope of Article 119 and has no other basis in Community law as it stands.[42] Therefore Article 119 does not effectively require an employer to organize its occupational pension scheme so as to take into account the particular difficulties faced by persons with family responsibilities in meeting the conditions of entitlement to such a pension.[43]

To summarize, the ECJ has interpreted Article 119 in a dynamic way and has been influential in challenging a number of rules which indirectly discriminate against part-time women workers either by excluding them from certain benefits or are more difficult for them to satisfy. On the other hand, Article 119 does not force the economic recognition of caring work by employers. In *Ruzius-Wilbrink*, in the social security sphere, an exacting attitude was also applied. This may be explained, however, by the fact that the discrimination against part-time workers in question which related to the calculation of the AAW invalidity benefit, was clear, and that the justification offered by the Dutch government was rather weak.

Additions for dependants

The Directive provides that there shall be no discrimination, directly or indirectly, in relation to additions to benefits for spouses. A failure to include additions to benefits for dependent spouses within the Directive would have allowed direct discrimination to continue, yet these additions in practice normally favour men (EC Commission, 1983, p.8). The European Commission argued that, where additions are granted, the spouses should be placed on an equal footing and that 'the concept of "head of household" is no longer in line with either the realities of society or the provisions of civil law' (1983, pp.8–9). Placing additions to benefits within the ambit of the equal treatment principle, however, inevitably raised the presumption that they would be found to be *prima facie* indirectly discriminatory against women (Prechal and Burrows, 1990, p.175). In acknowledging this, the Commission set out the circumstances in which, it argued, it would be justified to grant them, such as where the additions were given in the context of social benefits guaranteeing a minimum income. Additions to benefits that are proportional to remuneration would not be objectively justified, the Commission argued, since remuneration is not itself subject to additions for dependent spouses.

Including these additions within the scope of the equality principle reveals very clearly some of the complexities of achieving equality of outcomes in a social security system in which benefits to households are structured around particular assumptions about gender roles. Eliminating direct discrimination alone may simply create another form of discrimination. Here, formal changes are prescribed without displacing a system where one person receives benefit for two persons – that is, a system which reinforces the financial dependence of one partner on the other. Additions for dependent spouses have been the subject of three referrals to the ECJ, one of which involved an action by the European Commission against the Belgian state.

The first case, *Teuling*,[44] involved the complex interrelationship between two schemes for benefits for invalidity in the Netherlands; one an employee social insurance scheme (the WAO) and the other a national social insurance scheme (the AAW).[45] Under the employee social insurance scheme (the WAO), persons, regardless of sex and marital status, were entitled to a disability benefit set at a certain level. However, changes both to this law and to the national social insurance scheme (the AAW) were implemented, partly as a result of Directive 79/7/EEC. The WAO scheme's guarantee of a set level of benefit was replaced by benefit related to recent earnings. The AAW scheme, while extending benefits to married women for the first time, was reduced to 70 per cent of the statutory minimum wage. Under further legislation, supplementary benefits became payable to breadwinners (persons with dependent spouses or children) to bring benefit levels up to 100 per cent of the statutory minimum wage. These supplements were means-tested, taking account of the claimant's spouse's earnings and therefore, as a result of all these changes, Mrs Teuling suffered considerable loss as she was only entitled to 70 per cent of the AAW benefit (she did not qualify for the 30 per cent supplement because of her husband's earnings), and she was not at all entitled to a WAO benefit. She therefore claimed that this was indirectly discriminatory against women, contrary to Article 4(1) of the Directive. The justification given by the government for this change was the aim of guaranteeing a minimum subsistence income for households, and helping with the greater financial burdens of persons with families.

The ECJ decided that a system of supplements, as in this case, would be contrary to Article 4(1) unless it could be justified on grounds other than sex.[46] The Court referred to the Dutch government's aim to provide a minimum subsistence income to persons with no income from work, and stated that 'such a guarantee granted by Member States to persons who would otherwise be destitute is an integral part of the social policy of the Member States'.[47] Consequently, if supplements to this minimum subsistence benefit are intended, for beneficiaries with no income from work, to prevent the benefit from falling below the subsistence level for persons who, by virtue of having a dependent spouse and children, bear greater burdens than single persons, then these are justified under the Directive.[48] The Court did provide the qualification, for national courts to decide on, that the supplements must correspond to the greater burdens of the beneficiaries having a dependent spouse or children, they must serve to ensure an adequate minimum subsistence income for those beneficiaries and finally that they are necessary for that purpose.[49]

The Commission, drawing on its view of where additions for dependants would be objectively justified, as well as on the *Teuling* decision, brought an action against the Belgian state.[50] The Commission argued that the Belgian system of allocating unemployment and invalidity benefits was more fav-ourable to men than to women. The Belgian system divided claimants into three groups: group 1, which consisted mainly of men, included workers cohabiting with a partner, parent or child with no income; group 2 included workers living alone; and group 3 (mainly women) included workers cohab-iting with someone with an income. Within some limits the payments were related to previous income, and those in group 1 received the highest ben-efits, while group 3 received the lowest. The Commission argued that giving benefits based on previous income could not be said to be giving benefits on the basis of the needs of dependants and was therefore contrary to Directive 79/7/EEC.

The ECJ did not accept as an objective justification that the difference in the ratio of men to women between the three categories of beneficiaries is the product of a social phenomenon arising from the fact that fewer women are in employment than men. It was, however, more receptive to the Belgian govern-ment's argument that its national system is designed to provide, within bud-getary limits, each individual with a minimum replacement income taking into account the family status of the person. The Court reiterated that such an aim is an integral part of a Member State's social policy, and the recognition of the heavier responsibilities on families is a matter upon which Member States retain a reasonable margin of discretion.[51] The ECJ adhered closely to the *Teuling* judgement, characterizing the Belgian system, albeit one of *replace-ment income*, as having the character of a guaranteed minimum income.[52] The Court therefore found that the government, in controlling its social expendi-ture, was entitled to take account of the relatively greater needs of those persons with dependent spouses or children, and to reduce benefits because of an absence of dependent persons.[53]

The potential effects of a different result in the *Teuling* case leave a great deal to (optimistic) speculation. If the ECJ had found that the system of supplements was not objectively justified, the Dutch government could have been forced to reconsider the way in which the social security system gave benefits to single-earner households. This could have been an important thrust towards the creation of personal benefits.

The ECJ was in fact cautious in both this case and in *Commission* v. *Belgium*. The result of the latter decision is that rights accruing to women from their paid work, as regards unemployment and invalidity benefit, can be wiped out for most of them if they cohabit with a man who is also earning an income (Herbert, 1994). This has serious implications for the access of these women to personal income and may contribute significantly to enforced financial dependence upon men.

Further, it is now difficult to imagine a situation in which indirect dis-crimination could be proved in relation to a benefit, paid at low levels, whether or not it is intended as a minimum income scheme or as a replacement income scheme, which direct resources to single-earner households. The complete disregard of the fact that additions paid in respect of dependants in no way take account of their number or likely needs, but rather vary with the previous income of the breadwinner in the *Commission* v. *Belgium* case, means that the outlook is ominous for future enforcement of equality of treatment in this area (Banks, 1991, p.223). Yet dependants' additions in all countries are arguably indirectly discriminatory where they negatively affect women's employment incentives. The system of breadwinner supplements in the Netherlands, or the higher rates of benefits given to breadwinners in Belgium, or even the dependants' additions paid in both the UK and Ireland, can all contribute to making it more difficult for female partners of benefit claimants to enter paid work in anything other than in a marginal way, and thus reinforce financial dependence on male partners. The ECJ has already pronounced upon national social insurance schemes in the Netherlands (although not on employee social insurance schemes) and also on the unemployment and sickness social insurance scheme in Belgium. It is unlikely that challenges on these grounds from the UK or Ireland would be successful. In the UK contributory benefits are paid at flat-rate and relatively low levels. In certain circumstances those in receipt of contributory benefits can receive extra benefit from the income support (means-tested) benefit system. In Ireland levels of contributory benefits are a little higher than social assistance ones.

In November 1992 the ECJ in *Molenbroek*[54] confirmed these two decisions in all major respects. This case concerned the payment of pension increases for dependent spouses under the Dutch national social insurance scheme for old age pensions (AOW). The ECJ found that the pension given under the AOW has the character of a basic pension, in the sense that it is intended to guarantee a revenue equal to the social minimum, independently of whether or not the pensioner receives income from elsewhere.[55] The fact that, in some circumstances, the addition would be paid where it was not necessary to guarantee a minimum income did not affect, it stated, the necessary character of the means chosen to reach the purpose outlined above.[56] These decisions effectively represent a further narrowing of the scope of the equality principle.

A number of important themes have emerged from the discussion of the indirect discrimination concept in this field of EC equality law. First, there is the issue of the extent of redistribution, if any, required by the concept of indirect discrimination. It has been argued that the prohibition on indirect discrimination is a facet of a sameness approach, in the sense that different treatment of women in similar situations to men is not allowed, whether this is shown by sex-specific or sex-neutral criteria. For women in similar situations to men – such as women in employment – the prohibition on indirect discrimination has played an important role in challenging inequalities suffered by part-time workers. Where women are in dissimilar situations – for example, with respect to caring or financial dependency – the potential modifying effect of indirect discrimination is more limited. Of course, the pivotal issue here is the limited competence of EC equality law outside the employment-related sphere.

The second theme has been the strength of the concept of indirect discrimination in the references to the ECJ. Women who challenge indirectly discriminatory provisions related to paid work apparently have less difficulties in having their claims accepted than women challenging provisions related to the household and their social role as dependants and carers. Yet women face many problems gaining personal income from social security because of the qualitatively inferior social protection given their roles as carers. It is therefore of great importance, in terms of promoting women's access to personal income, that the prohibition of indirect discrimination is a strong legal standard to which social security systems should conform. This is all the more so given that social security rules are nowadays phrased in sex-neutral terms. Any limitation on the Directive's effectiveness to combat indirect discrimination is, therefore, a serious limitation in its ability to bring about real change for women.

The third theme has been the ECJ's ready acceptance of the characterization by Member State governments of the purposes of national schemes, even in the face of contrary evidence; this raises questions about the Court's commitment to 'equality' in anything other than a purely formal sense in certain areas of the benefit system. A problematic aspect of the ECJ's handling of the *Teuling*, *Commission* v. *Belgium* and *Molenbroek* cases is the way in which the Court ignored aspects of the schemes that were not in fact related to minimum income.[57] The supplements at issue in the Dutch schemes were not in fact necessary for all persons to bring households up to a particular level, since income could be gained from other sources. In the Belgium case the ECJ did not take proper account of the fact that the system in question was one of replacement income, even though the amounts were not generous. Again, these decisions hinged upon the ECJ's view of the limited EC competence in matters arising from the 'private' sphere of unpaid care work (and, indeed, financial dependence). Yet, as we have seen, women's place within the social security system, and the inequalities they face, cannot be adequately explained if one half of the picture is ignored. Women's paid work, as well as their unpaid care work, and financial dependency needs to be examined. Certainly, substantive equality for women can hardly be achieved without including both halves of this picture within the frame of reference.

IMPLEMENTING EQUALITY: LEVELLING UP OR DOWN?

In this section I consider the general question of whether equality in EC law means that equalization must be achieved by levelling up. Where the Directive has not been implemented or has only been partially or incorrectly implemented, and where persons have directly effective rights to enforce Article 4(1), we have seen that levelling up is the solution required by the ECJ in cases of both direct and indirect discrimination. Further, in implementing the Directive, a Member State may not recreate the discrimination complained of (Szyszczak, 1990, p.116; Curtin, 1988, p.25).

A disappointing feature of the text of the Directive is that it does not offer specific guidance on how Member States should implement equality of treatment (Hoskyns and Luckhaus, 1989, p.334; Curtin, 1988, p.36). Article 5 merely provides that:

> Member States shall take the measures necessary to ensure that any laws, regulations and administrative provisions contrary to the principle of equal treatment are abolished.

Are there then any grounds for arguing that is there a general obligation upon Member States in the Treaty or case law to level up provision, or to level up in a way that substantively guarantees equality of treatment?

Commentators have put forward a number of arguments to answer that question in the affirmative. First, Atkins and Luckhaus (1987, pp.120–1) argue that, since the Directive implements Articles 117 and 118, the improvement of living and working conditions is one of its most important aims. Fitzpatrick (1990) points to the Preamble of the Treaty, which refers to the 'essential objective of the constant improvement of the living and working conditions', which, he submits, is a crucial source for the purpose of interpreting Community legislation, albeit not a source of rights in itself. Article 117 also refers to the above aim and, while it cannot give rise to rights, the ECJ has stated that the objectives in this Article 'constitute an important aid in particular for the interpretation of other provisions of the Treaty and of secondary legislation in the social field'.[58] Although Directive 79/7/EEC is silent on implementation, both the preceding Directives (75/117/EEC and 76/207/EEC) contain references to the improvement of living and working conditions in their Preambles, and this leads Fitzpatrick (1990) to conclude that, since Directive 79/7/EEC was passed under Article 235, it is through the nexus between the principle of equal treatment and the essential objective of living and working conditions that this Directive has any constitutional basis in Community law at all.

These are indeed challenging legal arguments, and yet the ECJ has been prepared to accept levelling down where a Member State wishes to control its social expenditure, as we have seen in both *Teuling* and *Commission* v. *Belgium*. In effect the ECJ's statements as to the narrow scope of EC competence in Member States' social policy tends to refute the argument that equalization upwards is a significant objective in EC law (see below). The ECJ's decision in *Zaera*, recently confirmed by *Roks*,[59] is that Member States retain an (almost) absolute discretion over the level of social security benefits.

While the Court has made important statements regarding both the importance of the equality principle and improving living and working conditions, it has been reluctant to demand that 'equality' does not lead to levelling down, except in cases where Directives have not been, or have been partially or incorrectly, transposed into national law. Advocate General Van Gerven has argued that '[c]ommunity law does not preclude a reduction of such benefits, so long as those benefits are set at a level which is the same for men and women'.[60] He continued that taking any other view would be an undesirable interference in a sphere of policy in which it has been consistently held that Member States have a reasonable margin of discretion.[61] It is also worth quoting a paragraph of the ECJ's decision in the *Roks* case, in which the Court said:

> Community law does not prevent Member States from taking measures, in order to control their social expenditure, which have the effect of withdrawing social security benefits from certain categories of persons, provided that those measures are compatible with the principle of equal treatment between men and women as defined in Article 4(1) of Directive 79/7/EEC.[62]

Allowing Member States to withdraw benefits with little fear of breaching the equality principle is regrettable in view of the fact that, in implementing the principle of equality in their social security systems, Member States have often opted for nil-cost or levelling-down solutions (see Chapters 6 and 7). Levelling down may, while opening equality of access to benefits, in fact make it harder for women to claim benefits in their own right, and thus have a negative impact on women's financial independence.

The ECJ has had another opportunity to pronounce on whether or not equalization must be achieved by levelling up in *Smith* v. *Avdel Systems Ltd*.[63] At issue was how to equalize pensionable ages between men and women in the Avdel occupational pension in the wake of the *Barber* judgement on 17 May 1990. In *Barber* the ECJ held that Article 119 of the Treaty of Rome covered benefits from occupational pension schemes. On 1 July 1991 the Avdel scheme was equalized by raising the pensionable age for women to 65 years, with the effect that women who still wished to retire at the age of 60 would lose up to 20 per cent of their pension (a 5 per cent reduction of pension per year prior to pensionable age). In its judgement the ECJ isolated three time-periods:

1 prior to 17 May 1990 (the date of the *Barber* judgement);
2 between 17 May 1990 and 1 July 1991 (the date on which the Avdel scheme was equalized);
3 post-1 July 1991.

The Court held that, in relation to periods before the *Barber* judgement, there was no requirement on Avdel to ensure equality of treatment, so there is no requirement to retroactively reduce any advantages to women. With regard to the second time-period, between *Barber* and the equalization, there should be levelling up so that men should be able to retire at the age of 60. The reasoning is that the previously disadvantaged group (men) should be allowed to retire on a full pension at the same age as the previously advantaged group (women). However, once equalization had been effected, the Court held, Article 119 only requires that the rules should be the same for women as for men, whether this is achieved by levelling up or down. The Court stated that

> ... it follows that, once discrimination has been found to exist, and an employer takes steps to achieve equality for the future by reducing the advantages of the favoured class, achievement of equality cannot be made progressive on a basis that still maintains discrimination, even if only temporarily.[64]

This decision, as can be seen, represents no departure from the Court's jurisprudence and does nothing to prevent equality (as sameness) from being effected at the expense of women.

OVERRIDING EQUALITY

A thread running through the discussion on equality and Directive 79/7/EEC has been how, and in what circumstances, the equality principle has been overriden by other considerations, such as the needs of single-earner households, costs and budgetary constraints, and Member States' discretion in social policy. These are considered in turn below.

Needs of single-earner households versus challenging women's income dependence in households

The discussion of the cases relating to the payment of additions (or higher benefits) to persons in households with one earner and a dependent spouse and/or children has revealed two points. First, making rules sex-neutral will, in many cases, merely replace direct discrimination with indirect discrimination unless benefit structures are redesigned so that one person is no longer given benefits to meet the needs of other non-earners in the household. Second, it is apparent that the ECJ uncritically accepts the legitimacy of national policies aimed at compensating for the (greater) needs of these households. But social security benefits aimed at compensating for the 'burdens' of being a breadwinner are normally paid to men, and these normally exert a degree of negative control over a female partner's incentives to take up employment, both of which factors limit her access to personal income. There is a clear conflict here, and so we must ask whether, and in what circumstances, the needs of single-earner households should take precedence over a strict application of the equality principle to root out indirect discrimination.

There is clearly a delicate balancing of interests involved between, on the one hand, compensating for the costs of family responsibilities and protecting against the insecurity to which a household is subject once it loses its single earner and, on the other, a strict application of the equality principle (Laurent, 1986, p.161; 1987, p.514). In relation to means-tested benefits (or indeed flat-rate benefits paid at low levels), a strict application of the social minimum test, which is the European Commission's approach, could cause hardship, as any income, however small, entering a household, (such as a dependent spouse's earnings) would cause a withdrawal or reduction in benefits. To withdraw these additions for dependent spouses without other changes (such as the abolition of the aggregation rule), in the name of equality, could be to inflict hardship on to those households for whom the benefits plus additions are necessary to maintain a standard of living above the poverty line.

In effect, to do this would be to bring about full individualization, in which a person's claims from the social security system could only be in respect of themselves, and where both adult members of a household would have to separately satisfy the entitlement conditions in order to receive benefits. If both partners are unable to satisfy the conditions, to give households in which both partners are outside the labour market or in which one partner is engaged in employment generating a minimum income level, the same benefits as a single person seems unjust, since these households will have greater income needs. This may well also conflict with other policies, such as the desire to redistribute income towards families – and low-income families in particular.

Different considerations apply, it is submitted, with regard to earnings-related benefits and additions which are intended to maintain levels of previous earnings. The European Commission was of the opinion that these could not be objectively justified since wages take no account of family responsibilities (EC Commission, 1983, p.9). Earnings-related benefits and additions arguably impede women's access to independent income to a greater degree than flat-rate additions, or additions to minimum level benefits, in one significant respect. Additions to earnings-related benefits are likely to create stronger disincentives to women's employment, given that additions linked to a breadwinner's loss of income may be higher than the potential earnings of a dependent partner. The earnings of a dependent partner could therefore lead to a significant reduction in benefits – from, for instance, 75 per cent of previous earnings down to 60 per cent in the Belgian contributory pensions system. Moreover, additions to earnings-related benefits are also biased towards higher income groups.[65]

Additions for dependent spouses are common in the four systems considered in this book. In the short term, therefore, criteria need to be laid down as to the circumstances under which these additions should be paid in a way which minimizes women's financial dependency. I argue that additions should only be objectively justified in relation to minimum level flat-rate benefits on the grounds that, while they may still have disincentive effects upon women's employment, these effects are likely to be far less than in relation to increases to maintain a replacement income.

This proposal of course only represents a short-term answer to the conflicts involved between the needs of single-earner households, the application of the equality principle and the issue of women's financial independence in households. These conflicts can only really be resolved by more fundamental changes to the benefit structure, such as allowing both partners to receive individual benefits and permitting caring work to serve as an entitlement to adequate social insurance benefits.[66] My proposal is in the nature of 'damage limitation', since it does not challenge a structure in which one person receives benefit on behalf of other adults so that the creation of hardship for low-income households is avoided. This kind of change can, and probably should, only be brought about by legislative change.

Costs and budgetary constraints upon Member States

The cost issue runs like a thread through all the cases we have considered in relation to the Directive. This is inevitable given that any decision under the Directive (or indeed under Article 119) involves costs, whether they be on the state in relation to remedying past discrimination, or where women continue to bear the costs of discrimination or disadvantage. The ECJ has shown an ambivalent attitude towards imposing higher costs on Member States and disrupting the financial equilibrium of social security systems. In a number of cases, such as in *Dik*,[67] *Verholen*[68] and *Emmott*,[69] the Court has given decisions which would potentially entail high costs. It has also specifically rejected arguments that the financial equilibrium should not be disturbed, as in *Thomas*.[70] In the *EOC* case,[71] however, the ECJ put much emphasis on not disturbing the complex financial equilibrium of systems, as it did also in *Steenhorst-Neerings*[72] and *Roks*. A reluctance to precipitate higher costs may also have played a part in the *Teuling, Commission* v. *Belgium* and *Molenbroek* decisions.

The ambivalence in the ECJ's approach regarding the question of how a state should remedy past discrimination is, it is argued, revealed in the *Roks* decision. This case concerned the implementation of formal equality into the Dutch social insurance scheme for invalidity benefits (the AAW) which, as will be seen in Chapter 6, has been the subject of extensive litigation. In brief, the scheme originally discriminated against married women and, in equalizing the rules, an attempt was made to limit costs by introducing new rules of entitlement. It was the bringing into force of the new rules that was essentially at issue in this case. One of the questions asked by the national court was whether provisions such as those at issue, which in principle created *prima facie* indirect discrimination, could be objectively justified by budgetary considerations. The ECJ replied that:

> ... although budgetary considerations may influence a Member State's choice of social policy and affect the nature or scope of the social protection measures that it wishes to adopt, they cannot themselves constitute the aim pursued by that policy and cannot, therefore, justify discrimination against one of the sexes.
>
> Moreover, to concede that budgetary considerations may justify a difference in treatment as between men and women which would otherwise constitute indirect discrimination on the ground of sex ... would be to accept that the application and scope of as fundamental a rule of Community law as that of equal treatment between men and women might vary in time and place according to the state of the public finances of the Member States ... Community law does not prevent Member States from taking budgetary constraints into account when making the continuance of entitlement to a social security benefit dependent on conditions, the effect of which is to withdraw the benefit thereof

from certain categories of persons, provided that when they do so they do not infringe the rule of equal treatment as between men and women laid down in Article 4(1) of Directive 79/7/EEC.[73]

Can the containment of costs or exercising budgetary constraints in fact constitute legitimate objectives of social policies?[74] The Court's reasoning is, I would argue, rather ambiguous. While the Court appears to lay down a strong principle that budgetary constraints can never defeat the equality principle, it still reiterates its past case law in the dependants' additions cases. How might this be interpreted? The moral of this tale seems to be that, although costs cannot be an objective justification, Member States may create (alleged) indirect discrimination against women in pursuit of certain legitimate objectives, such as the needs of single-earner households. Despite the apparent strength of the initial pronouncements, this is indeed an important caveat to the supremacy of the equality principle.

The issue of social security costs is high on the current political agenda. The ECJ's decisions in social security over the last ten years have had as their background the new economic orthodoxy of welfare spending cuts and economic deregulation which effectively limits measures entailing financial commitments (Mazey, 1988, p.83). There continues to be debate about reducing the state's role in the social protection field in favour of greater individual provision, because of the 'demographic time bomb' and the rising costs of social security budgets. In this debate, as in the decisions of the ECJ, the costs issue is understood primarily in terms of putting greater costs on the state to meet the demands of equality. What is absent from this debate is the recognition that there are other costs which ought to be considered – most notably the costs of the status quo[75] which are defined here as being the costs to women of bearing discrimination, inequality and financial dependence on male partners. The costs of giving benefits (or indeed higher benefits) to women or compensating women for past discrimination are, however, repeatedly seen as lesser priorities.

Member States' discretion in social policy

In the *Roks* case, the ECJ held that making the continuance of entitlement to benefits subject to a condition (albeit *prima facie* indirectly discriminatory) applicable to both men and women, which has the effect of withdrawing from women, in the future, the rights which they derive from the direct effect of the Directive, shall not be contrary to the Directive.[76] This rather depressing decision was justified on the grounds that the setting and determining of access to rights to social security in the future remains within the sole competence of the Member States, by virtue of Articles 117 and 118 of the Treaty of Rome. The ECJ stated that Directive 79/7/EEC leaves intact the powers reserved by Articles 117 and 118 of the Treaty of Rome to the Member States to define their social policy and the nature and extent of measures of social protection, including those relating to social security and the way in which they are implemented.[77]

The Court's repeated assertion as to the wide discretion of Member States in social policy continues to be a significant stumbling block to the enhancement of social security rights through deployment of the equal treatment concept.[78] This has been particularly true of the dependants' additions cases, where, in the words of Docksey (1991, p.274), the Court has been 'too willing to limit the operation of the principle of equality' in cases relating to indirect discrimination and additions for dependent spouses. It is regrettable that, in the *Belgium* case and then later in *Molenbroek*, the ECJ incorporated within its test of objective justification the reference to the reasonable margin of discretion of the Member States (Herbert, 1994). By means of the principle of proportionality, this takes an important area outside of the scope of the ECJ's and national courts' review (Cousins, 1994, p.140).

Why is the ECJ so cautious? There may be a number of possible explanations. First, it may be that since the Directive was meant to begin the progressive implementation of the equality principle, the Court perceives its jurisdiction in this area as limited, so that it defers to national policy considerations and allows economic arguments full sway (Docksey, 1991, pp.275–6). The tension, contends Docksey, between the 'economic' and the 'fundamental rights' approaches has yet to be resolved in this area.

Second, with regard to the difference in approach between cases concerning with part-time workers and concerning additions for dependent spouses, the ECJ may not be prepared to accord women 'equality' where they claim it as 'workers'. Additions for dependent spouses, while included in the scope of the equal treatment principle, do in fact relate to an area which is largely excluded from the Directive. It may be surmised that women who are 'dependants' would not, in most cases, come within Article 2, and moreover benefits for dependants have largely been excluded from the scope of the Directive (such as in Articles 3(2) and 7(1)(b), (c) and (d)). Herbert (1994) argues that, apart from budgetary considerations and perhaps even more importantly than these, one key factor in the ascertainment of Member States' right of discretion is that the Court acknowledges that the implementation of *de facto* equality between men and women by suppressing indirect discrimination can involve calling into question basic options concerning the respective roles of men and women in couples and in working life. This places us, argues Herbert, directly before the (thorny) question of the individualization of women's rights in paid work.

Third, in the broader political context in which the ECJ operates, there seems to be a more pervasive battle about the perceived degree to which interference by the ECJ in national policy is acceptable. Two Member States have recently shown signs of 'rebellion' against the ECJ,[79] and tensions of this kind have been a feature of the relations between the Community and its Member States over the years. The ECJ is more likely to be 'interventionist' in areas where the competence of the Treaty is clearly laid out.

In broader political and institutional terms of possible relevance, in 1996 there is to be an intergovernmental conference at which the Member States will discuss the ECJ's role. The Court may well wish to tread carefully in advance of this conference so that its tailfeathers are not clipped too far back.

CONCLUDING REMARKS

Linda Luckhaus (1993, p.291) has incisively described the Directive as being 'structurally oriented towards paid work and paid workers'. Without question, this meets the original aim of the legislation, which was to eliminate differences in treatment affecting the increasing numbers of married women in the labour market. However, the gendered social reality and, in particular, women's lack of access to independent income in social security is a far more complex issue than abolishing rules which treat (all) married women as the dependants of their husbands. The issue of women's lack of financial independence, at least partly concerns the qualitatively as well as quantitatively inferior provision given to feminine risks (see Chapter 2).

The second observation relates to the ECJ's role in the face of the narrowness of the Directive's terms. The Court could play an important role in expanding these terms by some purposive interpretation. In the *Drake* case, in relation to the schemes covered by Article 3(1), the ECJ did show itself to be dynamic, but in more recent years it has retreated substantially. In relation to the Directive's personal scope, the ECJ has narrowed its scope. Cousins (1994, p.144) summed this up in the following way:

> ... the recent case-law of the ECJ has not only failed to promote a strong interpretation of the existing legislation but has weakened the potentialities of the Directive.

All these factors lead to fewer women being able to use the Directive to challenge the kinds of rule (such as those in means-tested benefits) which may affect them to a greater extent in the future. Again, in the words of Cousins (1994, p.143):

... women with childcare or other responsibilities who are living in poverty, who one might think most in need of equality of treatment, are, in fact, least likely to receive it under the Directive.

The sameness–difference model of the Directive does not allow challenge to the quantitatively and qualitatively inferior social provision accorded to benefits for female risks.

Three principal observations can be made regarding the equality principle in the Directive.

1   The prohibition on direct discrimination forces changes to the most obvious forms of discrimination against women. It is not always clear, however, how to assess instances in which the prohibition on direct discrimination leads to women-only rights or benefits being withdrawn.
2   The ECJ has a more exacting attitude towards discrimination against part-time workers than in relation to dependants' additions or breadwinner supplements. This too is linked to the employment-related ethos of the Directive.
3   A number of factors repeatedly take priority over a stringent application of the principle of equality.

It appears, therefore, that the Directive has limited potential in improving women's financial independence unless inequality is linked to rules affecting paid workers. In Chapters 6 and 7 I consider the implementation of the Directive in the four social security systems and offer observations as to how far women's financial independence has been advanced.

NOTES

1   An interesting line of enquiry, not pursued in this book, for reasons of space, is to compare the scope of the concept of indirect discrimination in EC sex equality law with other fields of EC law, such as in relation to the free movement of goods. On this issue, see Herbert (1990, pp.656–65) and the presentation by Sacha Prechal to the EC Specialist Workshop on Indirect Discrimination in Social Security, Hamburg, 19–21 May 1993. The report of the proceedings is cited as Bieback (1993a).
2   More generally on the concept of indirect discrimination in relation to the Directive, see Herbert (1990, 1994) and Prechal (1993). In relation to early decisions on the concept of discrimination in EC law generally, see in particular Herbert (1990, pp.656–65).
3   *Drake* v. *Chief Adjudication Officer*, Case 150/85 [1986] ECR 1995, at para. 34 of the judgement.
4   *State of the Netherlands* v. *Federatie Nederlandse Vakbeweging*, Case 71/85 [1986] ECR 3855, at para. 22 of the judgement.

5   *Borrie Clarke* v. *Chief Adjudication Officer*, Case 384/85 [1986] ECR 2865.
6   *Cotter and McDermott (No. 1)* v. *Minister for Social Welfare and Attorney General*, Case 286/85 [1987] ECR 1453.
7   *Caisses d'assurances sociales pour travailleurs indépendants 'Integrity'* v. *Rouvroy*, Case C-373/89 [1990] ECR I-4243.
8   This scheme is governed by Royal Decree No. 38 of 1967.
9   At para. 15 of the judgement.
10 At para. 13 of the Opinion.
11 At para. 14 of the Opinion.
12 Ibid.
13 Ibid.
14 Ibid.
15 In relation to Directive 79/7/EEC, the second theme can be seen most vividly in the ECJ's decision and Advocate General Tesauro's Opinion in *Thomas* (Chapter 4). The first theme is visible in *Commission* v. *France*, interpreting Article 2(4) of Directive 76/207/EEC (Chapter 3).
16 *Van Cant* v. *Rijksdienst voor Pensionen*, Case C-154/92 [1993] I-3811.
17 See *IBIS Review*, January 1994, pp.6–8, at p.7.
18 See 'A travail égal, pension inégale? Willockx a trouvé la parade', *Le Soir*, 9 February 1994.
19 Except of course those social insurance benefits given for the contingency of the loss of a breadwinner, either as the widow's or survivor's pensions common to all four countries, or as deserted wives' benefits in Ireland.
20 In her intervention at the conference, 'Equality of Treatment Between Women and Men in Social Security', Lincoln College, Oxford, 4–6 January 1994, Mme Clotuche (Directeur-Générale de la Sécurité Sociale in the Belgian Ministère de la Prévoyance Sociale) stated that only 14 per cent of women have a full pensions record as opposed to 60 per cent of men and that, on average, women have only 16 years of paid contributions.
21 Although, generally speaking, it would be preferable if this advantage were given to persons who have left the labour force to spend time in caring work, rather than to women, the former being a 'gender-sensitive' approach.
22 See 'A travail égal, pension inégale? Willockx a trouvé la parade', *Le Soir*, 9 February 1994.
23 *Roks and others* v. *Bestuur van de Bedrijfsvereniging voor de Gezondheid, Geestelijke en Maatschappelijke Belangen and Others*, Case C-343/92 [1994] ECR I-571.
24 At para. 33 of the judgement.
25 Rulings in the *Nolte* and *Megner* cases from Germany were expected in the autumn of 1995. Advocate General Léger delivered his Opinion in both these cases on 31 May 1995.
26 *Bilka-Kaufhaus* v. *Weber von Hartz*, Case 170/84 [1986] ECR 1607 (relating to an occupational pension scheme); *Kowalska* v. *Freie und Hansestadt Hamburg*, Case C-33/89 [1990] ECR I-2591 (relating to a severance grant in a collective agreement); *Nimz* v. *Freie und Hansestadt Hamburg*, Case C-184/89 [1991] ECR I-297 (a seniority classification system); *Arbeiterwohlfahrt der Stadt Berlin e V.* v. *Bötel*, Case C-360/90 [1992] ECR I-3589 (compensation for attending training courses).
27 *Kirsammer-Hack* v. *Nurhan Sidal*, Case C-189/91 [1993] ECR I-6185. Unusually, the ECJ, in this case, applied a rather narrow approach in defining the disadvantaged group (at paras 24–30), as well as to the question of objective justification, indicating that this would be satisfied where an objective was to lighten administrative and economic burdens on small firms (at paras 33–35).

28   *Ruzius-Wilbrink* v. *Bestuur van de Bedrijfsvereniging voor Overheidsdiensten,* Case C-102/88 [1989] ECR I-4311.
29   At para. 15 of the judgement.
30   *Rinner-Kühn* v. *FWW Spezial-Gebaüdereinigung,* Case 171/88 [1989] ECR 2743.
31   At para. 16 of the judgement.
32   At para. 17 of the judgement.
33   At para. 20 of the judgement.
34   On the tests of objective justification in EC equality law, see Hervey (1991) and Prechal (1993, pp.87–92).
35   At para. 36 of the judgement.
36   Ibid.
37   To recap, the test is that a Member State must establish that the means selected correspond to an objective necessary for its social policy and are appropriate and must be necessary to the attainment of that objective.
38   It needs to be borne in mind that the scope of the judgements will vary as to whether a provision is contrary to Article 119, which has horizontal direct effects, or a Directive, which has only vertical direct effects (that is, it only applies to the state), see Curtin (1990).
39   In *Kowalska* at para. 20 of the judgement.
40   At para. 21 of the judgement.
41   At para. 41 of the judgement.
42   At para. 42 of the judgement.
43   At para. 43 of the judgement.
44   *Teuling* v. *Bedrijfsvereniging voor de Chemische Industrie,* Case 30/85 [1987] ECR 2497.
45   See, further, the description of contemporary Dutch social security provision in Chapter 6.
46   At para. 15 of the judgement.
47   At para. 16 of the judgement.
48   At para. 17 of the judgement.
49   Linda Luckhaus (1988, pp.57–8) has suggested that, since in most cases benefits are paid to a man on the assumption that he will share the resources with his family, it could be argued that this is neither a suitable nor a necessary means for the protection of the dependent persons concerned against poverty. It is doubtful, however, whether the ECJ would accept such an argument, related to the possibility of women's and children's 'secondary poverty' in households.
50   *Commission* v. *Belgium,* Case C-229/89 [1991] ECR I-2205.
51   At paras 21–22 of the judgement.
52   At para. 23 of the judgement. The Court seems to have been influenced by the low levels of the payments in question, which did not differ markedly from those payable under 'Minimex', the safety net benefit (Banks, 1991, p.223). Advocate General Darmon was more explicit, stating at para. 13 of his Opinion that:

... the question is therefore, whether the payment of a sum of FB 29,198 for two people without any other income, or who have dependent children does not constitute a minimum income just as much as the payment of a replacement income.

53   At paras 25–26 of the judgement.
54   *Molenbroek* v. *Bestuur van de Sociale Verzekeringsbank,* Case C-226/91 [1992] ECR I-5943. This case is discussed in detail by Sohrab (1993a).

55 At para. 14 of the judgement.
56 At para. 18 of the judgement.
57 Ina Sjerps made this point at the meeting of the EC Network of Equality Experts in Hamburg in 1993: see Bieback (1993a, p.8).
58 *Giménez Zaera* v. *Instituto Nacional de la Seguridad Social y Tesoreria General de la Seguridad Social*, Case 126/86 [1987] ECR 3697, at para. 14 of the judgement. The ECJ recently confirmed that Article 117 is essentially in the nature of a programme whose objectives must be attained by a social policy to be defined by national authorities (*Sloman Neptun Schiffarts AG* v. *Seebetriebstrat Bodo Ziesemer der Sloman Neptun Schiffarts AG*, Joined Cases C-72/91 and C-73/91 [1993] ECR I-887). In *Sloman* the ECJ also held that Article 117 does not allow any judicial review of the social policy pursued by the Member States, at para. 27 of the judgement.
59 *Roks and others* v. *Bestuur van de Bedrijfsvereniging voor de Gezondheid, Geestelijke en Maatschappelijke Belangen and others*, Case C-343/92 [1994] ECR I-571.
60 *Ten Oever, Moroni, Neath and Coloroll*, Cases C-109, 110, 152 and 200/91, Opinion of 28 April 1993, at para. 60 of the Opinion.
61 The Advocate General confirmed this view in his Opinion in *Smith and others* v. *Avdel Systems*, Cases C-420/92 and C-28/93, Opinion of 4 May 1994. In this case, he reiterated that, as regards benefits based on rules in occupational schemes adapted to the principle of equal treatment which relate to periods of service after the entry into force of these new rules, EC law does not preclude a reduction of such benefits so long as benefits are the same for men and women (at para. 11 of the Opinion). Any other decision, he argued, would be tantamount to undesirable EC interference in a policy area falling within the competence of the Member States (ibid.).
62 At para. 29 of the judgement.
63 *Smith and others* v. *Avdel Systems*, Joined Cases C-420/92 and C-28/93, judgement of 28 September 1994, [1994] ECR I-367.
64 At para. 26 of the judgement.
65 I am grateful to Kirsten Scheiwe for this point.
66 I take up this theme in more detail in the conclusions.
67 *Dik and others* v. *College van Burgemeester en Wethouders Arnhem and Winterswijk*, Case 80/87 [1988] ECR 1601.
68 *Verholen and others* v. *Sociale Verzekeringsbank Amsterdam*, Joined Cases C-87/90, C-88-90 and C-89/90 [1991] ECR I-3757.
69 *Emmott* v. *Minister for Social Welfare and Attorney-General*, Case C-208/90 [1991] ECR I-4269.
70 *Secretary of State for Social Security* v. *Thomas and others*, Case C-328/91 [1993] ECR I-1247.
71 *The Queen* v. *Secretary of State of Social Security, ex p. Equal Opportunities Commission*, Case C-9/91 [1992] ECR I-4297.
72 *Steenhorst-Neerings* v. *Bestuur van de Bedrijfsvereniging voor Detailhandel, Ambachten en Huisvrouwen*, Case C-388/91 [1993] ECR I-5475.
73 At paras 35–37 of the judgement.
74 A representative of the UK government, present at the conference, 'Equality of Treatment Between Women and Men in Social Security', Lincoln College, Oxford, 4–6th January 1994, posed the question whether, given that Member States are collapsing under the weight of social security expenditure, maintaining sustainable levels of social security could be a valid social policy objective.
75 See McCrudden and Black (1994).
76 At para. 30 of the judgement.

77   At para. 28 of the judgement.
78   I am grateful to Linda Luckhaus for this point.
79   The two countries are the UK and Germany.   Since autumn 1992 there has been a constant stream of serious attacks directed at the ECJ's administration of justice, beginning with a speech by the Federal Chancellor, Mr Kohl.   It is apparently the Federal government's intention to promote publicity and political criticism against the ECJ and, if necessary, to take initiatives towards restricting the possibilities for cases from lower courts to be referred to the ECJ (see *EC Equality Network Newsletter*, Summer 1993, pp.43–4).

6   The Netherlands, Ireland and Belgium

The aim of this chapter is to consider the implementation of Directive 79/7/ EEC in three countries – Ireland, the Netherlands and Belgium. The central questions to be addressed are, first, what reforms have been enacted by these Member States to comply with the Directive? Second, what observations can be made about the impact of the reforms in promoting financial independence for women? The chapter is not intended as an exhaustive account of the changes brought about by the need to implement Directive 79/7/EEC, rather the objective is to capture the flavour of the changes in order to present some comparative insights. A threefold test is used as an analytic framework to assess how far implementation has advanced women's financial independence. Overall conclusions relating to the four systems under consideration, including the UK, are given in Chapter 8.

This chapter will provide a similar treatment of issues as that already carried out for the UK in Chapter 2, albeit in less detail. I will look at aspects of the gendered social reality in all three countries, concentrating primarily on women's labour market participation. For each of the three countries the discussion will be structured around four topics:

1   an overview of the national social security system;
2   a description of the inequalities facing women prior to the adoption of the Directive;
3   an outline of the legislative amendments passed and litigation in national courts;
4   a consideration of how far women's financial independence has been advanced.

I will highlight the extent to which direct discrimination has been replaced by indirect discrimination, and whether the social security system still retains the family/household as a determining factor in benefit allocation.

This chapter begins with a description of the analytical framework, followed by a consideration of some aspects of the gendered social reality in the three countries. The implementation of the Directive in the three countries is examined in turn – the Netherlands, Ireland and, finally Belgium.

ANALYTICAL FRAMEWORK

The focus of this chapter, as well as of Chapter 5, is a primarily legal one, and therefore, in examining the implementation of the Directive in the four social security systems, the book does not claim to offer a detailed empirical study. Rather, a threefold test is proposed as a framework to tackle the question of progress towards greater financial independence. The threefold test, representing various stages towards achieving women's financial independence, differentiates between:

- equality of access
- equality of opportunity
- equality of outcomes.

All three of these 'equalities' represent stages in achieving financial independence – that is, women being able to claim benefits, women being able to build up entitlements to benefits, as well as women actually receiving the type of benefits which are conducive to the achievement of financial independence, such as personal and non-couple-based means-tested benefits. I will now consider in greater detail each of the elements in the threefold test.

Equality of access represents a first stage in promoting women's financial independence – that is, can women actually claim benefits on the same terms as men? Are women, or indeed certain groups of women, barred from even claiming? Do different rules apply to them when they do claim? It may be that women, or specific groups of women, are not able to claim benefits, or are only allowed to do so if they are breadwinners. Further, in order to be able to claim, women may have to satisfy additional conditions. All these situations will be characterized as demonstrating an inequality of access.

The second stage is represented by equality of opportunity. This essentially asks whether there is a 'level playing field' between men and women in terms of gaining entitlements to benefits. Are there still rules or conditions which women, or particular groups of women, find harder to satisfy in practice, given the gendered social reality? In order to ascertain this, we need to consider such factors as the extent and type of women's labour market participation, the extent to which women live in couples (how many women are divorced or are single parents), the availability of childcare facilities, and women's earnings compared to men's. The impact on women of various benefit rules cannot be understood in isolation from these factors.

The third stage in the achievement of financial independence would be where equality of outcomes exists between men and women in terms of what benefits are actually received by women. This would not be evidenced by any such crude indicator as a 50–50 split between men and women claimants of any one benefit. Such a result would be impossible given that the current gendered patterns of employment and caring are likely to continue for some time. Rather, equality of outcomes would have two main characteristics. First, there would be a decrease in the sharp disparities that exist between men and women as claimants of social insurance benefits. Second, a focus on outcomes introduces the qualitative aspects in benefit receipt that have been emphasized throughout this book, relating to how different risks are provided for, whether by contributory or means-tested benefits, the connotations which attach to different benefit types, and finally to levels of benefits. Equality of outcomes will be evidenced by a qualitative, as well as quantitative, improvement in the benefits and (types of benefits) received by women.[1]

The boundaries between the three 'equalities' in this framework are not, in some cases, easy to distinguish. This is particularly true of the boundary between equality of opportunity and equality of outcomes. While it is straightforward to identify both whether there is equality of access and equality of outcomes, the notion of equality of opportunity lies, more fluidly, between the two. Equality of opportunity is nevertheless a useful concept, since it allows us to observe some of the processes by which equality of outcomes is not achieved.

The discussion of the implementation of the Directive in the three countries needs to be enriched by at least a partial understanding of the gendered social reality in the three countries, to which we now turn.

ASPECTS OF THE GENDERED SOCIAL REALITY IN THE NETHERLANDS, IRELAND AND BELGIUM

In this section, I consider aspects of the gendered social reality in the three countries, beginning with women in households, then women's labour market participation and finally a few remarks regarding gendered social security systems.

Women in households

In all three countries, most women (between 63 per cent and 73 per cent) are living as part of a couple, with or without children (Eurostat, 1992, p.33). On the other hand, both the number of divorces and of lone parents is increasing in the Netherlands and Belgium (ibid., p.41). In Ireland there is no legal divorce, but the numbers of women receiving social security payments as deserted wives rose dramatically from 6187 in 1981 to 16 314 in 1990 (Mangan, 1993a, pp.40–1). Lone parents across the three countries comprised around 10 per cent of all families in the 1980s (Pillinger, 1992, p.31). Finally, the birthrate has fallen in all three countries (EC Commission, 1992, p.8).

Women's labour market participation

There are a number of relevant factors to be noted, such as the proportion of women in the working population, their hours of working and age profiles, differentials between the earnings of men and women and the availability of childcare facilities. A number of these factors will be both described and presented below in chart form.

Rates of labour market participation

Of the three countries, women's labour market participation is highest in Belgium, at 52 per cent, with much lower levels in both the Netherlands (at 42 per cent) and in Ireland (at 38.5 per cent)[2] (Pillinger, 1992, p.12). This does conceal an important increase in women's labour market participation in the Netherlands, and recent research in Ireland shows that the increase in participation by women aged 25–34 (in particular married women) has been the most important single influence on changes in the composition of the Irish workforce in the past 20 years.[3]

Age distribution

Labour market participation varies considerably with age with the highest rates in all three countries achieved by young women (before they start having children). Later, participation declines and does not recover in any of the three countries. In the Netherlands almost 75 per cent of Dutch women around 22 years of age are in paid work, but by age 43 this figure has already fallen to 52 per cent (Eurostat, 1992, p.71). In Ireland women achieve the highest rates of labour market participation between 18 and 22 (at nearly 80 per cent), but by the age of 36 there are only just under 40 per cent of women in paid work (ibid.). In Belgium, activity rates are very high – at nearly 80 per cent – until women's late 20s but these rates fall steadily after the age of 30 (ibid., p.70).

Working hours

In order to understand the nature of women's labour market participation, we must also note the hours that are worked by women. In the Netherlands the numbers of women working for a few hours are significant, and in the fewest-hours categories the rates are double the EU average! 27 per cent of Dutch women work between 1–15 hours per week, 21.3 per cent of women work between 16–25 hours, 13.2 per cent of women work between 26–35 hours and 35.7 per cent of women work between 36–45 hours (Eurostat, 1992, p.95). Indeed, the Netherlands has the highest percentage of part-time employment as a proportion of total employment in the EU at just under 30 per cent, and part-time employment amounted to around 55 per cent of women's total employment in 1988 (Pillinger, 1992, p.35).

Part-time work in Ireland comprises a relatively small share of employment and is not characterized by the stark sex differences apparent in the UK. In Ireland 17 per cent of women's employment is part-time, while it is 11 per cent of men's (ibid.).

The distribution of women's working hours in Belgium reveals that most women work full-time: 56.2 per cent of women in paid employment work between 36–45 hours per week (Eurostat, 1992, p.95). Interestingly, this was also true of lone mothers with children aged 0 to 4 in 1985: 46 per cent worked full-time, 11 per cent worked part-time and only 17 per cent were out of the labour force (Pillinger, 1992, p.33).[4] In 1988 there were fewer women working part-time (5.1 per cent) at the very lowest hours thresholds of between 0–15 hours than in either the UK or the Netherlands. There were also 18.7 per cent of women working between 16–25 hours per week, which is comparable to rates in the UK and slightly below rates in the Netherlands (Eurostat, 1992, p.95).

Earnings

In the Netherlands women's gross hourly earnings as a percentage of men's in all industries in 1987 was 74.2 per cent, which was higher than women's equivalent earnings in the UK and Ireland (Pillinger, 1992, p.16). In Ireland in 1987–88 it was 67.1 per cent (which was the second highest differential in the EC, and around the same as the UK). In Belgium the equivalent figure was 75.3 per cent, which meant that, of the four countries, women's earnings compared to those of men were highest in Belgium (ibid.).

Availability of childcare

The extent of public day-care provision across the three countries varies considerably. Belgium has traditionally been one of the best providers in Europe, and in 1988 there were places for 20 per cent of children aged 0–2 and for 95 per cent of children aged 3–5 (Eurostat, 1992, p.52). In the Netherlands, in 1988, only 53 per cent of children aged 3–5 are in public childcare provision (ibid.), although this does represent a considerable improvement from the early 1980s. Finally, in Ireland in 1988, only 3 per cent of children aged 0–2 and around 55 per cent of children aged between 3–5 years were in public day-care (ibid.).

Observations on gendered social security systems

In all three countries there are obstacles blocking specific groups of women from achieving financial independence from social security. In Ireland and the Netherlands this has been by means of overt exclusions of particular groups of women from a range of benefits. In Belgium breadwinners have received the highest levels of the (partly) earnings-related benefits.

The principal mechanisms through which inequalities of opportunities exist vary between and across the four countries, taking into account the differences in the extent and level of women's labour market participation as well as the extent to which caring is compensated within the benefit system. A few observations are outlined by way of tentative hypothesis.

In the Netherlands significant numbers of women work part-time, and at low hours of part-time work, and so measures which discriminate against part-time workers will have an important impact on women's ability to build up social insurance rights. This is likely to be more true overall of the Netherlands and the UK than of Belgium and Ireland, where part-time work accounts for smaller proportions of total employment.

In Belgium most women in paid work are working on a full-time basis, and thus it would be expected that Belgian women would have equalities of outcomes in the social insurance system. However, the structure of social insurance benefits incorporates important needs-oriented elements, and this means that single-earner households receive higher benefits than single persons or persons cohabiting with an earning partner. Social insurance, therefore, still subsidizes a traditional hierarchical family model and disadvantages dual-earner couples, which in turn may impede alterations to the

traditional gendered division of labour (Scheiwe, 1993, p.7). Married female full-time workers in Belgium, who pay the same contributions as other
workers, have, over the years, seen their benefits reduced in favour of
greater support to single-earner households (Peemans-Poullet, 1993, pp.31–
3).

The Irish system is an unusual case in a number of ways. Women's low
labour market participation has meant that few women have been able to
build up their own entitlements to social insurance benefits. However, married men – as part of their contributions to the social insurance system – pay
for the contingency that they will abandon their wives. Where they do so,
married women may be able to claim a contributory benefit for deserted
wives. Second, an important Irish policy has been that mothers and carers
should not be forced to enter paid work, and an array of (means-tested)
schemes has been developed to provide for women looking after dependants. However, most of these schemes pay benefits at low levels of income,
may be difficult to claim in practice, and are liable to be withdrawn whenever a woman enters a marital, or quasi-marital, relationship. There are thus,
it is argued, clear inequalities of outcomes in terms of the qualitative nature
of the schemes which provide for female risks.

A number of inequalities of opportunities and outcomes are similar to all
four systems, although the emphasis may differ between countries. I now
turn to consider implementation of the Directive in the three social security
systems in turn.

THE NETHERLANDS

Overview

Labour market participation by married women was discouraged in the
Netherlands until the 1970s, and this was reflected in labour, tax and social
security legislation which penalized married women who engaged in paid
work (Sainsbury, 1993b, p.7). There were few incentives for married women
to enter the labour market at all or in anything but a marginal way (Sainsbury
1993b, p.6). Married women in employment received no tax allowances,
and unless they had breadwinner status they were not entitled to the minimum wage (Sainsbury, 1993b, p.6). In the social security field, married
women in paid work making social insurance contributions were denied a
series of benefits.

The absence of women from paid work until the 1970s, it is argued, partly
accounts for the relatively high level of the minimum wage and social

benefits, which were seen as necessary for male breadwinners to maintain family income (Roebroek, 1993, p.248). The construction of social security benefits and contributions revolved around the family as the norm, and around the notion of the family minimum (Sainsbury, 1993b, p.6). The social minimum was roughly equivalent to the net minimum wage for couples, 90 per cent for single parents, with lower rates for single persons and persons living at home (ibid.). The unit of contributions was also the household: the head of the household paid contributions on the basis of family income.

In the contemporary social protection system,[5] social insurance schemes are divided into national insurance schemes and employee insurance schemes, as well as a number of social assistance schemes. The level of benefits from the national insurance schemes and social assistance are based on a given level of the social minimum, which differs according to whether a claimant is a single person or whether she or he has dependants. Employees may also be entitled to benefits from employee insurance schemes – for instance, employees can claim from the ZW sickness insurance in their first year of incapacity. Benefits from these employee schemes are related to past wages; for example, under the ZW scheme employees are paid 70 per cent of their gross daily wages. Where employees are eligible for the national social insurance schemes, the latter benefits may be supplemented by wage-related benefits – as for example, the WAO employee scheme supplements payments from the AAW general scheme.

Social assistance schemes are wholly financed by general taxation; the main scheme is governed by the General Assistance Act (ABW). The ABW scheme provides for any Dutch person resident in the Netherlands who cannot meet his or her own subsistence needs (Pieters, 1990, p.195). Benefits under the ABW scheme are paid as a percentage of the national minimum wage (NMW), on a household basis, to couples at 100 per cent (or 50 per cent each), to lone parent families at 90 per cent, to single persons at 70 per cent, or to single persons sharing a house at 60 per cent.

Inequalities in social security

Prior to the early 1980s, married women suffered three main forms of inequalities of access to benefits in national social insurance schemes.

1. Married women were unable to claim benefits under the tax-financed unemployment benefit scheme, the *Wet Werkloosheidsvoorziening*, the WWV. Article 13(1), point 1, of the scheme excluded working married women who were not breadwinners (*kostwinster*).

2. Married women were excluded from claiming benefits under the *Algemene Arbeidsongeschiktheidswet* (General Law on Incapacity – AAW) until 1980.
3. Married women were unable to claim benefits in their own right under the national old age pension scheme, the *Algemene Ouderdomswet* (AOW). Furthermore, rules as to the reduction of benefits because of years of residence abroad differed between men and women.

Sex-neutral requirements, or conditions in the national social insurance schemes which obstruct women gaining access and entitlement to benefits (or to put it another way, inequalities of opportunity), have appeared in a number of guises. These include earnings thresholds (requirements that claimants have earnt over a specified amount in the last year), rules which make it more difficult for part-time workers to gain entitlement to benefits and, indeed, rules which give part-time workers lower benefits. These obstacles are compounded by the structure of the system which revolves around the family minimum and in which the most generous benefits are given to 'breadwinners'.

Employee insurance schemes also have a number of rules which effectively exclude women. First, earnings thresholds are built into a number of benefits, such as the ZW (the short-term employee sickness insurance) and the WAO (the long-term employee sickness insurance) and the WW (unemployment benefits), which have the effect of excluding many women. Second, the definitions of employee may also serve to exclude many women. In defining an employee (*werknemer*) under the above schemes, the law excludes certain categories of workers, such as homeworkers and other people who give 'personal services', when they earn less than two-fifths of the minimum wage (Holtmaat, 1989, p.484). Also excluded in practice are persons who undertake paid work for a family member, such as a daughter who works in her father's firm without an employment contract.[6] Another exclusion concerns persons who mainly perform household services in or for the household of their employer, when this work is performed for less than three days per week (ibid.). This rule chiefly affects mainly housekeepers, cleaners and childminders.[7] The assumption behind all these exclusions is that the women who work on the above basis do not need to be insured under a social insurance scheme, since they are deemed to be secondary earners already financially maintained by a breadwinner (ibid.).

Legislative amendments and litigation in the national courts

In the early and mid-1980s the Dutch government embarked on an important phase of social security reforms, prompted by a variety of factors, such as the complexity of the system, its rising costs in a time of economic crisis and the need to implement Directive 79/7/EEC (Sjerps, 1988, p.101).[8] In January 1987 a number of important new provisions entered into force, several of which levelled down social security provision.

Unemployment benefits

Originally, a benefit could be claimed under the WW scheme for six months, followed by a WWV benefit for two years, which, as will be recalled, excluded married women who were not breadwinners. After 1982 supplements up to the level of the social minimum for a family were no longer given with these benefits to unemployed breadwinners nor to unemployed persons over 35 years of age.[9] The government intended simultaneously to transpose the Directive into national law and merge the WWV unemployment benefit with the *Werkloosheidswet* (WW) scheme.[10] The merged benefit would no longer include the discriminatory wage-earner requirement in the WWV benefit. The merger of the two benefits was not in fact achieved on time, but the discrimination against married women was eventually repealed with retroactive effect to the 23 December 1984 by the Law of 24 April 1985 which entered into force on 1 May 1985. In order to secure funding for the change, the WWV benefits were reduced in duration for both men and women under 35 years of age (Barendrecht and der Wal, 1986, p.331).

This left the problem of those married women whose unemployment started before the entry into force of the Directive. This issue gave rise to two references to the ECJ – first, *FNV* in 1987 and then *Dik* in 1988 (see Chapter 4).[11] The ECJ held that women were to be treated in the same way as men as from the date of entry into force of the Directive, regardless of when they became unemployed. The referring court, the RvB Groningen, held that the lack of retrospection was contrary to the Directive and held it inapplicable.[12]

The duration of the new WW benefit now depends on factors such as age and duration of employment before the loss of employment. This means that young people or people who re-enter the labour market after periods out, such as women, are left at a disadvantage, although short periods of exit from the labour market to look after young children are partly compensated (see below).

Breadwinners receiving this benefit are entitled to receive supplements, under the *Toeslagenwet* (TW – Supplements Act) scheme, when their benefits fall short of the social minimum for a family (that is, 100 per cent of the statutory minimum wage). The level of the supplements depends on age and household composition and are means-tested on the income, but not capital, of a household (de Jong *et al.*, 1990, p.10).[13] All income from, or in connection with, employment of all members of the family unit, with the exception of dependent children, and any other possible income from possessions is taken into account in assessing means. This may exert a negative influence on a female partner's employment incentives, since any of her earnings are set against the benefit.

Sickness and incapacity for work

Married women had been excluded from claiming benefits under the AAW. The abolition of this exclusion led to a tightening of benefit rules, several aspects of which have been the subject of litigation alleging indirect discrimination against women. Changes to the employee invalidity scheme, the WAO, were also brought about in order to restrict the increase in public expenditure involved in allowing married women to claim the AAW (the WAO 'tops up' the national insurance scheme). The WAO's guarantee of benefit equivalent to the statutory minimum wage was substituted by an amount equivalent to a claimant's last wage.

The AAW scheme was amended by the Law of 20 December 1979, which came into force on the 1 January 1980 and which extended entitlement of benefits under the AAW to married women provided that their incapacity occurred after the 1 October 1975. The process of implementing equality in this benefit scheme proved very complex, and itself became a rich source of litigation in the Dutch courts (as well as in the ECJ).

Introducing a past income requirement The legislation of 1979 provided that, after January 1980, new claimants of the AAW, whose incapacity began after December 1979, had to satisfy a new requirement of having earnt a given level of income over a period of time. Transitional regulations were passed, allowing men and single women whose incapacity had started before this date to receive the AAW benefit under the old conditions. This same right was not, however, given to married women, who were still denied the AAW altogether if their incapacity started before 1975, and were subject to the income requirement if their incapacity started between 1975 and December 1979.

These regulations were repealed by a law in May 1989 because of a decision of the Centrale Raad van Beroep (CRvB)[14] of 5 January 1988 equalizing the conditions for married women whenever their incapacity started. The law of May 1989, however, still sought to limit claims by providing that persons whose incapacity started before 1979, who applied for benefits after 1989 (mainly in effect married women now entitled to the AAW), had to satisfy the income requirement. It was further provided that the AAW benefit was to be withdrawn from persons whose incapacity started before 1979 if they did not satisfy the income requirement.

A number of Dutch courts have examined whether income requirements are in general indirectly discriminatory against women. Their decisions have revealed inconsistencies and uncertainties, with courts in various cities coming to different decisions on different grounds. The Raad van Beroep (RvB) of Roermond struck down this requirement (Blom, 1993, p.99). The RvB Arnhem, which had upheld the part-time workers rule, struck down the income requirement on the grounds that while the aim of providing a threshold to limit insignificant benefit claims was legitimate, here the rule operated to exclude benefits even where benefits could not be considered insignificant.[15] The requirement was upheld by the RvB in Haarlem, but in this case the claimant had not actually lost any income from employment (Blom, 1993, p.100).[16]

Eventually, however, in June 1992 the CRvB decided that the income requirement was in fact indirectly discriminatory against women.[17] The court held that, while the aims of the requirement were legitimate (that is, to exclude insignificant benefit claims), the threshold itself was not suitable to achieve this goal (Prechal, 1993, p.92). However, the court also accepted the validity of the principle that loss has to arise from occupational income in granting an AAW benefit (Blom, 1993, p.101).

AAW benefit levels cut – greater resources to breadwinners   Changes in 1982 meant that the AAW was no longer to be paid at a level equivalent to the statutory minimum wage (SMW), but only at 70 per cent of this amount. Supplements were, however, to be provided to persons with a dependent spouse or child, to bring their benefit up to 100 per cent of the statutory minimum wage. These supplements, which were means-tested, could be argued to exert a negative effect on the incentives to take up part-time paid work of the dependent spouse (Schunter-Kleeman, 1992, p.45). These changes and the system of supplements, which favoured (male) workers with dependent spouses, were the subject in 1987 of the *Teuling* case.[18]

When the *Teuling* case returned to the referring court, the RvB Amsterdam found that the system of supplements was not justified under the grounds set out by the ECJ.[19] The court reasoned that, in many cases, the supplements did not arguably provide a minimum income and that, in other cases, the supplements were not necessary to provide such a minimum (Blom, 1993, p.91–2). First, a supplement did not guarantee a minimum in those cases where the claimant was a part-time worker who did not meet the income requirement, regardless of whether the worker had dependants or not. Second, the supplement was seldom necessary to provide a minimum income since many workers in fact received a benefit from the employee WAO scheme, which was not taken into account in calculating the AAW benefit.[20]

However, this decision was reversed on appeal to the Centrale Raad van Beroep (CRvB).[21] This court held that the purpose of the AAW was not to provide a minimum income but rather to provide a 'floor benefit' within the whole system of insurance against incapacity for work (Blom, 1993, p.93). The court deduced the legislator's aim as being to avoid a situation in which the WAO would support to a greater degree than the AAW because of the lowering of the benefit; this was, in the court's view, a legitimate aim (Blom, 1993, p.94). Further, the court held that the rules for part-timers were of no relevance to this case and that their legitimacy need therefore not be considered (ibid.). As noted by Blom (ibid.), it is 'striking' that the CRvB deduced a secondary purpose to the legislation wholly on its own initiative, and moreover that the court failed completely to apply the proportionality test.

Discriminatory rules against part-time workers in calculating benefit levels
Full-time workers who earned over the prescribed amount of past earnings in the AAW scheme, as well as the exempted categories (such as students and the low-earning self-employed), were entitled to a benefit linked to the minimum wage, but part-time workers only received benefits linked to their previous income. Part-time workers are the only group of workers who are not guaranteed a minimum subsistence income that is not dependent on previous earnings: for them their average daily wage is taken as the basic amount. Thus part-time workers, most of whom are women, receive lower benefits than other categories of claimants.

This method of calculating benefits for part-time workers was the subject of the *Ruzius-Wilbrink* reference to the ECJ.[22] Judgement was given in December 1989 and the Court held that these rules did indirectly discriminate against women. When the case returned to the national courts the rules were found to be justified. The RvB Groningen, the court which referred the questions to the ECJ, argued that the ECJ had not taken into account all the possible justifications for the legislation (Blom, 1993, p.95).[23] It continued that the aim of the AAW was not to provide a minimum subsistence income but to replace income from work lost through illness, and thus the treatment of part-time workers' earnings was in complete conformity with this aim (ibid.). With regard to the exempted categories, the court held that they affected such a small group that they did not alter the AAW's character. This decision was upheld on appeal to the CRvB, which held that the primary aim of the AAW is to replace occupational income, and the fact that the principle was not applied to full-time and part-time workers alike did not *prima facie* give rise to indirect discrimination (ibid., p.98).[24]

It will be recalled that, in its decision in the *Teuling* follow-up case, the CRvB argued that the AAW's primary goal was to provide a minimum income to those unable to work, while in this case the same court decided that the primary goal is the replacement of income. The CRvB, by regarding the purpose of the AAW benefit as either primary or secondary according to the facts of the case, created the situation where the purpose of the AAW is effectively brought outside the scope of review, and the principle of proportionality is circumvented.

To summarize, the national judgements subsequent to *Teuling* and *Ruzius* show a fundamental misunderstanding of the ECJ's objective justification test (Prechal, 1993, p.91). The judgement of the CRvB in the *Teuling* case, was according to Prechal (1993, pp.91–2), 'confused' and 'neglected almost entirely the seperate touchstones laid down' by the ECJ. As we have seen, the follow-up to *Ruzius* led to several divergent decisions of the lower courts before the CRvB finally found that the part-time workers rule was objectively justifiable (ibid., p.91). These cases show another 'precarious' problem, namely that of the national courts, after an ECJ judgement, searching for other possible justifications than were submitted to the ECJ (ibid., p.92).

In practice, there are still obstacles to women's entitlement to benefits under the AAW scheme. Married women have not been awarded AAW as frequently as married men or single women: almost 40 per cent of claims by married women non-breadwinners are rejected, which is not true of the claims of married men (Sainsbury, 1993b, p.21). To claim a benefit under the AAW a person must have received earned income during the preceding year equal to 48 times the minimum daily wage, thus excluding many part-time workers (ibid.). Supplements to breadwinners are also paid under the Supplements Act (TW) with benefits for sickness and incapacity. It will be recalled that these may exert a negative influence on a female partner's employment incentives, since her earnings are set against the benefit.

Old age pensions

The *Algemene Ouderdomswet* (General Law on Old Age – AOW) was reformed by the Law of 23 March 1985, taking effect from 1 April 1985, to allow married women to be able to claim pensions in their own right. In the early 1980s the AOW represented a strange combination of harsh discriminatory measures against married women, but also a more inclusive construction vis-à-vis women, since even persons without income are covered by the old age benefit (Sainsbury, 1993a, p.75).

Verholen[25]   Because the 1985 reform was not made retrospective, married women were still being denied full pensions because of the effect of past discriminatory rules. This was challenged by three women on the basis that the lack of retrospection perpetuated the discriminatory effect of the earlier rules beyond December 1984 – the date the Directive entered into force. The ECJ rejected the Dutch government's argument that to accord married women the same treatment as men after December 1984 would be to give the Directive retroactive effect, in view of the fact that the AOW scheme is based on the progressive acquisition of rights. Cousins (1992a, p.62) has argued that this ruling may mean that any person who was excluded from social insurance prior to 1984 on discriminatory grounds will now have to be treated as though he or she was insured.

The referring court, the RvB of 's-Hertogenbosch decided, on the basis of the ECJ's decision, that only one of the three women involved was actually entitled to invoke Directive 79/7/EEC, as only she fell within its scope. However, the difference in treatment between claimants was deemed to be in violation of the equality principle Article 26 of the Covenant of Civil and Political Rights and Article 1 of the Dutch Constitution and therefore invalid.[26]

On appeal to the Centrale Raad van Beroep, this court decided that there was no violation of Article 26 of the Covenant, so that only those persons who had been in the labour market were entitled to equality of treatment under Directive 79/7/EEC.[27]

Supplements for dependants – Molenbroek   Pensions under the AOW scheme are now paid individually to both spouses in a married couple or a cohabiting heterosexual or gay couple over 65 years of age. Where only one partner is over 65, he or she receives a benefit of 50 per cent and a 50 per cent supplement for the dependent spouse (unless the latter requests that it be paid directly to them).[28] The supplement is subject to a reduction of 2 per cent for every year in which the dependent partner was not insured in the AOW scheme. Until 1 April 1988 these supplements had been paid without regard to the dependent partner's income. Since April 1988 the dependent partner's income will, within certain limits, affect the level of the supplement. The supplements are paid without regard to the income of the partner over 65 (the non-dependent partner). In fact many people receiving these benefits do have an overall income far higher than the minimum level, due to occupational pensions or income from other sources such as investments (Blom, 1993, pp.101–2). The rule introduced in 1988, which reduces the level of the dependant's supplement because of a dependent partner's earnings, can be argued to be indirectly discriminatory against women, since more women than men will see their overall benefit reduced because of a spouse's earnings.

Three RvBs considered the presumption of indirect discrimination in these supplements before a question on this issue was eventually referred to the ECJ (see below). The RvB Haarlem considered that it was irrelevant that, in practice, the supplements were often not needed to provide a minimum income, even where this is purportedly the aim of the benefit scheme.[29] The RvB Arnhem stated that the supplement system should be tested for suitability and necessity, according to the principle of proportionality, but did not actually apply this test on the grounds that, if the system were held in violation of the Directive and had therefore to be struck down, a vacuum would be created in the benefit scheme (Blom, 1993, p.103).[30] This is a rather astonishing decision, given that EC law clearly states that, in a situation such as this, discriminatory rules must not be applied, and the previously disadvantaged group is entitled to be treated on the same terms as the advantaged group (ibid.). The RvB Roermond held that while the system of supplements was legitimate, since they were not often necessary for their purpose, the system could not be justified (ibid., p.103–4).[31] Further, the court rejected the argument that the supplements were justified because an additional aim of the law was to provide a 'floor benefit' in comparison to other sources of income (ibid., p.104).

The apparently indirectly discriminatory nature of the dependants' supplements, in view of 1988 changes, was the subject of a reference to the ECJ in *Molenbroek*.[32] It will be recalled that the plaintiff in this case, a married man, argued that the rule relating to the income of the dependent partner was indirectly discriminatory against women in the hope that the pre-1988 situation would be reinstated in which he was financially better off. He argued that the AOW benefit supplements are not in fact necessary to provide a minimum subsistence income. The ECJ, on the other hand, accepted the Dutch government's argument that, since the purpose of the AOW scheme was to provide a minimum level of income, the rules could be objectively justified.

How far has financial independence been advanced?

The Dutch system is now characterized by significant equality of access to benefits for women. This was achieved by removing the exclusions against married women claiming benefits under the AAW in 1980, the AOW in 1985 and the WWV in 1985. Contributions to the general insurance schemes were individualized in 1985 (Sainsbury, 1993b, p.20). However, these reforms do not appear to have significantly advanced equality of outcomes for women. This highlights the difficulties of implementing substantive social change within the context of deep structural inequality (Kaplan, 1992, p.158).

The family minimum still shapes the construction of several benefits (Sainsbury, 1993b, p.22). The TW (Supplements Act) still gives breadwinner supplements, and it is unlikely that these could be found to be indirectly discriminatory against women, given the ECJ's rulings in both *Commission v. Belgium* and more recently in *Molenbroek*. The reforms of the 1980s were characterized by a considerable levelling-down of benefits, thereby increasing the numbers of people finding themselves falling more quickly below the level of the social minimum. This implies a greater role for social assistance, which is itself predicated on the family model (Sjerps, 1988, p.104). In fact, between 1970 and 1985 there was a 100 per cent increase in recipients of social assistance, from 299 000 to 606 000 persons (Room *et al.*, 1989, p.168). Married persons become ineligible for social assistance benefits where their spouses are employed, and where their spouse is claiming means-tested benefits they will have strong incentives to leave employment or not to seek paid work (Sainsbury, 1993b, p.22). This, as we have also seen in relation to the UK, means that women's opportunities of gaining an income that is not mediated through the hands of a male partner are limited.

Moreover, in 1984 the Dual Wage Earner Act was passed, which gives both spouses the same basic tax allowance. This change by decreasing the tax burden on single breadwinner families and raising it for double-earners discriminates against working women (Kaplan, 1992, p.158). Many women in part-time work have, it seems, seen their small incomes dwindle, and over 10 000 left their part-time jobs once the new system came into force (Sjerps, 1988, p.101). The husband's privileged position is maintained because a woman's entry in the labour market sets her earnings against a deterioration in her husband's tax position (Sainsbury, 1993b, p.20).

Implementing equality of access to benefits in a situation of structural inequality may at times produce unintended effects. One such unintended effect is that extending benefits to men for the first time, to comply with a prohibition on direct discrimination, in fact changes the nature of a benefit and thus leads to a levelling-down for all. This is what has happened with the widow's benefit under the AWW scheme.[33] This benefit, aimed at compensating for the loss of a breadwinner, had been given at relatively generous levels and without a means-test. Since the benefit was extended to men on the same terms by a court decision in 1988,[34] these payments become too generous, in the sense that men would be receiving them even though they may already have access to adequate levels of income. Now the AWW is in the process of being reformed, so that the payments are partly means-tested, which may also have a negative impact on women.

This suggests that 'grafting' equality of access on to schemes which are based on certain assumptions about gender roles produces less than equality of results. The case of the widow's benefits is the flipside of the situation that inequalities of opportunity remain even when women are allowed to claim social insurance benefits, where these benefits are geared to the worker in a 'standard employment relationship'. Arguably, equality of outcomes seem to necessitate a greater rethinking of benefit structures, including issues of how entitlements are built up, adequacy and the (changing) purpose of schemes. This might be better suited to a legislative, rather than a judicial, role.

The creation of sex-neutral rules does not, as already observed, lead to equal outcomes because of the interaction with the gendered social reality – that is, the structural inequality between men and women. In other words, bringing about equality of access in relation to social insurance benefits, without also modifying the conditions of entitlement to those benefits to adapt them to two (as opposed to one) gender role, only benefits 'exceptional' women, to borrow Rubenstein's phrase (1990, p.89). Thus, rules that are directly discriminatory are easily replaced by (sex-neutral) rules which indirectly discriminate against women. This can be observed especially with regard to the thresholds and earnings rules which regulate access to social insurance benefits. Married women may now claim these benefits but, because the increase in women's labour force participation in recent years has been in part-time work,[35] the effect of equality of access is likely to be blunted.

As part of the official policy that every person should achieve economic independence, the '1990 initiative' was launched. Prior to this, cohabiting and married men who were unemployed or the victims of industrial injury were entitled to receive supplements to their benefits from the *Toeslagenwet* (TW) scheme if their benefits were below an acceptable minimum for their families and themselves (Bussemaker *et al.*, 1993, p.1). Since 1990 this TW supplement has no longer been paid to anyone reaching the age of 18 in or after 1990. Thus, for both members of a couple to gain benefits, each partner must be available for work. There is just one exception to this rule, and that is for women who have a child, or children, under 12 years old, who are not required to be available for work (ibid.). This change has been criticized on at least two grounds (ibid.). In the first place, why is the exemption clause only for women with children under 12? Because it is taken for granted that she will look after the children when they are young, policy-makers argue that caring responsibilities are being taken seriously. But, argues Bussemaker (1991, p.56), in practice this can mean an affirmation of the separation between 'men's work' and 'women's work'. In the second place, the women affected by being forced into availability for work will probably be anything but prepared for employment, argue Bussemaker *et al.* (1993, p.2), since they are mainly in the lowest wage categories.

Care tasks have remained firmly within the private sphere. Public childcare facilities are not widely available, and the main type of care offered is in the form of playgroups which operate on a part-time basis and cater for pre-school children of who are $2^{1}/_{2}$ years or older (Sainsbury, 1993b, p.22). This may be different in the future; the government promised to expand existing childcare facilities by 52 000 places over the 1990–94 period through the release of extra funds (Bussemaker *et al.*, 1993, p.3). Some steps have been taken towards collectivizing care in the social security system, notably by credits for unemployment benefits. The 1987 changes to the employee social insurance scheme for unemployment benefits also included the intro-duction of a childcare credit system enabling claimants to lengthen the period of unemployment for which benefits are paid. For every child under six years of age a parent can count the whole period of childcare towards extending the duration of benefit, and for every child between 6 and 12 years a claimant can count half of this period (Article 42(5)–(8) of the Unemployment Insurance Act (WW)).

Summary

While equality of access has been achieved for Dutch women, there remain inequalities of opportunity and of outcomes. The many female part-time workers are excluded by even modest income thresholds, even without taking account of the definitions of 'employee' that exclude many other women from the employee social insurance schemes. Inequalities of oppor-tunity and outcomes remain strong in the Netherlands. It is to be regretted that Dutch courts did not properly apply the ECJ's decision in *Ruzuis-Wilbrink*. It will be recalled that the CRvB held that the primary aim of the AAW benefit scheme is to replace occupational income, and the fact that this principle was not applied to full-time and part-time workers alike did not *prima facie* give rise to indirect discrimination. The household structure of benefits (the social minimum for the family) and breadwinner supple-ments make women less likely either to gain access to benefits at all or gain income that is not mediated through men. This also may have negative implications for women's employment incentives. New means-tested ele-ments such as the post-1988 rule taking account of a dependent partner's earnings in paying the supplement to the AOW old age pension scheme, have been introduced into social insurance schemes. Sjerps (1988, p.104) argues that the reforms of the 1980s moved in the opposite direction to individualization and in fact moved further towards a system constructed around breadwinner benefits.

IRELAND

Overview

Ireland has been characterized as a 'strong male breadwinner' system – that is, historically the Irish social security system has been based on a rigid model of the household containing a male breadwinner and female dependant (Lewis, 1992, p.162). The social welfare system assumed that the few married women who were in the labour market were secondary earners and accorded them lesser entitlements to benefits on the assumption that they did not really need them (Cousins, 1993, p.6). Moreover, it was believed that a man's duty of support towards his family should not be interfered with by allowing women their own entitlements to benefits (Daly, 1989, p.67). Until the 1970s, on marriage, a female contributor to the social insurance system received a marriage grant which closed her contribution record. If she took paid work after marriage she had to start a new contribution record, resulting in many women only having patchy and inadequate contributions (Cook and McCashin, 1992, p.33). The view of women's rightful place, as expressed in Article 41 of the Constitution, also meant that lone mothers, whatever the reason for their single state, have received social welfare benefits (Daly, 1989, p.67).

In employment, women also suffered inequalities of opportunities. Until the 1970s it was common for women to leave paid work, and in some cases to be forced to leave paid work, upon marriage. A marriage bar operated against women in the civil service until 1977 (Lewis, 1992, p.163). Until the 1960s unemployment was merely a theoretical concept as far as women were concerned. Married women who have engaged in paid work have faced exceptionally harsh tax treatment in terms of high marginal tax rates, very low tax-free allowances and very low levels of childcare provision (ibid.).

The Catholic corporatist nature of the Irish state is crucial to understanding the role assigned to women. It was believed that, since the family predated the state, the latter had no right to interfere with the family as long as it fulfilled responsibilities and cared for the welfare of its members (McLaughlin, 1993, p.206). The principle of subsidiarity allowed the state to intervene only if the family's capacity to care for its members was exhausted or when it was socially necessary (ibid., p.207). Women were the key to maintaining the family's role as the welfare provider. These beliefs came to be embodied in Article 41 of the Irish Constitution of 1937. Article 41(1) (2) stated that 'the State recognises that by her life within the family home, woman gives to the state a support without which the common good cannot be achieved'. Article 41(2) therefore pledges that the 'State will endeavour to ensure that mothers shall not be obliged by economic necessity to engage in paid labour to the neglect of their duties in the home'.

There are social insurance schemes in Ireland for the risks of old age, sickness and invalidity (with special schemes for industrial injuries and occupational diseases), maternity, unemployment, and for the loss of maintenance following separation between spouses, but only where the deserted wife has not remarried and is not cohabiting (Pieters, 1990, pp.156–64). Virtually all income earners between the ages of 16 and 66 years of age are compulsorily insured, although social security cover for the self-employed is limited to widow's and orphan's benefits and old age pensions (Mangan, 1993b, p.109). Regulations in April 1991 extended full insurance cover to part-time workers earning over IR£25 per week.

Short-term social insurance benefits, such as disability benefit, unemployment benefit and maternity benefit, require that claimants have paid a certain level of contributions since entering the social insurance system, as well as 39 weeks of contributions in the last full tax year before the claim. The contribution requirement for the long-term invalidity pension is 260 weeks (five years), as well as 48 weeks of contributions in the last full tax year before the claim. In relation to the widow's contributory pension and the deserted wife's benefit, claimants must have paid, or been credited with, contributions over a longer period (Pieters, 1990, p.156). Provision for old age is divided between the retirement pension, the old age contributory pension and the old age non-contributory pension. Eligibility for the old age contributory pension depends on having started to pay insurance contributions before the age of 56, a minimum contributory period of 156 weeks and an annual minimum average of at least 20 weekly contributions (Döring, *et al.*, 1994, p.13). The old age non-contributory pension is paid to persons over 66 years who satisfy a means test.

Contributions are credited to persons when they start work, and these help them to qualify for short-term benefits, such as against the risk of unemployment and maternity, as soon as they have paid 39 weeks of contributions. This only applies to the first time a person starts work. Credits towards social insurance benefits are given to persons in receipt of certain benefits, including the single woman's allowance, the lone parent's allowance, the carer's allowance or persons on part-time work schemes for the unemployed.

Both flat-rate and pay-related benefits are paid in the Irish system, although the latter have been greatly reduced in scope in recent years (Mangan, 1993b, pp.109–10). Additions for dependent spouses and children can be paid with both social insurance and social assistance benefits. Additions vary from between 50 to 60 per cent of the basic benefit. Dependants are allowed to earn IR£55 per week before the allowance is reduced or withdrawn. Only one half of the child addition will be paid where the married parents live together and where the claimant's spouse is not considered to be an adult dependant (Pieters, 1990, p.157).

There are a number of social assistance schemes which provide for a wide variety of contingencies, as well as a general safety-net social assistance scheme, the supplementary welfare allowance (Pieters, 1990, p.164). Many of the social assistance schemes, such as the deserted wife's allowance, the prisoner's wife allowance, the single woman's allowance, and the widow's and orphan's non-contributory pensions, all provide income to women and are all subject to a cohabitation rule. A carer's allowance, introduced in 1990, is paid to carers looking after pensioners and certain other categories of persons.[36] The lone parent's allowance, also introduced in 1990, was designed to replace a number of the allowances payable to unmarried mothers, deserted wives, widows and widowers and other lone parents with at least one dependent child.

Inequalities in social security

Married women suffered from a number of specific forms of inequalities of access to benefits:

1   Lower rates of contributory benefits were paid for shorter periods (312 days instead of 393 days).
2   Wives were considered as dependants if they were living with their husbands, regardless of actual dependency, but husbands could only be classed as dependants if they were incapable of self-support and wholly maintained by their wives.
3   They were ineligible for means-tested unemployment assistance, except where their husbands were wholly or partly maintained by them and were incapable of self-support, and where they had at least one dependent child. Ineligibility for unemployment assistance had the consequence of excluding married women for certain programmes for the long-term unemployed (Callender, 1988, p.8).
4   Additions to benefit for dependent children were paid for children who were 'normally resident' with the beneficiary, and children were regarded as normally resident with their father.[37]
5   The prescribed relatives' allowance was not paid to an elderly person where he or she was cared for by a person being maintained by their spouse.[38]
6   Women social welfare claimants were often denied benefits on the basis

of answers to questions about childcare and family responsibilities. In order to determine claimants' availability for work, women – but not men – were routinely asked questions such as 'Who will mind the children?' or 'Who will cook the dinner?' (ibid., p.5).

Legislative amendments and litigation in the national courts

Ireland's implementation of the Directive was 'prolonged, controversial and litigious' (Cook and McCashin, 1992, p.35). In the early 1980s public debate was concentrated on the earliest possible implementation of the Directive and, initially at least, there was little consideration of its potential consequences (Callender, 1988, p.1). In 1982 warnings began to be articulated that implementing the Directive could bring major financial losses to low-income families depending upon how the system of dependants' allowances was modified (ibid., p.3). There were indeed few potential beneficiaries since, at that time, only 15 per cent of women were both married and working (ibid.).

Initial reforms

Three minor reforms were passed between 1978 and 1982 (Callender, 1988, p.2, note 1). First, the government lifted the ban on widows and single women applying for unemployment assistance. Second, the duration of unemployment benefit for married women was doubled from 26 to 52 weeks in 1979, but benefit was still paid for 65 weeks to other claimants. Third, in May 1982 the requirement that married women must have at least one dependant in order to qualify for unemployment assistance was abolished (by s.8, Social Welfare Act 1982). This change was prompted by a case seeking to challenge the constitutionality of this rule: *Conway* v. *Minister for Social Welfare* (ibid., p.7). In May 1982, before the date set for the hearing, the government removed the rule about having at least one dependant before being able to claim. This change affected separated wives, but did not remove the discrimination from against all other married women (ibid., p.8).

The major reforms of 1985–86

The most important changes were finally effected in two stages, but after the date of entry into force of the Directive on 22 December 1984. The equalizing benefit changes only took effect in May 1986, with the provisions relating to unemployment assistance and the redefinition of dependency only taking effect from November 1986. The process of implementation gave rise to litigation because Ireland was in breach of the Directive in two respects. First, between December 1984 and mid-May 1986 Ireland continued to discriminate against married women. Second, the system of transitional payments introduced in November 1986, amounted to a perpetuation of discriminatory treatment of female claimants who would not qualify for such payments (Whyte and O'Dell, 1992, p.306).

Equalizing benefit rules, part I – 1985   The Social Welfare (No. 2) Act 1985 brought about four major changes:

- abolition of reduced rates of benefit payable to married women under the unemployment benefit, disability benefit, invalidity pension and occupational injuries schemes
- payment of unemployment benefit to married women for the same duration as other claimants (s.6)
- eligibility of married women to claim unemployment assistance
- provision allowing for the revision of the conditions governing the payment of additions for adult and child dependants under the social insurance and assistance schemes (ss. 3, 4).

The first Cotter and McDermott *action*   Although the 1985 Act repealed the discriminatory provisions of the 1981 Act, in particular those relating to the amount and duration of married women's entitlement to unemployment and other benefits, the reforms only came into force on 15 May 1986.[39] Further, the retrospective effect of the Act was very limited; only those married women who had been in receipt of unemployment benefits within the 78 days prior to 15 May 1986 were entitled to benefit from the reforms (Curtin, 1988, p.18). This meant that all those married women who ceased to receive unemployment benefits between the period of 23 December 1984 and 15 February 1986 were unable to avail themselves of the equalizing provisions.

The limited retrospection had provided the basis for the first *Cotter and McDermott* case[40] in 1987, in which two married female claimants sought to establish their directly effective rights to equal treatment from December 1984 (see Chapter 4). The ECJ's decision meant that married women could receive the higher rate of unemployment benefits from 23 December 1984 until their entitlement expired, and this would have to be for the longer period of 393 days. This case was very controversial, as the Irish government strenuously defended its decision not to give full retrospection, on the grounds that this would cost over IR£200 million and would disrupt public finances which were already in difficulties (Reid, 1990).

Equalizing benefit rules, part II – resolving the thorny issue of dependency additions The issue of how to bring about equality in dependency additions had been evaded because it was seen as too complex in that there seemed to be no clear way to bring about equal treatment (Callender, 1988, p.4). The system of paying dependent additions to husbands even where their wives were not actually dependent on them had developed in the 1950s when so few married women were in paid employment that it was administratively simpler to assume that all were full-time housewives (ibid.). Moreover, policy-makers in this high unemployment society were reluctant to encourage married women into the labour force, either as workers or as registered unemployed (ibid., p.3). In any case this system worked to the general financial advantage of those families where the husband was receiving benefits and where the wife was employed, who were generally low-income families. All these factors meant that 'very few people had any interest in changing' the system (ibid., p.4).

To level up by assuming that all married men were dependent on their wives, when 85 per cent of married men were in paid work would have been absurd. In the end the only reform that seemed possible was to make the payment of the addition subject to a criterion of actual dependency, and in reality most married women are financially dependent on their husbands (ibid., p.5).

In relation to child additions, several possible reform options were canvassed, all of which were in some way problematic (ibid.). The option eventually chosen was to give each parent half the relevant addition where each partner was in receipt of a benefit payment. This did not affect the overall amount of benefit payable to unemployed couples, but did mean substantial losses for claimant fathers with wives in employment.

In November 1986 a commencement order was brought into effect to provide that additions could only be paid, irrespective of sex, for adult dependants in situations of actual dependency, and that additions for children were to be paid on the basis of equality between male and female claimants. In 1986 this principle was also extended to the means-tested unemployment assistance.[41] The Minister for Social Welfare had announced that some 40 000 married women would benefit from the proposed changes to the additions, at a cost of IR£16 million per year (ibid., p.9). Gainers would be families in which the man was working and the wife was already receiving a benefit payment, or where she would be entitled to benefits for the first time (ibid.). Losers were families where the father was in receipt of benefit and where the wife was either working and earning over IR£50 per week (about 9000 cases) or also receiving a benefit payment (about 8000 cases) (ibid.). Losses were estimated to be in the region of 20–26 per cent of a couple's combined income (ibid.). This reform was very controversial because it resulted in some significant reductions in benefit – as much as IR£50 per week for many families (Whyte and O'Dell, 1992, p.305).

The system of transitional payments – a further source of litigation: Cotter and McDermott (No. 2)   In 1986 regulations were enacted to try to cushion the potentially large financial losses to families brought about by the equal treatment reforms. Initially these transitional regulations were only intended to last one year, but were extended every year until 1991 (SIPTU, 1992, p.1). In fact the compensatory payments only partially offset the losses experienced by some families (Whyte, 1988, p.42). The transitional regulations contained a variety of measures which cushioned the losses of male breadwinner claimants by restoring the full level of the child dependant's additions and additional benefits, and by applying an earnings rule of IR£50 per week on the adult dependant's additions before the dependent status of spouses would be affected (Callender, 1988, p.12).

In anticipation of the ECJ's decision in the first *Cotter and McDermott* action, the two female claimants brought a second set of proceedings in February 1987, claiming payment of benefits (including the transitional payments) which they had been denied. Hamilton P, the presiding judge, accepted the applicants' claim for unemployment benefit (and pay-related benefit), but rejected all the other claims, including those for the transitional payments.[42] In rejecting the claims for the child dependant's additions, Hamilton P observed that since the implementation of s.4 of the Social Welfare (No. 2) Act 1985 in November 1986, the applicant suffered no more discrimination on grounds of sex or marital status. Prior to that time the regulations favoured men over women, but Hamilton P expressed the view that this was a 'reasonable attempt to deal with the question of entitlement'. But, as Whyte (1988, p.45) rightly argues, it is not adequate to conclude that these regulations are otherwise reasonable if they discriminate directly on grounds of sex. Although Hamilton P accepted that there had been discrimination on the grounds of sex, he denied the applicants' claim for relief by invoking a rule limiting the retrospective effect of judicial decisions.[43] He also declared that, since Mrs Cotter's husband was at all relevant times in full-time paid employment, it would be

> ... unjust and inequitable to pay to the applicant an adult dependant's increase when ... her husband was not financially dependent on her and it would be unjust and inequitable to require the people of Ireland to pay her such an increase.

The ECJ, referred to again on this matter, held conclusively that national principles of law may not reduce the effectiveness of directly effective rights under Directives[44] (see Chapter 4). On 6 June 1991 it was announced that the parties to *Cotter and McDermott* had settled the dispute.[45] It was estimated that there remained many thousand married women who had not been paid enough social welfare payments between December 1984 and November 1986 (Whyte and O'Dell 1992, p.313). In 1992 Regulations provided for the payment of arrears over a three-year period (1992–94):[46] married women in receipt of certain benefits at any time between December 1984 and November 1986 were to be paid the difference between the reduced rates and the full rates applicable at that time. Married women were also to receive adult and child dependant's additions in arrears, but they had to demonstrate that their husbands were wholly or mainly maintained by them during that period – a condition which did not apply to men at that time.

Although the payment of arrears has already begun, several problems still remain (SIPTU, 1992, pp.3–4). First, arrears are being paid at 1984–86 values with no account taken of subsequent inflation. Second, a test of actual dependency is applied to women in relation to the dependant's additions, which clearly contravenes the ECJ's ruling in *Cotter and McDermott (No. 2)*. Retrospectively assessing their claims to unemployment assistance is likely to cause enormous problems (Whyte and O'Dell, 1992, p.313). Third, instead of extending the post-1986 transitional payments to women, in line with ECJ case law, these payments have been stopped for men. Fourth, the government is allocating £IR62 million to cover the arrears, even though it stated in evidence before the ECJ that full arrears would cost £IR240 million. On the other hand, if the government were forced to allocate more funds to the arrears payments, in the current cost-cutting economic climate, this could prompt cuts elsewhere in the benefit system to finance them (ibid.). These regulations have led to further national litigation challenging the loss of purchasing power and the withdrawal of transitional payments from all claimants in July 1992.[47] In addition, the European Commission is considering whether to activate infringement proceedings against the Irish government under Article 169 of the Treaty of Rome.

How far has financial independence been advanced?

The implementation process in Ireland has been described as:

> … an ill-prepared attempt to implement the Directive at the least possible cost to the State, followed by a panic-stricken effort to alleviate the worst effects of this policy. (Callender, 1988, p.14)

The changes were 'achieved at the expense of many families on inadequate welfare incomes who suffered a reduction in those incomes consequent on the redefinition of adult dependant' (Whyte, 1988, p.58). Equality by levelling down has hit some of the most deprived and marginalized families in Irish society (Cook and McCashin, 1992, p.38). It has been argued that the November 1986 changes and the consequent financial losses to many families caused 'a "backlash" against women for "looking for equality" and "bringing down men's payments as a result"' (Callender, 1988, p.13).

Conversely, the changes did result in a 'redirection' of welfare income to other claimants – mostly married women – and they had the potential of improving the situation of other groups, such as families on unemployment assistance or supplementary welfare allowance, relatives caring for pensioners and, paradoxically, some unemployed men (Whyte, 1988, p.58). Further, it is unlikely that there would have been sex equality reforms in the social security sphere without Directive 79/7/EEC (Mangan, 1993c, p.72). Ireland's membership of the EU, and EC legislation and institutions, have in general provided an opportunity to accelerate changes in policies for women (Conroy Jackson, 1993, p.78; McLaughlin, 1993, p.225).

Returning to the issue of women and financial independence, implementation by levelling down has involved the introduction of new rules into the social welfare system which have tended to reduce women's access to personal income. Despite the 1986 reforms marital status was retained as a condition affecting entitlement in three means-tested schemes: unemployment assistance, disabled person's maintenance allowance and supplementary welfare allowance (Whyte, 1988, p.42). Normally, the reforms should have allowed married women to claim these means-tested benefits and incidentally increase household income because of this. However, to limit the expenditure increase implied in the reform, s.12 of the Social Welfare (No. 2) 1985 Act provided that, where a husband and wife were both in receipt of social welfare and one or both was in receipt of unemployment assistance, the combined income of the household would be 'capped' so that it would not exceed what would have been paid to them before the equal treatment reforms, even though a wife could now claim under her own name (ibid., p.51).

The 'capping' provisions did not initially apply to cohabiting couples but, in the *Hyland* case,[48] a married couple successfully argued that this was contrary to the constitutional guarantee to protect marriage. As a result the government extended the 'capping' provisions to cohabiting couples in the Social Welfare (No. 2) Act 1989, re-enacted in s.27 of the Social Welfare Act 1992 (Whyte, 1992, p.146), so that the position of unmarried couples has now been assimilated to that of married couples for most welfare schemes.[49] The extension of the 'capping' provisions does mean that the Irish system is moving further away from a policy of individual rights and fewer derived rights (Mangan, 1993c, p.75).

After nearly ten years of the Directive being in force in Ireland there remain a number of problems concerning its incomplete implementation, a few of which will be discussed. A number of benefits still apply different rules to men and women: unemployment benefit, death benefits, widow's and child dependant's allowances and rules relating to social insurance contributions. As stated earlier, the saga regarding arrears for the reduced payments of unemployment benefit is still to be resolved and, moreover, complaints continue about discriminatory questioning in relation to assessing availability for work. Since the implementation of the equality reforms, the Department of Social Welfare maintains that all its staff have been instructed to pose such questions to both married men and women (Callender, 1988, p.7) and has rejected the demand that these questions should not be asked at all. Despite the assurances, significant reservations remain; even where these questions are asked of both men and women, the perceived impact, significance and consequences of the replies are still likely to differ between men and women (ibid.). Difficulties of proof in these cases have, however, been a major obstacle in resolving this problem.

In addition, rules exist that impede equality of opportunity, although they are unlikely to be successfully challenged on present interpretations of Article 4(1) of the Directive. First, the household basis of the means test means that wives are less likely to be able to claim social assistance in their own right or on behalf of a household. Some 23 per cent of married women, as opposed to 82 per cent of men, work outside the home. Wives' smaller possibilities of claiming social assistance in their own right has implications for their access to the state-sponsored employment scheme for the long-term unemployed, since the opportunity to participate depends upon having received some unemployment assistance (Whyte, 1988, p.55).

Second, although the treatment of part-time workers was significantly improved in 1991 by the lowering of the earnings threshold for contributions to IR£25 per week, part-time workers still suffer some indirectly discriminatory treatment in that there are a number of exemptions to full social insurance cover which affect women more than men. The most important of these is the exemption for persons employed by their spouse or for persons who work with a self-employed spouse.

Third, although the transitional payments have now been phased out, the earnings ceilings, which continue to allow part-time and very low-paid workers to be classed as 'adult dependants', remain. As elsewhere, the spouse earnings disregard on benefits could have the effect of decreasing women's incentive to work in other than atypical, and therefore low-paid and non-unionized, work with few legal protections (Callender, 1988, pp.12–13). Potentially it could encourage the creation of jobs which yield income just below this level (ibid.). In 1992 a report by the Irish National Economic and Social Council concluded that the current treatment of households acted as a disincentive to the participation of married women in the employment market, while encouraging participation in very low-paid jobs (Cousins, 1993, p.12). In fact it has created the strange situation that a married woman earning between IR£25–55 per week can be both fully covered by social insurance in her own right and also be a dependent spouse of her husband, entitling him to benefit for her.

Although equality of access seems to have been largely achieved, as in the Netherlands, there remain inequalities of outcome. Equality of opportunity exists in a formal sense, but it remains to be seen how far the lowering of the PSRI earnings threshold to IR£25 per week brings more women into the social insurance system as fully insured persons in their own right. The short-term disability benefit is the only contributory benefit in which male and female claimants are roughly equal:[50] in 1992 51 per cent of claimants were women (against 48 per cent in both 1988 and 1984). It is interesting that, in 1992, the numbers of women claimants of this benefit, who were also in receipt of additions for adult or child dependants, exceeded the number of men, while in 1984 only 246 women received this benefit with an addition as against 25 600 men. In 1992 women comprised 34 per cent of unemployment benefit claimants, and 35 per cent of invalidity pension claimants,[51] 37 per cent of old age contributory pension claimants and 23 per cent of contributory retirement pension claimants. On the other hand, in the same year, women comprised 96 per cent of the claimants of the means-tested lone parent's allowance and 77 per cent of the means-tested carer's allowance.

Ireland provides extensive support to women in their caring role, although normally by means-tested benefits.[52] A high percentage of lone parents are, for instance, in receipt of social assistance benefit payments.[53] Although there is a contributory benefit for deserted wives, many women have difficulties gaining entitlement to this benefit because of the difficulties in proving how the relationship ended – that is, that the husband left of his own free will or the wife had just cause to leave him (Ward, 1990, pp.62–3). The carer's allowance, introduced in 1990, is means-tested on a household basis[54] and paid at a low level of social assistance.[55] Further, like the UK invalid care allowance, this allowance requires high levels of disability and need of attention on the part of the cared-for person (Glendinning and McLaughlin, 1993, p.37).

There are, however, doubts as to how far these benefits provide women with financial independence. First, social assistance, it will be recalled, is a quantitatively as well as qualitatively inferior type of social security protection in terms of allowing women access to personal income. Although Ireland's caring benefits do keep women out of poverty, they do not bear the qualitative advantages of receipt of contributory benefits. Further, the co-habitation bar not only necessitates intrusion into claimant's personal lives, but also means that attempts to enter into other relationships force financial dependence on men, in the form of withdrawal of personal benefit.

Second, these benefits may be evidence of a wider policy to prescribe and sustain the place of women as mothers in the home. Conroy Jackson (1993, p.83) argues that the first social assistance allowance for lone parents was introduced as a wage for housework and childcare to act as an incentive for women not to have abortions once the 1967 UK Abortion Act liberalized potential Irish access to abortion. The unmarried mother's allowance provided 16 years of payments, but disqualified claimants from registering as full-time unemployed, did not provide credits for contributory benefits, and any part-time work taken combined with this benefit did not allow women to build up a contributions record for other benefits (ibid.). Further, a co-habitation bar was attached to this benefit (ibid.).

The Directive precipitated quite fundamental reforms in the Irish system. The changes to the treatment of married couples, and the consequent desire to limit public expenditure, stimulated a significant change to the way in which unmarried cohabiting couples have been treated. This in turn has led to a recognition that the treatment of households within the social welfare system generally needs to be further thought out. Consequently, in May 1989, in the wake of the *Hyland* decision and the extension of the 'capping' provisions to unmarried couples, the government appointed a Review Group to examine the social welfare code as it affects households.[56]

There are a number of worrying trends in Ireland that also run counter to advances in women's financial independence. First, conditions of entitlement to benefits under social insurance have been tightened in recent years. The number of contributions required to qualify for certain benefits have been increased, with the effect of restricting entitlement to those persons in regular employment for longer periods (Mangan, 1993b, p.110). In 1987, for instance, contributions were raised to qualify for short-term benefits (Oorschot and Schell, 1991, p.204). Income tests have been introduced for benefits for deserted wives (Mangan, 1993b).

Second, in recent years the Irish social welfare system overall has moved towards household-based payments (Mangan, 1993c, p.68). Unemployment assistance is now a much more important benefit for the unemployed than contributory unemployment benefit (ibid., p.69). In fact this trend has been underway since Ireland joined the EC in 1973: all subsequent improvements for one-parent families, for instance, have involved means-tested provision (ibid.). The extension of the scope of household-based, means-tested benefits means that there is little point in married women applying for certain benefits in their own right; however, failure to gain entitlement to benefits means that they do not receive credited social insurance contributions, which in turn has negative implications on future personal entitlement to pensions and other benefits (ibid., p.75).

Summary

Important inequalities of opportunity and outcome for women remain in the Irish social security system. The implementation of the Directive was effected at the least possible cost, although this may have been expected in a country with low female labour market participation and high unemployment. Litigation in relation to the Directive has been dominated by battles over compensation for past discrimination – in the form of the continuing saga over transitional payments – rather than challenges to current inequalities of opportunity. A number of changes brought about to implement the Directive have regrettably extended the means-testing net. On the other hand, the lowering of the threshold to the social insurance system for part-time workers – a reform unconnected to the Directive – may significantly improve the personal entitlements to contributory benefits for a number of women.

BELGIUM

Overview

The Belgian social security system developed along two principal lines (Ferrera, 1993, pp.86–9; also, Denis, 1986). First, until recently, social security schemes were fragmented along occupational lines. Second, the Belgian system evolved along the lines of the structural subdivision in society between the three ideological pillars – the Catholic, liberal and socialist. The social security system, in which benefits have been linked to maintaining previous levels of wages, have accorded higher rates of benefits to breadwinners. Family allowances, which were introduced as early as 1921, were linked to employment.

Social insurance provides for the risks of sickness, unemployment, old age and invalidity, and family allowances.[57] Since 1974 a number of measures have sought to control the 'crisis' of the increasing costs of social security expenditure (Denis, 1986, pp.40–1). These measures have included the encouragement of early retirement and the lowering of the pensionable age, increasing the number of benefits providing only a minimum income, expanding the income base on which contributions are paid and a greater probing of family resources before benefits are paid out. Recently, the government has tried to reduce expenditure in unemployment and sickness benefits, attempting in the autumn of 1993, for example, to negotiate a 'social pact' to freeze wages and reduce social security benefits. Political turmoil ensued, and the government announced a 'global plan' on employment, competitiveness and social security.[58] This plan contains a number of short-term measures aimed at reducing the budget deficit and comprises: a reduction in family allowances; a narrowing of entitlement to unemployment insurance for school-leavers; and the levying of a 'solidarity' contribution on statutory and occupational pensions.

Benefits in Belgium are index-linked, and social insurance benefits are partly earnings-related (Pieters, 1990, p.19). However, there are elements in the structure of social insurance benefits that favour redistribution towards low-earners – in which category women are overrepresented – such as minimum levels at which benefits are paid (Scheiwe, 1993, p.7). Maximum amounts of social insurance benefits soften the earnings and contribution-related aspects of social insurance that tend to give men higher benefits because of their higher earnings (ibid.).

Social insurance benefits, as well as some means-tested benefits, are structured according to household composition. Heads of households receive more generous levels of benefits than other groups, such as single persons or persons living with another worker. The unemployment insurance system is a good example: benefit is paid at 35 per cent of a previous wage, plus a 5 per cent allowance, plus a 20 per cent adjustment allowance for the first year of unemployment. After the first year of unemployment, the benefits of non-heads of households are reduced, while heads of household retain the 60 per cent of lost salary level for however long they are out of the labour market (Pieters, 1990, p.30).

Old age pensions under the social insurance system are given as either 75 per cent or 60 per cent of the average wage over the period between the claimants' 20th birthday and when they attain pensionable age. The higher rate is paid where the insured person is married, provided that his or her partner has no income from work, income maintenance (a family pension) or is entitled to a single person's pension (ibid.). A full minimum old age pension is paid for a full insurance career of 40 years for women and 45 for men (Döring *et al.*, 1994, p.14). Women who have worked all their lives part-time cannot claim a full pension, as part-time work is counted proportionately (ibid.).

The survivor's benefit is relatively generous, giving 80 per cent of the pension the deceased person would have received, with entitlement ceasing on remarriage. This is subject to the surviving spouse being over 45 years of age, or with a dependent child or being 66 per cent incapable of work (Pieters, 1990, p.28). Under the general employees scheme, as well as the scheme for the self-employed, divorced spouses are entitled to a survivor's pension corresponding to the years the marriage subsisted, and paid upon attaining pensionable age, independently of whether or not the ex-spouse is receiving their pension (ibid.).

For several benefits, such as unemployment and sickness insurance, co-habitation has been classed equally to marriage (Scheiwe, 1993, p.7). However, important benefits are still reserved for married partners, such as survivor's pensions, higher child allowances for widows, a pension in the case of death of the insured through an accident at work, and finally in access to the higher rate of old pension benefit (ibid.). Family allowances are payable in respect of dependent children, and are normally given until children reach 16 years of age, with payments increasing in relation to the number of children in a household (Pieters, 1990, p.32).

There are four branches to the social assistance scheme, including family benefits, the 'Minimex' (*minimum d'existence*) and a guaranteed income for the elderly. The Minimex is given to persons with insufficient resources, who are either over 18, or married, or unmarried with at least one dependent child (ibid., p.33). Benefits vary depending on whether claimants are part of a couple or are single persons and are means-tested. In 1992 an important change was made to the Minimex benefit, allowing a single-parent family to receive the same rate as a couple and thereby acknowledging the greater needs of a lone parent compared to a single person living alone (Scheiwe, 1993, p.7). The guaranteed income for the elderly provides benefits, roughly equal to the minimum subsistence level, to all residents in Belgium who have attained pensionable age and who have insufficient means.

Inequalities in social security

In Belgium, married women's inequality of access to major insurance benefits was less explicit than in the Netherlands and Ireland – or indeed in the UK – prior to 1975. In practice, however, the most generous levels of social insurance benefits were given to (male) workers with a spouse of the opposite sex with no income from employment or other sources. Married women were rarely able to gain access to, for instance, unemployment and sickness benefits, nor to old age pensions.

Unemployment insurance, under the Royal Decree of 13 October 1971, gave (male) worker-heads of household 60 per cent of their previous wage for the entire duration of their unemployment, while other claimants' benefits were reduced to 40 per cent of previous wages after one year of unemployment.[59] Worker-heads of household were defined, by a ministerial decree of 4 June 1964, as married workers with spouses or cohabitees of the opposite sex exclusively engaged in household tasks (De Vos, 1990a, p.544). The benefit rates for men and women were different, with women's payments being lower.[60]

Claimants could be excluded from unemployment insurance benefits where their unemployment had lasted a very long time or where it had occurred 'abnormally' often (see Article 143 of Royal Decree of 20 December 1963; Van Droogenbroeck and Denis, 1986, p.48). The majority of persons excluded in this way were women (94.8 per cent in 1982), even though they only represented about 53 per cent of the unemployed in that year (Van Droogenbroeck and Denis, 1986, p.48). From November 1984 onwards, the criteria for exclusion specified that, in suspending benefit, consideration had to be given to whether the claimant lived in a household with another worker, and further that these criteria cannot be applied to the detriment of a 'head of household' (*chef de ménage*) (ibid.).

Finally, the unemployment benefits given to compensate for the move from full-time to part-time work were paid at a lower rate to women until 1982, when the discrimination was abolished (ibid., p.49).

The sickness and invalidity scheme considered a married woman to be her husband's dependant unless she was herself an insured worker under the scheme (ibid., p.50). The same was not true of men who were only considered dependants in the most exceptional cases – for instance, where a married man was incapable of work for one year (ibid.).[61] Where both members of a couple were entitled to benefits, dependants would be considered to be those who were under marital or paternal authority, or the claimant would be the oldest of the two (ibid.). Women received lower rates of benefits until 1 January 1981; the daily indemnity for invalidity for persons with no dependants was 608 BF per day for men and 508 BF for women (ibid., p.52).

Retirement pensions are paid at two rates: either at 75 per cent or 60 per cent of annual average wage earned over a working life of 44 years for men and 39 years for women. The higher rate was only paid to married men with dependent spouses, who were always considered to be 'heads of households', while women could only receive the 60 per cent (single person's) pension rate (ibid., p.53).

Helper-wives of self-employed workers had no social security rights under the social security scheme for self-employed workers set up in 1967 (ibid., p.57).

Cash benefits for children have been strongly employment-related in Belgium, being paid according to a particular order of persons, starting with fathers, stepfathers and then only mothers. Part-time employees were excluded from these benefits until 1981 and, even since then, they must work 20 hours per week or 16 full-time days per month to qualify (Scheiwe, 1993, p.5). In 1970 a residual scheme was introduced to pay child benefits to categories of women otherwise excluded – predominantly lone parents – but this is means-tested (ibid.).

Women also experienced problems in proving their entitlements to benefits; they were required by the administration to prove they had dependants and were 'heads of households' by means of birth certificates and so on, while men were taken at their word (Van Droogenbroeck and Denis, 1986, p.46).

Legislative amendments and litigation in national courts

The first step towards implementing Directive 79/7/EEC was taken by the Law of 29 June 1981. Article 16(1) stated that, in relation to the general social security scheme for employees, in fixing social benefits and the conditions under which they are given, no distinction should be made between insured persons who find themselves in the same situation.[62] Article 29 provided that, in conformity with its obligations under the Directive, the necessary measures would be taken with regard to sickness and invalidity insurance, family benefits, pensions and unemployment insurance. In particular, changes would be made to the concepts of 'head of household' and 'dependant', differences in the conditions under which benefits are given, to differences in proof and to differences in the way in which benefits are calculated.

Belgium was, however, in breach of a duty not to take measures which tend towards discrimination between the adoption of the Directive and its entry into force. This arose from changes to the payments structure of unemployment and sickness insurance (see below).

Unemployment benefits

Until the passing of the Ministerial Decree of 24 December 1980, the higher 'head of household' rate for unemployment benefits was only paid to workers cohabiting with a spouse of the opposite sex who was exclusively occupied with household tasks (Van Droogenbroeck and Denis, 1986, p.46). As a result of a complaint to the European Commission by the Comité de Liaison des Femmes, the government changed this provision to make it formally sex-neutral (Ward *et al.*, 1992, p.81). However, in effect, the outcome was just the same: in 1980 a 'worker-head of household' was redefined as:

1   a worker married and living with a spouse who has no income from employment or other income;
2   a worker cohabiting with a person of the opposite sex who has no income from employment or other sources;
3   a worker living with either one or more children (for whom they receive family benefits) or certain relatives (such as parents, parents-in-law, a son-in-law or a daughter-in-law).

The higher rates were still overwhelmingly paid to men, and the lower rates to workers living with another worker were overwhelmingly paid to women (Van Droogenbroeck and Denis, 1986, p.47).

The European Commission took over the complaint of the Comité de Liaison des Femmes and, after a few years, it initiated infringement proceedings against Belgium (Ward *et al.*, 1992, p.81). The Commission sent its considered opinion to the Belgian government that indirect discrimination existed whenever an apparently neutral measure affected one sex disproportionately, arguing that the concept of 'head of household' could not be regarded as neutral (ibid.).

The claimant categories were subsequently remodified by the Belgian government in the Royal Decree of 8 August 1986. The reference to 'head of household' was removed and the following categories created:

1   unemployed persons living alone;
2   unemployed persons with family responsibilities;
3   unemployed persons without family responsibilities.

The second category of claimant – unemployed persons with family responsibilities – is still paid the highest benefits, with the third category receiving the lowest benefits. Ward *et al.* (1992, p.81) described the change in the following way: 'this is ... both completely different and exactly the same'. In fact, the reference to 'family responsibility' in categories two and three refer to the presence of a dependent spouse or cohabitee, since unemployed persons who cohabit with another adult with earnings from employment are not considered to have 'family responsibilities', however many children live with them (De Vos, 1990a, p.545).

The European Commission was not satisfied with the 1986 changes and pressed ahead with its infringement proceedings. The ECJ gave its ruling in May 1991, in which it refused to interfere with the Belgian government's discretion in its social policy.[63] The claimant categories in the unemployment insurance, as well as in the sickness scheme, therefore remain unchanged.

Sickness and invalidity benefits

The Royal Decree of 16 May 1980 redefined 'dependants' in a gender-neutral fashion, as either the spouse of the worker or a person with no income of their own, regardless of their sex, who looks after the worker's home (Van Droogenbroeck and Denis, 1986, p.50). This reform was forced on the government by two court decisions, in which the previous law was held to be sexually discriminatory, contrary to equality before the law guaranteed in Article 6 of the Belgian Constitution (De Vos, 1990a, p.537).[64]

Before 1986 two levels of benefits were given: first, 65 per cent of lost salary for those with dependants and, second, 43.5 per cent of lost salary for those without dependants. By a Royal Decree of 30 July 1986 the latter category was subdivided on the lines of the unemployment insurance into:

1   persons living alone or only with persons whose income is below certain limits (receiving 45 per cent of lost salary);
2   other claimants with no dependants (receiving 40 per cent of lost salary).

A decree of 16 May 1980 recognized the principle of equal treatment for men and women in so far as they are dependants in the sickness/health care scheme. It was provided that a married man could also be considered as a dependant and, further, that a dependant could be any person (male or female) staying at home and taking responsibility for the housework. Lastly, where parents do not live together, children would be the 'dependant' of the parent actually looking after them.

The dispensing of the waiting period for health benefits, previously accorded to women, was extended to male claimants where they have given up employment to look after a child at home, provided that this is done within three years of the child's birth (Royal Decree of 23 October 1981; Van Droogenbroeck and Denis, 1986, p.51).

In 1985 the Cour du Travail de Bruxelles held that it was contrary to both Article 6 of the Constitution and Article 4(1) of Directive 79/7/EEC that the body dealing with the administration of the sickness and invalidity scheme did not cover the costs of wigs for male employees suffering from the side-effects of chemotherapy treatment (De Vos, 1990a, p.538).

Pensions

A number of reforms have been made in the pensions sphere. First, the Royal Decree of 31 December 1983 extended to men the possibility of safeguarding pension rights when they left employment to undertake childcare (Van Droogenbroeck and Denis, 1986, p.51).

Second, since the passing of Law of 15 May 1984 the higher rate of pensions (75 per cent) may be paid to either married men or women with dependent spouses (ibid., p.53). The effect of this reform can readily be seen in the claimant statistics.[65] In 1985 no married women received pensions at the household rate (*le taux ménage*) in the general scheme for employees. By 1987 there were 141 married women receiving pensions at the household rate, rising to 418 married women in 1992. However, although the increase in married women receiving the household rate pension since 1985 has been of the order of 400 per cent, in fact as a proportion of all persons receiving the household rate in 1992, they are a small minority in the order of 0.15 per cent. Married women are well represented among married persons in receipt of the single person's rate of pension. In 1992 there were 228 755 married women receiving the lower rate as against 187 027 married men.

There may in fact be a disincentive to both partners claiming pensions based on their own contributions. If both spouses receive a pension (two payments of the single persons rate – 60 per cent), the spouse with the better contribution or earnings record – normally the husband – can obtain the head of household rate if the other spouse renounces their pension. This may be financially advantageous since the 15 per cent lost may be far less in monetary terms than the extra 15 per cent gained by the head of household spouse (Van Droogenbroeck and Denis, 1986, p.54).

Third, in cases of divorce, since 20 September 1984 men have been able to gain a pension based on a wife's contributions, by pension-splitting (ibid., p.55).

Fourth, in changing its differential retirement age, Belgium opted for a 'flexible' age – that is, men and women can retire at any time between the ages of 60 and 65 (Law of 20 July 1990) (De Vos, 1990b, p.361). However, a number of problems remain despite the reform. Although the pensionable age was changed, the age limits for access to other benefits were not altered, and so women who are incapable of work through illness or who are unemployed, and who have retired early, will lose their rights to these benefits at 60 (ibid.). This means they will have to claim their retirement pension or be without income, even though women have far fewer contributory years for pensions than men. Male workers will, however, be able to choose for the five years between 60–65 whether to claim unemployment or sickness benefits or the retirement pension (ibid.). The guaranteed minimum income for the elderly continues to be payable only to women from age 60 and to men from age 65.[66] The ECJ's decision in *Van Cant*[67] in July 1993 forced the Belgian government to make some changes to the pensions law (see Chapter 5).

In creating the 'flexible' age of retirement the number of contributory years to build up a pension remained the same, and meant lower pensions for men if they chose to retire at an earlier age than previously. The ECJ held that, once the pension had been equalized, then all the conditions for that pension also had to be equal between men and women. This created problems for the Belgian government because it recognized that formal equality could make it more difficult for women, with far fewer contributory years, to qualify. A compromise appeared to be reached in February 1994, when a technical change was made to the system to conform with the ECJ's judgement, without lengthening the years required for women to qualify for a pension. It was announced that the legal pensionable age for men would be reset to 65 years, and it was expected that this could be done without actually decreasing men's realistic ability to gain full pensions (see Chapter 5).

Contributions

Helper wives of self-employed workers with no income of their own were exempted from the requirement to pay contributions. The Tribunal du Travail of Huy held that this was contrary to Article 6 of the Constitution (De Vos, 1990a, p.538) .[68] However, the Tribunal du Travail of Liège came to a different conclusion on the grounds that the legislator wished to compensate the husband for the fact that he could not gain access to a survivor's pension based on his wife's insurance record (ibid.).[69] By a Law of 13 June 1985 this exemption for helper spouses was finally revoked to bring the law into conformity with Directive 79/7/EEC, and to bring helper spouses within the social insurance system (ibid.).

Married women, widows and students could also be exempted from the requirement to pay contributions from their self-employment if their annual income was below certain limits (ibid.). This exemption, which meant that these persons stayed outside the social insurance system, was challenged by a married man, and was referred to the ECJ in the *Integrity* case[70] (see Chapter 5). The ECJ held that married men were entitled to have the same rules applied to them as married women.

How far has financial independence been advanced?

The process of implementing the principle of equal treatment into the Belgian social security system has been described by the Belgian Ministry of Employment as being essentially one of 'equalization' (quoted in Scheiwe, 1990). Many of the equality of access measures passed have benefited men by extending to them advantages hitherto only accorded to women, such as qualifying for health insurance as a dependant, the right to a survivor's pension and to retain entitlements in the event of a break in employment in order to bring up the child. Equality of access measures were also passed in areas not covered by the Directive, such as family benefits and survivor's benefits (Van Droogenbroeck and Denis, 1986, p.42). Scheiwe (1990) is especially critical of the pension changes since, in her view, the reform has caused benefits to be redistributed in favour of men, partly with the contributions paid by women.

Equality of access, as we have already seen in relation to the Netherlands and Ireland, does not necessarily bring with it equality of opportunity or outcome. A number of factors explain this. First, the structuring of benefits towards earnings-related benefits, giving higher benefits to worker-heads of households, is a very strong obstacle to women achieving equality of outcomes in terms of financial independence. Married women, for instance, continue to receive lower benefits for the same contributions.

Second, Van Droogenbroeck and Denis (1986, p.42) argue that, although many instances of direct discrimination against women have been eliminated, forms of indirect discrimination – in particular those linked to the family status of workers – have been compounded. Yet, because the ECJ has consistently left such a wide field of discretion to Member States in determining their social policy, challenge has been singularly unsuccessful.

Third, derived rights have been extended to men, and this can be criticized on the basis that – while it may be fair on an individual level – this extension reinforces the extent to which financial dependence on a spouse acts as a criterion for benefit entitlement.

Finally, the scope of the household-based means test in social assistance has also been widened in terms of the numbers of people falling within it. This also has negative consequences for women's access to personal income. The numbers of recipients of the nationally guaranteed 'Minimex' (*minimum d'existence*), for instance, rose 363 per cent, from 9436 persons in 1976 to 43 774 persons in 1986 (Room *et al.*, 1989, p.168).

In terms of litigation under Directive 79/7/EEC, this law has been less widely used in Belgium than in the UK and the Netherlands. A number of factors have been cited to explain this:[71]

1   the complexity of the Belgian social security system;
2   the traditional refusal of Belgian courts to review acts of legislature, so that courts have declined to hold legislative acts to be discriminatory even when they contravene the constitutional provision outlawing discrimination;
3   insufficient awareness among judges, lawyers and claimants of the contents, invokability and implications of EC law;
4   the strength of the unions, which have considerable expertise in social

security but which have concentrated on achieving change through the legislative process and collective bargaining rather than through litigation. The absence of class actions has also been a factor in the preference for the mechanism of collective bargaining.[72]

In Belgium a significant proportion of women's labour market participation – higher than all the other three countries – is on a full-time basis. In considering the contribution of a sameness approach to equality to the strategic issue of advancing women's financial independence, it was argued that 'sameness' would benefit women in the social insurance system who most closely fit the 'standard employment relationship'. The discussion of the Belgian system suggests that this assertion needs to be more nuanced. It appears that, even where many women are in a standard employment relationship, a sameness approach will still be limited where the broader structure of the system itself gives the highest rates of benefits to breadwinners. Further, given the weakness of the prohibition on indirect discrimination, the Directive is unlikely to be able to force change to this structure, even though this inequality of opportunity and outcomes relates to the classic risks of unemployment, sickness and old age covered by Article 3(1)(a) of the Directive.

On a more positive note, it is worth looking at how far unpaid care work is compensated by the social security system, to throw further light on the equality of opportunity of women in building up entitlements to contributory benefits. In each of the social insurance sectors, years in which women have left the labour market to look after children are not counted in the requirements of years for entitlement to benefits (Van Droogenbroeck and Denis, 1986, p.56). The conditions as to years allowed for crediting and the age of the children vary from sector to sector (ibid.). Further provisions were introduced in 1990. Certain periods of childcare since 1990 can count in calculating the seniority required to gain entitlement to early retirement benefits (Scheiwe, 1993, p.7). Under unemployment insurance some periods of caring for a child under six years of age can be counted as actual working days (ibid.). Up to ten days' unpaid leave for important family reasons are treated as paid employment under social security provisions.

As in the Netherlands and Ireland, the implementation of the Directive in Belgium brought about equality of access for women, but no significant progress towards achieving equality of opportunities or outcomes. An important factor explaining this is the structure of payments of social insurance benefits, which give higher rates (which are at least partly earnings-related) to breadwinners. Although this is now defined in sex-neutral terms, the interaction of these rules with the wider gendered social reality means that it is women workers who in practice receive lower levels of benefits and for shorter periods of time. Women's ability to gain the same levels of social insurance benefits – and personal income – as men is compromised. The spread of the means-testing net in Belgium also contributes to an undermining of women's access to personal income.

In the following chapter, the implementation of the Directive in the UK system is examined in detail, with concluding remarks offered as to how far the Directive has advanced women's financial independence in that country.

NOTES

1   Earlier in this book I discussed the concept of substantive equality and what this could mean in terms of equality in social security. Substantive equality, as I have described it, is similar, although not identical, to the idea of equality of outcomes in this analytical framework. The former – substantive equality – refers more directly to the end goals to be borne in mind in policy and legislative changes to the social security system, such as the idea of the 'inclusion model'. Equality of outcomes, in the sense used in Chapters 6 and 7, focuses less on normative goals and more on the specific outcomes of these goals.

2   It has been argued that existing measures of labour market participation miss out some forms of paid work, such as childminding, and some workers, such as publicans' wives and farmers' wives (Bond, 1993, p.30).

3   'Female Employment up 40% in 20 Years', *The Irish Times*, 27 August 1993, p.6.

4   This is striking in comparison to the UK, the Netherlands and Ireland where only between 5–7 per cent of lone mothers with children aged 0–4 worked full-time, and between 69–74 per cent were economically inactive (Pillinger, 1992, p.33).

5   In relation to the Dutch social security system, see generally MSAE (1990) and de Jong *et al.* (1990). The author gratefully acknowledges the generous and invaluable help received from Judith Blom in understanding the Dutch system and in following recent developments.

6   Articles 4–5 of the ZW, WAO, WW and KB, 24 December 1973, Staatsblad 1973, 629.

7   Article 6(1)(c) of the ZW, WAO and WW schemes.

8   For a detailed account of the retrenchment in social security in the Netherlands during the 1980s, see Chapter Six of Cox (1993) and Chapter Four of de Jong *et al.* (1990).

9   Law of 29 December 1982, Staatsblad 1982, 737.

10 Prior to 1987 the WW scheme provided a very short-term insurance scheme for employees who became unemployed. Once the WW benefit became exhausted, the unemployed could claim a benefit under the WWV scheme, financed out of general taxation, which was linked in part to a person's last wage. On expiry of this benefit, unemployed persons can claim a means-tested benefit under the RWW scheme linked to the minimum wage.

11 *State of the Netherlands* v. *Federatie Nederlandse Vakbeweging*, Case 71/85 [1987] ECR 3855; *Dik and others* v. *College van Burgemeester en Wethouders Arnhem and Winterswijk*, Case 80/87 [1988] ECR 1601.

12 RvB Groningen, 3 June 1987, *NJCM Bulletin* 12–5 (1987).

13   The breadwinner provision in the WW scheme was abolished when the Toeslagenwet (TW), the Supplements Act, came into force from 1 January 1987.

14   The Raad van Beroep (RvB) are the first tier in the court system to deal with social security cases. Appeals from here go to the Centrale Raad van Beroep (CRvB), which is the highest court of appeal in social security matters (see MSAE, 1990, Chapter 11).

15   RvB Arnhem 13 September 1990, RSV 1991, 83.

16   RvB Haarlem 5 January 1990, RN 1990, 105.

17   CRvB 23 June 1992, NJB 1992, p.313. It will be recalled that, in *Roks*, the ECJ confirmed that national legislation which makes the granting of benefits subject to a gender-neutral income requirement, which affects more women than men, in the Law of May 1989 is contrary to Directive 79/7/EEC.

18   *Teuling* v. *Bedrijfsvereniging voor de Chemische Industrie*, Case 30/85 [1987] ECR 2497.

19   RvB Amsterdam 29 December 1987, RN 1988, 1.

20   The WAO provides a benefit of 70 per cent of the previous wage, and so represents a higher benefit than the AAW for those employees who earn over the minimum wage. Claimants would receive an AAW benefit, topped up by the WAO to 70 per cent of their previous wages, but even if the WAO gave a higher benefit than the subsistence level, the AAW supplement was still payable.

21   CRvB 19 April 1990, RN 1990, 103.

22   *Ruzius-Wilbrink* v. *Bestuur van de Bedrijfsvereniging voor Overheidsdiensten*, Case C-102/88 [1989] ECR I-4311.

23   RvB Groningen 10 April 1990, *NJCM Bulletin* 1991, 531. In a later decision this court reasoned in a similar vein: see RvB Groningen 23 January 1991, RN 91, 158. The RvB Arnhem in an earlier case had accepted that the AAW's main aim was to replace income (24 October 1990, RSV 1991, 58), although in its judgement the court had mixed up together all the different aims put forward in the various proceedings (Blom, 1993, pp.96–7). This court also found that the exemptions did not interfere with these general principles. Yet another court, the RvB Roermond (12 March 1991, RN 1991, 18), found that the rules for part-time workers were discriminatory (ibid. p.97). It reasoned that, while the aim of the law was to replace income, a court had to test whether the law's aim was in fact achieved. The exempted categories raised doubts about this, and some of these categories were not very different from part-time workers.

24   CRvB 6 June 1991, *NJCM Bulletin* 1991, 531.

25   *Verholen and others* v. *Sociale Verzekeringsbank Amsterdam*, Joined Cases C-87/90, C-88/90 and C-89/90 [1991] ECR I-3757.

26   RvB 's-Hertogenbosch, 15 November 1991, RSV 1992/192, 1992/193, 1992/194.

27   CRvB 26 January 1993.

28   Previously the benefit for heads of household consisted of 70 per cent for the claimant plus a 30 per cent supplement. The 50–50 split was brought about by the Law of 23 October 1993, Stb. 1993, 592, in force from 1 February 1994.

29   RvB Haarlem, 21 August 1989, RSV 1990, 130.

30   RvB Arnhem, 21 December 1989, RSV 1990, 163.

31   RvB Roermond, 8 November 1989, RSV 1990, 160.

32   *Molenbroek* v. *Bestuur van de Sociale Verzekeringsbank*, Case C-226/91 [1992] ECR I-5943. The referring court was the RvB Amsterdam 24 July 1991, RvR 109.

33   This reform was brought about by a court decision interpreting a UN Covenant and not on the basis of Directive 79/7/EEC which, as will be recalled, excludes survivor's benefits from its material scope (Article 3(2)).

34 By a decision of the Centrale Raad van Beroep of 7 December 1988, based on Article 26 of the UN Covenant on Civil and Political Rights of 1966.

35 See de Jong *et al.* (1990, p.20).

36 See, further, Chapter 3 of Glendinning and McLaughlin (1993).

37 Article 5 of the Social Welfare (Normal Residence) Regulations 1974 [S.I No. 211 of 1974].

38 The eligibility conditions for this allowance were so extensive that as little as 3-4 per cent of full-time carers actually received it (see Glendinning and McLaughlin, 1993, Chapter 3).

39 Social Welfare Act 1986, s.2 and Social Welfare (No. 2) Act 1985 (s.6) (Commencement Order) 1986 [SI No. 173/1986].

40 *Cotter and McDermott (No. 1)* v. *Minister for Social Welfare and Attorney General*, Case 286/85 [1987] ECR 1453.

41 SI No. 365/86 Social Welfare (No. 2) Act 1985 (s.6) (Commencement Order) 1986.

42 [1990] 2 CMLR 141.

43 A later decision decided to the contrary: the 1989 case of *Carberry* v. *Minister for Social Welfare* [1990] 1 CMLR 29. Barron J held that plaintiffs are entitled to rely retrospectively on the ECJ's ruling in *McDermott and Cotter (No. 1)* and gain entitlement to adult dependency additions which were refused to them.

44 *Cotter and McDermott (No. 2)* v. *Minister for Social Welfare and Attorney General*, Case C-377/89 [1991] ECR I-1155.

45 It appears that three further actions were also settled: *Harvey and others* v. *Minister for Social Welfare* and *Austin and others* v. *Minister for Social Welfare* were representative actions seeking to extend the relief given in the *McDermott and Cotter (No. 1)* action to 550 women. *Lang* v. *Minister for Social Welfare* concerned unemployment benefit.

46 SI No. 152 of 1992.

47 In April 1994 actions were begun in the High Court by 1800 married women seeking arrears of benefits (see *The Irish Times*, 12 April 1994). These cases are supported by the Free Legal Advice Centres (FLAC). There are essentially two heads of claim:

1. residual child and adult dependent allowances not covered by the 1992 regulations
2. transitional payments which were introduced for married men only in 1986 and which were stopped in 1992. (Letter from Mary Johnson, solicitor, FLAC, 6 April 1994).

48 *Hyland* v. *Minister for Social Welfare* [1989] 2 CMLR 44.

49 Implemented by ss 45, 48 Social Welfare Act 1991 and ss 17–19 Social Welfare Act 1992.

50 I have calculated these percentages drawing on the information in the yearly *Statistical Information on Social Welfare Services*, produced by the Department of Social Welfare, Dublin, for the years 1979–80, 1984, 1988 and 1992.

51 It appears that women are, however, gradually increasing as a proportion of claimants of invalidity pension, from 30 per cent in 1984 to 31 per cent in 1988 to 35 per cent in 1992, although it is unclear whether this has been affected by the equal treatment reforms.

52 The Irish social assistance system, as we saw earlier, supports unpaid care work in a number of ways, albeit at low levels of income, including through the carer's allowance and the lone parents allowance and a range of social assistance schemes that give some protection to women with no breadwinner.

53 Two reports discuss in detail the situation of lone mothers in Ireland. See Millar *et al.* (1992) and McCashin (1993).

54   The second most common reason for not awarding a carer this allowance is because they fail the household-based means-test; this was responsible for 31 per cent of unsuccessful claims (see Glendinning and McLaughlin, 1993, pp.40–1).

55   Since the carer's allowance does not carry entitlement with it for a range of other benefits, such as mortgage relief, special needs additions etc., carers may be better off on other social security benefits. This may contribute to the low take-up of this benefit (Glendinning and McLaughlin, 1993, p.41).

56   This Report is discussed in detail by Whyte (1992) and Cousins (1993).

57   See generally on the Belgian social security system, Denis (1986).

58   See European Industrial Relations Review, No. 239, December 1993, p5.

59   The Cour de Cassation in 1973 in the case of *Office National de l'Emploi c. Samerey* (3e ch. 24 January 1973) held that this was not contrary to Article 6 of the Constitution because the system which in fact gave men and women different benefits was a reflection of the fact that female workers, on average, earned less than male workers (Jacqmain, 1989, pp.68–9).

60   For an overview of the differences in treatment between men and women, see ABFJ (1975, pp.81–99).

61   In the case of *Chareau et Hamachep* c. *Union Nationale des Fédérations des Mutualités Professionnelles* (Cour du Travail de Liège, 5e ch, 4 January 1974) the court said that the difference between men and women in defining dependency is based on the totality of Belgian civil law provisions relating to the family, and was not therefore contrary to Article 6 of the Constitution (Jacqmain, 1989, pp.69–70).

62   See, further, 'Egalité entre Hommes et Femmes' (1990) Bruxelles Ministere de l'Emploi et du Travail, Secretariat de la Commission du Travail des Femmes.

63   *Commission* v. *Belgium*, Case C-229/89 [1991] ECR I-2265, (see Chapter 5).

64   Tribunal du Travail de Bruxelles (19e ch.) 22 June 1979, *Defays* c. *Alliance Nationale des Mutualités Chrétiennes*, JTT 1979, p.238; Tribunal du Travail d'Anvers (7e ch.) 26 June 1979, *Van Camp* c. *INAMI*.

65   I gratefully acknowledge the help given by the Ministère de la Prévoyance Sociale, Direction Générale des Etudes Financières et Statistiques in providing the relevant statistics.

66   A 60 year-old man recently challenged the fact that he could not claim the elderly person's guaranteed income when a woman in his situation would have been able to (see Court of Arbitration, 27 January 1994, judgement 9/94; *Newsletter of the Network of Equality Experts*, Spring 1994, p.37). His claim was successful.

67   *Van Cant* v. *Rijksdienst Pensioenen*, Case C-154/92 [1993] ECR I-3811.

68   Trib. Trav Huy, 23 October 1981, *Inasti* c. *Rappe et Decoeur*, JTT 1982, p.199.

69   Cour Trav. de Liège, 28 May 1985, RG 9805/82.

70   *Caisses d'assurances sociales pour travailleurs indépendants 'Integrity'* v. *Rouvroy*, Case C-373/90 [1991] ECR I-4243.

71   See Report of the EC Network of Equality Experts, Meeting of April 1991, Warwick University, Belgian representative Hans Gilliams.

72   See also 'Table Ronde Autour des Acteurs de l'Application des Directives', (1990) *Revue du Travail*, (4–6), pp.681–99.

7   The UK

In the preceding chapter I considered the implementation of Directive 79/7/EEC in the Netherlands, Ireland, and Belgium. I have now come full circle by returning to a discussion of the UK in terms of the changes made to the UK system to comply with the obligations under the Directive in order to answer the question 'How far has women's financial independence been advanced?' In a sense the discussion in Chapter 2 has already revealed the answers. What this chapter offers is an analysis of the progression towards the contemporary system.

In the mid-1970s many women's opportunities to build up personal entitlements to contributory benefits, or to establish themselves as claimants of means-tested benefits, were limited. It will be recalled that the 'married women's option', in relation to contributions for social insurance benefits, forced married women into financial dependence on their husbands, in so far as their ability to build up their own entitlements to these benefits were significantly limited. Moreover, married and then, later, cohabiting women were unable to claim means-tested benefits on behalf of themselves and their (male) partners. The cohabitation rule withdrew social assistance benefits from women as soon as they entered into a cohabitation arrangement with a man. In the same decade the two new non-contributory benefits, the invalid care allowance and the non-contributory invalidity pension, both contained and reinforced assumptions of the (rightful) financial dependence of married and cohabiting women on their partners.

Here, I consider the equalization reforms passed before the enactment of the Directive, and offer some conclusions as to how far women's financial independence in the UK has been advanced.

STEPS TOWARDS EQUALITY PRIOR TO THE ADOPTION OF THE DIRECTIVE

The UK is unusual, in comparison to Belgium, the Netherlands and Ireland, in that the reforms whose impact on increasing women's financial independence in social security was the most significant had been passed prior to the adoption of the Directive. The four 1975 reforms are considered below, the most important of which were the abolition of the married women's option and the introduction of home responsibilities protection (HRP).

First, the married woman's option was abolished for all women marrying after April 1977.[1] To recap, the option had forced married women to choose between either paying full contributions in exchange for reduced unemployment and sickness benefits as well as a single person's pension at 60 years of age or paying very small contributions in exchange for a dependent wife's pension at 60 years (provided their husbands were over 65 and claiming a pension) and forfeiting the right to unemployment and sickness benefits.

Second, home responsibilities protection (HRP) was introduced to safeguard the entitlements to the basic state pension of persons who take years out of the labour market to engage in caring work (care of children under 16, or care of an elderly or incapacitated person). HRP does not, of itself, give entitlement to benefits, in the same way as paid contributions or credits, rather it reduces the number of required contributory years over a working life (normally 39 years for a woman). But someone can only benefit from HRP protection where they have a minimum working life of 20 years – in other words a substantial career.

Third, short-term benefit rates for men and women were equalized by the Social Security Pensions Act 1975 (Luckhaus, 1983, p.325). Previously only married women who were also breadwinners could gain the same rate as married men.

Fourth, the married women's 'half test' was partially abolished by the Social Security Pensions Act 1975. Before this reform, married women had not been not entitled to a Category A pension unless, in addition to other conditions, either their marriage occurred after the age of 55 or, alternatively, they had paid contributions for at least half the years between their marriage and attaining pensionable age. The 1975 Act removed the additional conditions for women reaching pensionable age on or after 6 April 1979.[2] Women who reached pensionable age prior to this date were still caught by this rule and could still therefore be denied a Category A pension.[3]

To summarize, a number of significant reforms were passed in 1975, the most important of which, it is argued, were the abolition of the married women's option and the introduction of HRP. The abolition of the 'option' brought equality of access for married women into the contributory benefit system. The introduction of HRP can be seen as a major step towards equalizing outcomes between men and women with regard to pensions. However, at the same time as these reforms were passed, two new benefits were introduced which denied married and cohabiting women equality of access altogether – the non-contributory invalidity pension and the invalid care allowance.

LEGISLATIVE REFORMS POST-1979: TWO STEPS FORWARD, ONE STEP BACK?

A number of reforms were made to the UK system in order to comply with the obligations in Directive 79/7/EEC, whose implementation period expired in December 1984. These reforms related to four areas:

1 additions payable with contributory benefits;
2 the non-contributory invalidity pension;
3 the invalid care allowance;
4 the principal means-tested benefits – supplementary benefit and its successor, income support.

The most common reform has been to accord equality of access alone. Moreover, rather than levelling up, in many cases the extension of benefits to women on the same terms as men has been followed by narrower entitlement conditions for all. This section considers the four areas of reforms in turn, with discussion focusing on two questions: how far have equalization reforms been undermined? and what inequalities remain?

Additions to contributory benefits for dependants

Prior to the Social Security Act 1980 married women could only claim additions to short-term benefits – invalidity benefit and the non-contributory invalidity pension (NCIP) – for dependent husbands or children where their husbands were incapable of self-support by reason of infirmity (Luckhaus, 1983, p.332).[4] Married men, on the other hand, were automatically entitled to an addition for a dependent child, as well as for a wife if her earnings fell below a specific threshold (ibid.).

The 1980 Act brought a number of reforms to the rules governing the payment of these additions, although the implementing regulations only came into effect in November 1983.

Additions for children

The 1980 Act provided that married women would be treated in the same way as married men in claiming allowances for dependent children, but only at a certain point in the future (1984). Between 1980 and 1984, women could only claim the addition if their husband's total weekly income was less than the amount of the addition, which at £1.70p per child from November 1979, was of little practical importance (Atkins, 1981, p.17). In any case, what had been given with one hand was soon taken away. By November 1984 the phasing out of these additions with short-term benefits was complete.[5] Women can now claim dependency additions on the same terms as men, but these additions only exist for long-term benefits.

Additions for spouses

From November 1983 onwards, when the implementing regulations came into effect, married women were able to claim additions for dependent spouses with short-term benefits on the same terms as married men. Additions are payable as long as the total weekly earnings of the dependent spouse do not exceed the amount of the addition.

In relation to long-term benefits, however, between 1980 and 1984 married men and women were still treated differently (see Atkins, 1981, p.18). Married men could receive the addition as long as their wives did not earn over £45 per week and, where they did, the addition was gradually reduced along a taper. Married women, on the other hand, could only receive the addition if their husbands earnt less than the amount of the addition, which was £14 per week and, where husbands earned over this amount, the addition was immediately withdrawn in its entirety. This difference in treatment was justified by the government on cost grounds, as well as by invoking the derogation in Article 7(1)(d) of the Directive (ibid.).

Since November 1984 married men and women have been able to claim the additions for dependent spouses on the same terms, with just one exception. A married woman claiming an addition for her dependent husband, paid with a Category A retirement pension, must show, on top of the usual conditions, that immediately before reaching pensionable age she was already receiving an addition for him with unemployment, sickness or invalidity benefits.[6] Reform of this discriminatory rule has been resisted on the grounds that this provision falls within the derogation in Article 7(1)(d) of the Directive, which covers additions for dependent wives with certain long-term benefits.[7] In Chapter 4 we saw that the ECJ, in July 1994, found that this difference in treatment does indeed fall within the derogation in that Article.[8] In a White Paper of 1993, however, the UK government has promised to eliminate this difference in treatment by abolishing this extra requirement on the same timescale as the equalization of pensionable ages (that is, between 2010 and 2020).[9]

To summarize, a number of changes were brought about by the 1980 Act to achieve equality of access with regard to claiming additions with contributory benefits. Their impact has been far from significant. Hoskyns and Luckhaus (1989, p.330) have summed up their effect by saying that 'men with high-earning partners lost entitlement while some married women with low-earning partners gained access for the first time'. Additions with short-term benefits for children were withdrawn for all claimants, and it may be wondered how far the reforms to long-term benefits have promoted equality of outcomes, given that far fewer women than men qualify for contributory benefits in the first place.

The reform of the non-contributory invalidity pension

In 1975 the government introduced a non-contributory invalidity pension (NCIP), which was designed to provide income for persons who had been unable to build up sufficient contributions for invalidity benefit (IVB), due to inadequate contact with the labour market (Ogus and Barendt, 1988, p.144). The NCIP was similar in scope to IVB, although paid at a less generous level. Initially, married and cohabiting women were excluded from claiming this benefit (Atkins and Hoggett, 1984, p.168) but the need was later perceived to extend NCIP to persons primarily engaged in unpaid caring work, such as 'disabled housewives' (ibid.). The criteria used to define the incapacity of this group, brought into force in 1977, were 'crude and discriminatory' (ibid., p.145). In order for married and cohabiting women to receive the NCIP they had to show, in addition to incapacity to work (the test for all claimants), that they were incapable of performing normal household duties.[10]

In fact the organization of the contributory invalidity benefit and the non-contributory NCIP meant that many disabled women were denied benefits altogether. Having paid reduced contributions in the past they could not claim Invalidity Benefit, and because of insufficient incapacity they could not pass the 'normal household duties' test (ibid., p.168). As neatly summed up by Richards (1979, p.70):

... the net result is that the housewife who would be in paid employment were she not disabled, and the housewife who would be running her home and looking after her children were she not disabled, both suffer discrimination, in different ways.

The official justification for the 'normal household duties' test was the familiar one that most married women did not take paid employment and were financially dependent on their husbands (ibid., p.69). Since NCIP had been intended as an income-replacement benefit, rather than as compensation for disability, it appeared inequitable to give benefits to married women who would not, in any case, be in the labour market (ibid.). The government argued that it would be unfair to other claimants of NCIP if disabled housewives were able to claim the benefit while still doing household duties and being supported by husbands (ibid.). On the other hand, where a wife was not able to carry out her normal household duties – which was her part of the marriage 'bargain' – then presumably it would be legitimate for the state to intervene in the form of providing benefits. It is worth quoting an official policy document from 1974, which argued that:[11]

> ... some housewives are so disabled that not only would they be incapable of doing a paid job, but they are unable to cope with the household work which is their working contribution to the family ... a wife with this degree of incapacity can have a most serious impact on the household budget. ...The economic value to the household of the wife's work is beyond dispute. The housewife's disablement can lead to higher expenses for laundering, ... domestic help and so on ...

The government was put under pressure to eliminate the discrimination against married and cohabiting women contained in the normal household duties test. In 1983 it published a white paper outlining options for reform, entitled the *Review of the Household Duties Test*. The simplest of the reform options canvassed would have been to abolish the test altogether, but this was rejected on the grounds that it would cost an estimated £250 million per year to fund (Ogus and Barendt, 1988, p.145). A second option could have been to concentrate on lost earning potential and impose some test of recent employment activity, but this was also considered too costly, as well as too difficult to apply in practice (ibid.). In the end the preferred solution was to apply an objective measurement of the degree of disablement, through methods already used in the industrial injuries and war pensions schemes (ibid.).

Introducing a new benefit: substituting direct discrimination with indirect discrimination?

The Health and Social Security Act 1984 abolished NCIP in November 1984, and replaced it with a new benefit, the severe disablement allowance (SDA). To qualify for SDA a person has to fulfil several conditions:

1 non-eligibility to contributory invalidity benefit;
2 proof of long-term incapacity for work (28 weeks);

3 onset of incapacity for work prior to a claimant's 20th birthday or, if later, a demonstrable 80 per cent threshold of disability.

The change to a new benefit did not significantly improve women's equality of opportunity in gaining the SDA. The condition of the 80 per cent loss of faculty meant that only 20 000 of the 240 000 women unable to claim NCIP became eligible for the new benefit (Kidd, 1989, p.69). Official statistics show that, even after the introduction of the new benefit, the numbers of claimants remained broadly the same. Luckhaus aptly described this outcome in the following terms: 'the intellectual game is to come up with the same trump card each time you shuffle the pack' (1987, p.39).

Luckhaus (1986a, pp.163–8) has made the case very forcefully that the SDA has in fact substituted indirect discrimination for direct discrimination. The main mechanism through which the indirect discrimination occurs, argues Luckhaus, is the requirement that those over 20 years of age have a loss of function of 80 per cent (ibid., p.163). It was acknowledged in the 1983 Report that the age bar in SDA would disproportionately affect married women in the group of disabled persons, since the overwhelming majority of people who become disabled whilst of working age, but who lack an adequate contribution record, are in fact married women (ibid.). There has as yet been no challenge to the SDA on the grounds that the 80 per cent threshold combined with the age bar indirectly discriminates against women. An ideal test-case litigant could be a married woman over 20 years of age, with an inadequate contributions record (preferably not through choice), who became disabled while in paid employment and was forced to give up employment for this reason (ibid.).

Successful challenges to the transitional regulations under the Directive

When the SDA was introduced, transitional regulations were passed to protect the entitlements of persons already receiving NCIP.[12] These regulations effectively gave recipients of NCIP a passport to receipt of the severe disablement allowance. A married woman, Mrs Clarke, who had been unable to claim NCIP and who was also unable to claim the new benefit, claimed that these regulations perpetuated discrimination beyond December 1984, the date on which equality should have been implemented. The ECJ agreed with her and held that the regulations were contrary to the Directive.[13] The UK government took a narrow view, however, of the effect of this decision and decided not to find and pay the other approximately 2 million women who would have been entitled to the SDA on the same basis as Mrs Clarke (Hoskyns and Luckhaus, 1989, p.331).

Some years later, s. 165A of the Social Security Act 1975 was passed, which requires persons to actually make a claim for a benefit in order to establish entitlement. The effect of this provision in relation to the SDA, combined with the transitional regulations passporting claimants from NCIP to SDA, was such as to make it impossible for women who were denied the SDA after 1984 to demonstrate entitlement to NCIP for any period in the past. Knowing that the normal household duties test would have debarred them, many women realized there was little to be gained by making a claim for the NCIP; however, this failure to make a claim prejudiced them later in seeking to establish entitlement to the SDA. The *Johnson (No. 1)* case[14] did successfully challenge the combined discriminatory effect of these rules.

To summarize, the abolition of the discriminatory normal household duties test brought about equality of access for married and cohabiting women, yet, by a sleight of hand, this advance was undermined by the setting of a high disablement threshold into the new sex-neutral benefit. Although women in fact, comprise the majority of SDA claimants, the design of this benefit clearly demonstrates the UK government's grudging attitude towards implementing the Directive.

The extension of the invalid care allowance

An invalid care allowance (ICA) is paid to both male and female carers of working age, who are 'regularly and substantially engaged' in looking after a severely disabled person, defined as a person receiving one of several benefits (see Chapter 2). When ICA was first introduced in 1977, women living with a man as wives or cohabitees were barred from claiming. Underpinning this exclusion were two principal assumptions (Groves and Finch, 1983, p.152). First, it was assumed that women – and married women in particular – are the 'natural' carers in the domestic setting. Second, it was assumed that married women's earnings, if any, are marginal to the security of the domestic group. On the basis of this, it was not considered necessary to compensate these women for leaving the labour market since their partners were believed to maintain them financially. The original design of ICA can be regarded as an excellent case study of how state policies 'support and promote gender-related patterns of caring' (ibid., p.149).

Despite the fact that the government repackaged NCIP into the severe disablement allowance, it refused to do anything about the discrimination in the invalid care allowance. A coalition of interest groups determined to force a change to this rule brought a test case – the famous *Drake* case – which challenged this discrimination under Directive 79/7/EEC (see Harlow, 1992, pp.345–6). On the eve of the ECJ's judgement in 1986, the government extended invalid care allowance to married women. Further, all the 126 000 backdated claims were met in full all the way back to December 1984 (Ogus and Barendt, 1988, p.169). This represents a rare example of genuine levelling up by the UK government in response to the obligations under Directive 79/7/EEC.

The extension of ICA can be seen as a victory for the campaigning groups in the UK as well as a publicity 'coup' for the Directive.[15] However, as we saw in Chapter 2, ICA, even in its extended version, is not a widely paid benefit, being very difficult to claim because of its link with attendance allowance (or the care component of the disability living allowance), with its narrow eligibility conditions. It will be recalled that only an estimated one in ten carers investing the requisite number of hours actually receive the benefit (Glendinning, 1992, p.167). A number of other rules, which will be discussed below, in effect cancel out the benefit of claiming ICA for many persons on the lowest incomes.

First, in April 1988 the rules for the receipt of the severe disability premium to income support (IS) were changed. In brief, no one may receive this premium if another person is already claiming ICA for looking after them. This means that where a person gives up employment to care for a disabled person, and where the cared-for person is in receipt of a severe disability premium, one of these two benefits (the ICA or the premium) will be withdrawn.

Second, ICA is paid subject to an earnings rule, albeit without a means test. The least well-off who are claiming income support, or who are family members of income support claimants gain no advantage from ICA because their income support is reduced by the same amount. These rules may also have the effect that claimants receiving ICA, income support and the carer's premium with income support of £10 might be worse off financially, where receipt of ICA causes a significant reduction to the whole value of the other benefits.[16]

Third, an adult dependent addition is paid at the same level as ICA, and only one of these can be given. Overlapping benefits regulations also prevent a person in receipt of a widow's pension from receiving ICA. In cases where there is eligibility for both, the higher of the two benefits is paid.

To summarize, although the symbolic value of the government's climbdown in the *Drake* case is still worth savouring, the actual outcomes produced by the eventual reform were not of great importance relative to the numbers of actual carers in the UK. This is all the more so, given that, in a number of situations, receipt of this benefit does not improve the incomes of the carers in the poorest households. Extending the ICA to married and cohabiting women has given many women a degree of personal income and undoubtedly constitutes some recognition of the value of their work. However, in terms of my threefold test, the extension of ICA may not constitute a move towards equality of outcomes, given that, in its qualitative aspects, this benefit can promote marginal labour market participation on the part of carers, and the low levels at which the benefit is paid may reinforce the financial dependence of carers on their partners or on cared-for persons.

Supplementary benefit: the exclusion of married or cohabiting women

In the post-war period, married (and cohabiting) women were unable to claim national assistance and its successor, supplementary benefit, because of the claiming partner rule. Heterosexual couples were treated

> ... not simply as a claimant and dependant but as an indivisible unit, as one. This meant that their needs and means were aggregated and only one could claim. That one had to be the man (Hoskyns and Luckhaus, 1989, p.328).

In 1978 the government published *Social Assistance*, a major review of the supplementary benefits scheme, in which the question of how to bring about equality of treatment was tackled. Several equalization options were proposed, including individualization or disaggregation, the free choice of the couple, the main breadwinner being the claimant, or lastly choosing a nominated breadwinner on the basis of a recent full-time paid work record. The individualization option was rejected immediately on cost grounds, as was the free choice of the couple, and the option preferred was to 'nominate' a breadwinner.

The 1983 'nominated breadwinner' regulations

The Social Security Act 1980 removed the bar on married and cohabiting women from claiming supplementary benefit and amended the rules on the aggregation of resources so that a couple's resources could be treated as belonging to either the man or the woman, whichever was to be the claiming partner.[17] This reform of supplementary benefit was justified in official quarters largely on the basis that married women should not be treated as if they did not work when in fact they did (Luckhaus, 1990, p.662). In 1983 'tortuously worded and enormously complex' regulations[18] were drawn up to set out the conditions under which a nominated breadwinner would be ascertained (ibid., p.657).

In the main, the 1983 regulations provided that the nominated breadwinner (or claiming partner) would be the member of the couple who was already the claiming partner in relation to other social security benefits (see

Luckhaus, 1983, pp.327–30). However, other conditions could be invoked to allow a partner to become the claimant where they could demonstrate substantial reasons for absence from employment. The 1983 regulations did entitle some women to claim supplementary benefit for the first time, but in the overwhelming majority of cases men continued to be the claimants as before (Luckhaus, 1990, p.656).

'Free choice' undermined by subsequent rules

S.22(5) of the Social Security Act 1986, which came into effect in April 1988, finally allowed either partner to claim, with the decision being left to the couple. But the potential impact of this positive development has been undermined by a more recent change (Luckhaus, 1990, p.660). Income support now includes the rule that a person is barred from claiming where their partner is in full-time work, defined since April 1992 as 16 hours per week ('the full-time work exclusion rule'). Linking entitlement to income support to the labour market participation of both partners arguably negates equality of opportunity because of the very different nature of men's and women's labour market participation (or the 'gendered social reality') in that greater numbers of women than men will have partners working over 16 hours per week. This rule may indeed also exclude claims from a number of men whose female partners are working over 16 hours per week, but if the latter's employment is low-paid there would be a strong incentive for women to give up their (low) paid work. As a consequence, it is suggested, fewer women will be able to gain access to personal income, which bears negatively on their choices and on their power within their relationships.

The full-time work exclusion rule does therefore go a long way towards neutralizing the free choice accorded in 1988. Indeed, Luckhaus (1990, p.665) argues that this rule now performs the exclusionary function formerly served by the claiming partner rule. Statistics from the late 1980s show that, in 19 out of 20 cases, it is male partners who are the claimants on behalf of couples, although the proportion of women has slowly crept up (Lister, 1992, p.42). Rules such as the full-time work exclusion rule, combined with the widening of the social assistance net, mean that the negative impact on women's employment incentives and their limited access to personal income is spread to an even wider group of women.

Summary

In implementing the Directive the benefits given with one hand (equality of access) have been undermined by the other hand (rules which, in practice, undermine equality of opportunity). Although most rules in the UK system are sex-neutral, women suffer sharp inequalities in outcomes not only in terms of benefits received, but also in terms of the qualitative aspects of risk provision. The sex-neutral rules of the UK system, interacting with the gendered social reality, leave many women with little financial independence.

HOW FAR HAS FINANCIAL INDEPENDENCE FOR WOMEN BEEN ADVANCED?

In October 1995 the ECJ found that Mr Richardson is entitled, under Directive 79/7/EEC, to the right to free prescriptions from the age of 60, the state pension age for women.[19] While not wishing to deny the importance of the *Richardson* case, neither at the individual level nor in terms of the potential benefits for a wider group of men on low incomes, it does throw into sharp relief one of the central questions of this book: to what extent has the Directive promoted financial independence for women?

The implementation of Directive 79/7/EEC has been primarily characterized by giving equality of access to women for a range of benefits without also equalizing their opportunities to gain these benefits in practice, or by equalizing outcomes between men and women. To refer back to one example, equalizing access to dependency additions paid with contributory benefits increases the levels of income that women personally receive but, where no other changes are made – such as to entitlement structures – the numbers of women benefiting from this equalization of access is likely to be modest.

In many cases, in implementing the Directive, what has been given with one hand has been taken away, at least partially, by the other. While not claiming that the primary purpose of taking benefits away has been to deliberately undermine 'equality', if the effects of subsequent rules are considered, equality of opportunity has clearly been undermined as demonstrated by the examples below:

- The equalization of access of married women with regard to claiming dependant's additions for children with short-term contributory benefits was followed by the abolition of short-term benefit additions in respect of children for all claimants.
- The equalization of access of married and cohabiting women to the ICA may be cancelled out for many claimants at the lowest levels of income.
- The discriminatory NCIP was repackaged into the sex-neutral severe

disablement allowance (SDA), to which women have equality of access, yet the numbers of claimants of the new benefit remained at similar levels.

- The free choice of a couple as to who will claim, on behalf of both, income support, is undermined by the full-time working partner exclusion rule.

In regrettably few cases has the government fulfilled its obligations under the Directive by a genuine levelling-up of provision for women. The best example of a genuine levelling-up remains the extension of the invalid care allowance in the wake of the ECJ's decision in *Drake*. On the other hand, as we have seen above, for carers in low-income households receipt of ICA may not be financially advantageous, thus undermining the receipt of personal, albeit low, income for carers.

The argument has consistently been made in this and preceding chapters that bringing about equality of access without also modifying the rules on entitlement to benefits is unlikely to achieve equality of opportunity or outcomes. Women and men are in structurally different positions in terms of what benefits they receive, their levels and the type typically provided for them. Rules which are equal in terms of access, but which interact with the gendered social reality – that is, patterns of labour market participation and the financial dependence of women in households – cannot produce equal outcomes.

The reforms in the UK which have most advanced equality of opportunity and outcomes, it is argued, were passed before the adoption of the Directive. The first such reform was the abolition of the married women's option for women marrying after April 1977 which had a comparable effect to that of the Directive in the Netherlands, Ireland and Belgium in requiring that women claiming paid work-related benefits be treated on the same terms as men for the first time. This change has therefore had a significant impact on enabling women to receive personal income from the contributory benefits system.

Second, the introduction of home responsibilities protection (HRP) has helped to preserve the personal entitlements to the basic state pension for those women with at least 20 years of paid-work earnings exceeding the lower earnings limit. HRP cannot, by any means, protect the entitlements of all women workers, yet arguably it has an important role to play in cushioning those women who combine paid and unpaid work over their lifetimes, and ultimately in allowing them to gain access to personal contributory benefits. Arguably the introduction of HRP is one of the few examples of a reform in the UK which promotes equality of outcomes. Its impact is nevertheless limited because of the requirement of at least 20 years' contributions rule.

Prospects for the kind of legislative reforms that would advance women's financial independence are rather bleak in the UK. Official policy is set on widening the means-tested net, as well as on eroding the contributory benefits system, with all its attendant dangers for women's ability to gain personal income. The review of social security in the mid-1980s, which was hailed as the most comprehensive since Beveridge, in fact contained:

> ... no re-appraisal of the objectives or functions of social security in the light of changes in employment and in access to employment. The basic model remains the full-time (male) worker who requires income maintenance for short spells of unemployment or sickess, or for longer spells of disability or retirement. (Millar, 1989, p.316)

While government policy in the 1980s and early 1990s extols the independence of the individual from the welfare state, the dependence of women on men in households is, to say the least, tacitly accepted.

Implementation of the Directive in the UK, and subsequent pressure on the government to equalize outcomes between men and women, in fact owes a great deal to the active work of a number of welfare rights groups and independent bodies, such as the Child Poverty Action Group, the Birkenhead Resource Unit, law centres, as well as bodies such as the Equal Opportunities Commission (EOC). The struggle, if it can be called that, now appears to have shifted to the judicial forum, both at the level of the national courts and at the supranational level of the ECJ. Litigation strategies using Directive 79/7/EEC have had notable successes, such as the *Drake* and *Thomas* cases, but these are rare.

This chapter completes the critique of EC equality law in the field of statutory social security. I have hinted frequently that far-reaching changes are needed to substantially alter women's lack of access to independent income, and that such changes are more appropriately brought about by legislation. In the conclusions I propose four normative criteria with which to assess strategies to promote women's financial independence.

NOTES

1   Although the numbers of married women still exercising the option is decreasing every year, it still applied to 25 per cent of employed married women in 1987 (Micklewright, 1990, p.9).

2   The 'half test' was finally completely abolished with effect from 22 December 1984, by s.11 of the Social Security Act 1985 (Ogus and Barendt, 1988, p.201). The after-effects of this rule have, however, continued to disadvantage some women (see the cases *R(P) 4/88* and CP 31/1989, unreported).

3 See, for instance, the case of CP 72/1983.
4 See *R(S) 11/79*.
5 S.13, Housing and Social Security Act 1984. These were abolished, according to Ogus and Barendt (1988, p.339), as a first step in a policy to reduce differences in the level of family support between short-term beneficiaries and those in employment.
6 S.45(1)(a), Social Security Act 1975.
7 In *R(P) 3/88* a Commissioner accepted that this rule could not be challenged because it falls within the derogation in Article 7(1)(d).
8 *Bramhill* v. *Chief Adjudication Officer*, Case C-420/92 [1994] ECR I-1086.
9 *Equality in State Pension Ages*, Cmnd 2420, London: HMSO, December 1993, at para. 3.10 (p.24).
10 S.36(2) of the Social Security Act 1975, and SI 1975/1058, regulation 12(A)(2), inserted by SI 1978/1340.
11 *Social Security Provision for Chronically Sick and Disabled People*: HC Paper, 31 July 1974, para. 43.
12 Regulation 4(b) of the Social Security (Severe Disablement Allowance) Regulations 1984 (SI 1984, No. 1303).
13 *Clarke* v. *Chief Adjudication Officer*, Case 384/85 [1987] ECR 2865.
14 *Johnson (No. 1)* v. *Chief Adjudication Officer*, Case C-31/90 [1991] ECR I-3723.
15 The ICA campaign also demonstrates very clearly the importance of raising public awareness about equality issues (Kidd, 1989, p.98). At the time Mrs Drake won her case more than 90 000 claims had been received, and others were being received at a rate of 2000 per week (ibid.). There was regrettably a lack of official enthusiasm in the aftermath of the decision, which may have hampered the processing of subsequent claims (ibid.). Department of Social Security headquarters, for instance, delayed the arrival of important documents in local offices and withdrew a central brief on staff training, causing considerable confusion among local officials and fostering an understanding on their part that this regulation did not share the same importance as other matters (ibid.).
16 See, further, Barlow and Lamb (1990, pp.18–19).
17 Married and cohabiting women were also unable to claim the main family benefit, family income supplement (FIS). FIS was technically outside the scope of the Directive (see *R(FIS) 2/88*), but the 1980 Social Security Act also amended this rule in relation to FIS, apparently to maintain consistency between the two benefits (Luckhaus, 1983, p.330). FIS did still contain the condition that the claiming partner had to be in full-time employment, which meant that fewer women could claim (ibid.). FIS was eventually replaced by family credit in 1988, which in fact is normally paid to women.
18 Supplementary Benefit (Equal Treatment) Regulations 1983 (SI 1983, No. 1004).
19 Judgement of European Court of Justice not yet reported.

8   Conclusions

In 1972 a research conference was organized in Vienna by the International
Social Security Association on the theme of women and social security. It is
worth quoting in full the introductory remarks of the proceedings of the
conference in order to demonstrate that, after more than 20 years, many of
the difficult questions raised have still not been resolved, although the
language of debate has changed:

> Against the changes in the social role of women and more especially in the light
> of their increasing participation, in particular of married women, in the labour
> force, existing social security arrangements are being scrutinised and questions
> posed as to their pertinence and adequacy in relation to the needs of women for
> social security protection as workers, wives, mothers, widows. Should provision
> for men and women be identical? For example, should the age at which the
> retirement pension may be drawn be the same, or what differentiation is justified
> and acceptable? To what extent and in what ways should social security cover-
> age be extended to the 'housewife' who, temporarily or for a longer time, is not
> involved in the labour force? Should social security be assured to women,
> particularly to non-working women, through their husbands' insurance record,
> or should they have an independent status within social security? In case of
> widowhood or divorce, what is the appropriate role of the social security sys-
> tem? (ISSA, 1973, p.1)

Directive 79/7/EEC was the last of the 'strong' social policy Directives
passed in the equality sphere (Hoskyns and Luckhaus, 1989, p.321). The
equality Directives passed in the 1970s were largely characterized by an
equality-as-sameness approach linked to the workplace. It was recognized
that equality policies also needed to take account of family responsibilities
and how this affected labour market participation, but very little further
legislative action has been taken in this direction due to the sustained oppo-
sition of certain Member States.

   Directive 79/7/EEC remains, therefore, the primary equality instrument
in the field of statutory social security schemes. The hopes for going beyond
a strictly employment-related principle of equality at the EC level are cen-

tred on the European Court of Justice (ECJ) interpreting this instrument in a dynamic way. This may, however, be too much to expect from the Court, since in the social security area it has been more cautious than in the sphere of employment. I will return to the interpretative role of the ECJ later.

There are a number of positive aspects to Directive 79/7/EEC. At the very least, requiring formal equality has a strong symbolic value, and 'even crude legal instruments can be important to weak and disadvantaged groups in society and can give them at least some purchase in the political process' (Hoskyns, 1985, p.73). The Directive was passed at a time when the overt forms of discrimination against married women, both in terms of employment and social security, were beginning to sound a jarring note. The 'mood' of the 1970s has been captured in the following way by Brocas *et al.* (1990, p.5):

> ... since 1975... certain basic questions concerning women's rights in social security have come to the fore and various new goals have been defined. Recognition of the new role played by women in economic, social and cultural development had led to a questioning of the old standards and attitudes, which by then no longer matched the reality. As regards social security, the movement which was getting under way aimed to secure equal rights for the new generations of women wishing to take up paid employment on the same terms as their male counterparts.

Equality in EC law was intended, at least in part, to remove the 'barriers' or 'restrictive' practices which obstructed women (Hoskyns, 1985, p.78). Arguably, it was also realized that, given the increasing numbers of women in the labour market, married women could no longer be assumed *a priori* to be the financial dependents of their husbands (Hoskyns and Luckhaus, 1989, p.333).

As shown in Chapters 6 and 7, the Directive has indeed been instrumental in removing overt forms of discrimination against married women in a range of benefits. Mazey (1988, p.82) has succinctly characterized EC equality law as having 'doggedly chipped away at the vast edifice of sexist practices and policies' over the years.

Yet the Directive has not been a vehicle to achieving equality of outcomes for women in terms of their greater access to independent income. Why is this the case? The answer to this question relates to the vision of equality contained within the Directive.

Equality in Directive 79/7/EEC is seen through a 'sameness–difference' lens. Women are to be accorded the same treatment when they are the same (where they are workers) and different treatment when their social role is different from men's (where they are carers and dependants). This is first and foremost a limited version of the equality principle because it does not encompass within it the reality of inequality.

It is a vision, however, that seems to be widely shared. It is interesting in this regard to consider the definition of equality offered in a report produced on behalf of the International Labour Organization relating to progress towards equality of treatment for women in social security (Brocas *et al.*, 1990). Brocas *et al.* (1990, p.109) define equality in this sphere as meaning three things:

1   For women exercising an occupational activity, whatever the nature of that activity and the economic sector in which it is carried out, social coverage should be identical to that enjoyed by men.
2   The same rules should be applied to both men and women insofar as they are in the same employment situation.
3   Rules should be adjusted when a category of workers experiences specific needs arising from a particular situation.

The equality offered here gives women access to the pre-existing structure, except in the (limited) cases in which it is clear that they diverge (such as maternity), and here they can be treated differently.

This vision, it has been argued, fundamentally misses the point that existing structures ought to be changed to 'include' women and their gendered life patterns within them. Only this can substantially improve the disadvantages facing women in the 'gendered social reality'. It is unrealistic to expect most women to adopt masculine life patterns, since caring work still has to be done. Equality, as seen in the Directive, does not allow for challenges to the privileged benefits accorded to masculine life patterns.

I have shown that the complex picture of the inequality that women face in gaining independent income goes far beyond instances of 'sex discrimination' – that is, deliberately treating women unfavourably on the grounds of their sex. Important elements in this complex picture are the qualitatively and quantitatively inferior provision given to feminine risks, as well as to the rules and policies within the social security system which reinforce traditional gender roles and therefore women's financial dependence on men.

What is needed to alter this gendered social reality is a far more radical understanding of equality; one which, at the very least, is rooted in a conception of existing inequality. This understanding, or model of equality, would not simply conform to the prevailing standard, but rather demands far-reaching changes along the lines of an 'inclusion model' (Bacchi, 1991a, p.2).

But the vision of equality in the Directive is flawed in terms of altering the gendered social reality in three important respects. First, the Directive offers women equality in access to male risks. The prohibition on discrimination in the Directive means that women must be able, formally at least, to have the possibility of claiming employment-related social insurance benefits on the same terms as men (whether by eliminating direct discrimination or by attacking sex-neutral rules which have a disadvantageous impact on part-time workers). At a conceptual level this does not challenge the link between social insurance benefits and therefore qualitatively, and often quantitatively, superior benefits and paid work.

Second, the vision is limited because women's employment patterns often do not secure them full personal entitlements to social insurance benefits. This is no minor difference because masculine and feminine risks may be provided for rather differently, and I have shown that feminine income-loss risks receive qualitatively and quantitatively inferior provision. Women cannot compete on the same terms as men for these benefits, in view of the inequalities in the labour market as well as women's income dependence on men in households, and so outcomes are unlikely to change. At the heart of the Directive's vision is the creation of a level playing-field, where each person theoretically has the same opportunity of access to social security, but without actually bringing into effect any of the necessary fundamental changes to the system.

Third, although the Directive prohibits direct and indirect discrimination, removing rules which treat men and women differently is essentially a negative way of bringing about equality. What is needed is some positive redistributive step based on a notion of inequality. EC equality law does not currently offer redistribution as a general rule, but rather is premised on existing cultural and social divisions (Ellis, 1991, pp.206–7; see also Hoskyns and Luckhaus, 1989, p.333).

Although the Directive is fundamentally limited in some respects, I have suggested a number of ways in which its scope could be expanded by more dynamic interpretation. For example, the notion of 'worker' could be uncoupled from exit from the labour market by reason of a risk in Article 3(1); the notion of worker could reflect more realistically women's contemporary employment patterns which alternate periods of paid work with periods of unpaid work; in determining which schemes offer protection for the risks in Article 3(1)(a) attention should be paid to how protection for the Directive's risks is given in practice; finally, in interpreting the prohibition on indirect discrimination, the ECJ has taken much of the bite out of this concept in the social security sphere and should apply a stricter standard of the objective justification test.

Were the ECJ to be more courageous it could adopt a more ends-oriented interpretation of the equality principle. Glimpses of this are occasionally seen – as, for instance, in the *Dekker* case in which the ECJ grasped the nettle of pregnancy discrimination, boldly stating that, since only women can become pregnant, discrimination against them on grounds of pregnancy can only be direct discrimination. Ends-oriented interpretation should take account of the inequalities facing women. New evaluative criteria would, it seems, be needed, and work should be done to develop these. The discussion of the *Integrity* case in Chapter 6 would suggest that one evaluative criterion of a more ends-oriented interpretation could be the extent to which rules perpetuate systems in which women, or certain categories of women, are kept outside of the social insurance system and are forced to depend upon derived benefits.

In relation to discussions about costs, and the extent to which these considerations negate not only the principle of equality but also the extent to which compensation is given for past discrimination, a missing dimension is a recognition that women bear the costs of inequality in terms of their financial dependence on men. Ignoring this reveals, at best, a misplaced complacency about income-sharing between men and women in households, while at worst it shows a fundamental deprioritizing of women's interests in an adequate level of personal income.

It is not the intention to dismiss the relevance of all costs arguments – after all, we do live in a world of finite resources. It may well be true that political reality dictates that where women are to be compensated for past discrimination this is achieved by cuts in other parts of the benefit system, making all benefit claimants, who are by and large the poorest members of society, financially worse off. The argument is, however, that, at the very least, the costs for women of continuing inequality should be explicitly acknowledged. To assume that it is only the bringing about of equality which entails costs is dangerously deceptive. This also suggests that equality reforms need to be thought out very carefully, and this may be best achieved by legislative, as opposed to judicial, means.

A number of common themes were observed in the implementation of the Directive in the four countries, none of which gives cause for jubilation or optimism for the future. In all these countries the Directive has brought about equality of access but has failed to stimulate equality of outcomes. The argument here is that the Directive has apparently been unable to tackle the deeper issues of structural inequality that limit women's access to independent income. Implementing equality of access alone into entitlement conditions, for instance, tends to substitute indirect discrimination for direct discrimination. A sex-neutral 'gloss' can easily be painted on to systems in which higher benefits go to (male) claimants with dependent partners doing the caring work, as is the case in the Netherlands and Belgium. It is therefore regrettable then that the prohibition on indirect discrimination in Directive 79/7/EEC is rather weak in this area, due in large part to the ECJ's unwillingness to intervene in Member States's social policy.

The inability of the Directive to tackle the deeper issues of structural inequality can be explained both by its own flaws and external factors. Fundamentally, the Directive has two principal flaws. First, its sameness approach is limited because, as has been seen, men and women are in very different social situations and treating women like men only benefits a privileged few. This is especially true of countries such as the Netherlands and Ireland, where women's labour market participation is very low compared to men's and where, as in the Netherlands, much of women's employment is part-time rather than full-time.

A sameness approach to equality has also meant that men have acquired benefits previously only given to women. In Belgium, for instance, the Directive prompted 'equalization' in men's favour. In the Netherlands and in Ireland some survivor's benefits have also been extended to men, despite their exclusion from the Directive. This move to a widening of derived entitlements is, I would argue, a further undermining of progress towards the individualization of benefits. Nevertheless it is, of course, 'unfair' that men should be unable to benefit from their wives' contributions, and moreover the granting of derived entitlement to men undermines the idea of the man as the (only) 'provider' for a household.

The Directive's second principal flaw is its tendency to give equal treatment to women who experience the classic-work related benefits. Cook and McCashin (1992, p.35) have argued that the Directive appears to be geared towards countries in which significant numbers of women are in paid work, but not to countries such as Ireland in which female labour market participation is low. However, even in a country such as Belgium where significant numbers of women are employed full-time, where the inequalities are embedded within a sex-neutral structure of payments, the Directive was spectacularly unsuccessful in attacking this because of the ECJ's reluctance to intervene in national policy.

The four, at times interrelated, external factors explaining the Directive's inability to attack structural disadvantage are the widening of the means-testing net, the continuing prevalence of benefits structured on a household basis, the pattern of implementing equality by levelling down and finally the lack of collectivization of caring within the social insurance system.

First, in the UK, as in the Netherlands and Ireland, the scope of social assistance has been widened (Room et al., 1989, p.168). Belgium is the only country of the four in which there is a continuing adherence to the principle that social insurance schemes are preferable to social assistance, although, even in Belgium, there was an increase in the numbers claiming the Minimex benefit (Room et al., 1989, p.168).[1] The widening of the means-tested net in all four countries may be attributed to a variety of factors. In the first place there has been a general increase in both the young and long-term unemployed, and in many countries these groups exhaust or have never built up social insurance rights (Oorschot and Schell, 1991, p.198). Second, it is common for lone parents to be reliant on social assistance, and there has been an overall increase in their numbers (Oorschot and Schell, 1991, pp.200–2). Third, there have been cuts to social insurance schemes, such as decreases in the levels of benefits, as well the tightening of entitlement conditions (Oorschot and Schell, 1991, p.203). Finally, means-tested elements have been introduced into already existing social insurance schemes, or new means-tested schemes have been created (ibid.).

A second significant factor limiting equality of opportunity is that women's access to independent income is undermined by benefits which are structured around a household's needs or a household minimum, since this is associated with higher benefits for (male) primary earners. The Dutch and Belgian systems, in particular, continue to retain this structure in the payment of benefits, although arguably this can also be seen in the UK and Ireland, given the wide scope of means-tested benefits in the former and the extent of adult dependant's additions in the latter. This may have been exacerbated by the general increase in the numbers of claimants receiving social assistance, as well as the introduction of means-tested elements into social insurance schemes. In relation to the latter, the Belgian unemployment and sickness insurance scheme takes account of other income in a household in relation to the category of claimant who cohabits with another worker (ibid., p.207).

Employment disincentives for women may be stronger in systems such as the Dutch and Belgian, where certain social insurance benefits are at least in part earnings-related. In Belgium, where a woman's husband is in receipt of an unemployment insurance benefit her earnings may have to be high to cushion the loss of 20 per cent of his past salary, which is the difference between the rates of the workers with and without family responsibilities. In contributory systems with flat-rate benefits, such as the UK and Ireland, women probably have greater incentives to enter employment although this, of course, depends on the levels of the additions to the flat-rate benefits. In Ireland, for instance, the high level of the adult dependant's addition at IR£55 may well contain strong disincentive effects on the employment of female partners.

Third, the changes in all four countries, albeit to varying degrees, have been accompanied by cost-cutting and the narrowing of entitlement conditions and the scope of benefits. Cost-cutting reforms have often also entailed the introduction of means-tested elements into social insurance benefits (ibid., p.205). This may be for two reasons. First, the period during which the Directive was implemented was characterized by fears of over-spending in the social security sphere. Second, equality for women is not high on political agendas, especially when it implies increased expenditure. Two examples of levelling-down are worth highlighting. In the Netherlands the levelling-down of provision concentrated greater resources on male breadwinner/female dependant households. The capping provisions in Ireland have in effect limited benefit increases in households in which one or both partners is in receipt of social welfare (means-tested) payments.

Fourth, none of the four countries has taken great strides towards the collectivizing of care, in the sense of recognizing unpaid care work in the building up of entitlements to contributory benefits. Small steps have, however, been taken in all four countries. In the UK carers are credited towards the basic state pension through home responsibilities protection. In Ireland persons receiving one of the several care-related benefits are credited with contributions for social insurance benefits. The Belgian system gives some 'credit' in the building up of pension rights for periods out of the labour market to engage in care. In the Netherlands the introduction of credits towards unemployment benefits for those who have left full-time work in the labour market to care for children under 12 years is a small step in the right direction.

A worrying aspect of the implementation of the Directive which has emerged is that the Directive's concepts may not have been properly accepted by national courts. This has been noted several times; for instance, in the treatment of the findings of objective justifications in the Dutch courts, and in the understanding of the meaning of equality in the two decisions considered by the UK courts. In the Irish courts there was a deliberate attempt to restrict married women claiming the transitional payments, although this was thwarted by the ECJ. It is particularly regrettable that national courts have not always correctly applied the indirect discrimination test, since social security rules are largely sex-neutral, and challenges to rules which, in practice, still limit women's access to independent income must be in terms of their indirectly discriminatory effects.

Current and future social security trends do not bode well for improvements in women's lack of access to independent income from the social security system. In all the four countries there have been cuts in contributory benefits and a marked spreading of the means-tested net, albeit to varying degrees. Political discourse in both the UK and the Netherlands, while stressing that individuals should be independent from the welfare state, do not spell out the consequences of this for women's dependence on men in households.

Can the Directive still be used to challenge inequalities? Arguably, it could be used to challenge forms of indirect discrimination in access to social insurance schemes, such as earnings thresholds. In the UK, the lower earnings limit excludes 2.25 million working women from the contributory benefit system (Lister, 1992, p.27; see also Chapter 2). It could be argued that this threshold constitutes indirect discrimination against women. Assuming the *prima facie* difference in treatment were to be accepted, the justifications offered would probably be that any reduction in the thresholds could decrease the number of part-time jobs, since employers would not wish to take on the extra burden of paying contributions for employees, or indeed could raise the administration costs of benefit authorities. If this question were referred to the ECJ, there is a strong likelihood that such an objective justification would be accepted. The ECJ could, for instance, refer to its statements in the *EOC* case in 1992 relating to not disturbing the 'complex financial equilibrium' of national social security systems.

To counteract an excessive pessimism, however, it is worth recalling two cases which show a positive judicial approach to this issue. First, the Centrale Raad van Beroep, the highest Dutch court on social security matters, found that an earnings threshold in the invalidity benefit, the AAW, did indirectly discriminate against women. Second, there was a successful challenge in the UK to rules in national employment protection legislation which placed a higher burden on part-time workers in satisfying the thresholds of periods of continuous employment necessary to bring an action of unfair dismissal against employers.[2] This higher threshold excluded a higher percentage of women workers. The government argued that changing the qualifying thresholds would put an increased burden on employers, which would lead to a decrease in the number of part-time jobs. The House of Lords in March 1994, refusing to accept this justification, found that the rules were in breach of EC equality law.

Returning to an issue raised earlier – the role of the ECJ – two points are worth considering. First, because of the stagnation in the legislative arena, the development of EC equality law has shifted to the judicial sphere. Although in some cases the ECJ has not disappointed those who believed in its promise, in many others it has interpreted the law narrowly. These instances highlight most clearly the limitations of reform on a case-by-case judicial basis. To what extent should we be expecting radical changes to be brought about by courts interpreting equality or anti-discrimination laws? Although this is an important question, realistically, however, there is little choice, particularly from a UK perspective.

This book has implicitly pressed for women to gain greater financial independence by according greater economic recognition to caring work, to be achieved by 'gender-sensitive' rights. These rights are aimed to advantage women but, because of their sex-neutrality they also offer benefits to men.

I argued in Chapter 1 that equality lawyers must be ready to develop proposals for reform to be put before the legislature. I offer four normative criteria with which to assess strategies to further women's access to independent income, and which draw upon the insights gleaned so far. The criteria, which may be overlapping in some respects, derive from the discussion of the three questions I set out at the very beginning of this book. Taken as a whole, I would argue that, where these criteria are satisfied, women are likely to have greater power and choices than is currently the case. I shall summarize the criteria up by presenting four questions, before considering each in detail in turn:

1   Would a reform proposal give personal benefits at an adequate level?
2   Would a reform proposal conceptualize caring as 'activity' and 'work'?
3   Would a reform proposal have the positive features of social insurance?
4   If the reform proposal gives women employment incentives, are these incentives to take up jobs which offer adequate income?

The first criterion relates to the adequacy of personal benefits. Financial independence comprises a number of strands. The first is that social security is paid on the basis of personal rights to benefits. These rights belong to an individual, they have been acquired by a person's own contributions (in whatever form that contribution is), they are paid to individuals without taking account of another person's resources, and they contain no link of financial dependence on another adult. The last-mentioned condition should, it is argued, prevent maintenance from ex-partners (which may be paid to help with the costs of bringing up children) from being seen as independent income. Maintenance, I would argue, may in practice reinforce women's lack of choices and power vis-à-vis their ex-partners, while at a conceptual level it fails to challenge the implicit links between caring and financial dependence on men.

Second, associated with the idea of financial independence is that of the adequacy of benefits. One aspect of the qualitative inferiority of current provision in the UK for feminine risks is the low level at which the benefits for these risks are paid. The current level of benefits is not merely a paltry recognition of socially valuable work, but, by not offering the possibility of self-support, it may also encourage financial dependence on another adult.

A third way in which financial independence can be judged draws upon the concept of equality of outcomes from the analytical framework used to assess implementation of the Directive in the four countries. The concept of equality of outcomes, it will be recalled, has two main characteristics. In the first place, there would be a decrease in the sharp disparities that exist between men and women as claimants of social insurance benefits, and second, there would be a qualitative, as well as quantitative, improvement in the types of benefits received by women.

The second criterion focuses on caring as activity and work. Caring has very different meanings for men and women. Graham (1983, pp.24–5) has argued that while, for men, financial dependence and poverty are the costs of being cared for, for women it is giving care that can lead to financial dependence and poverty. This difference is significant not only in terms of women's lesser income because of the time they invest in unpaid caring work, but also because of the implications this lesser income has on women's choices and power within their relationships.

Women often fall into the category of 'dependants' in social security systems, either as persons for whom dependants' additions are paid or as recipients of derived benefits. What is to be understood from this description? Primarily, a dependant is a non-earning and non-working member of the household. What this description obscures then is the volume of services (such as care for children, and sick and elderly persons, as well as domestic work) provided by women, who are generally by no means 'inactive' when not working full-time in the labour market. In the words of O'Kelly (1985, p. 82):

> ... [a]t present married women, who perform the bulk of [caring] tasks, are generally regarded as being dependants of their husbands, although ... the concept of dependency is particularly inappropriate to them since they provide services on a substantial scale.

Further, the concept of 'dependants' in both the social security and income tax system is used to justify the argument that a 'breadwinner' (or male single-earner) has greater income needs. Yet it is forgotten that the breadwinner does gain the advantage of having a partner at home to pursue tasks with a significant monetary value (ibid.).

In political terms it is crucial that being outside of the labour market is not seen as analogous with 'inactivity'. The caring and other unpaid work done by women involves skills and a significant time, emotional and physical investment – and therefore carries a high price tag. This price tag becomes immediately obvious as soon as a monetary value is attached to this work. In the UK, for instance, it has been estimated that the value of unwaged care work is equivalent, in terms of care workers' wages, to approximately £24 billion – a sum approaching the cost of the entire National Health Service (Taylor-Gooby, 1991, p.101).

Two conclusions should be drawn from this. First, women who are 'dependent' on men are usually engaged in activities, such as caring and domestic work, with a significant social and monetary value. Second, caring should be seen as 'work', and not as 'inactivity' or 'non-working', in any strategy to advance women's access to independent income. To see caring as inactivity or non-working is fundamentally to negate a crucial part of the process of social reproduction – one that is, arguably, as important to society as paid work in the labour market.

The third criterion relates to the preference of social insurance over social assistance schemes. I have consistently argued in this book that there are significant qualitative and quantitative differences between social insurance and social assistance benefits. Atkinson (1993, pp.12–15) has summarized a number of the major weaknesses of means-tested benefits:

1   Social assistance implies high marginal tax rates which may create a poverty trap with a dampening effect on work incentives and incentives to save, and suffering from a perceived lack of fairness.
2   An extension of the household as the benefit unit both goes against the trend towards independence and has inherent implications for women's employment incentives.
3   There are problems of incomplete take-up in relation to means-tested benefits.
4   Means-tested benefits entail higher administrative costs than social insurance.

A further criticism of social assistance benefits that I have made in this book is that the household basis of the means test has the capacity to lead to a denial of benefit for many women. Conversely, the qualities of social insurance benefits are that they are personal, they are paid directly to claimants, and they are associated with active participation in society. Further, social insurance benefits have fewer problems with take-up, and they exert less negative control over the employment incentives of a claimant's partner.

In any strategy to promote women's financial independence, therefore, social insurance would need to play the leading role. As currently organized, however, such schemes present women with enormous difficulties in access to benefits. In brief, these are created by earnings thresholds, requirements as to years of contributions, as well as the fact that caring does not count as a contribution for benefits. Nevertheless, the qualities of social insurance, in terms of the personal nature of rights, are significant and therefore worth using as the foundations of a reformed system.

The last criterion highlights the tensions between independent income and employment incentives. A common argument voiced in discussions of non-labour market measures which could provide women with greater independent income is the danger that these may encourage women to remain outside the labour market, thereby further entrenching women into their traditional caring role.[3] This line of reasoning deserves critical analysis for two reasons.

First, we have already seen that labour market participation cannot be seen as the panacea for all the problems which affect women in terms of lack of independent income.

Secondly, we need to think carefully about what sort of employment women are in practice being encouraged to take up. In the UK at least, many women are encouraged into employment which is part-time or low-paid or both. Benefit rules themselves play a part in this, in the form of the proverbial carrot and stick. The stick is represented by the threat of benefit withdrawal where claimants are not actively seeking work, or where they set conditions on the jobs they will accept beyond the 13-week period of grace which claimants are allowed. The carrot is represented by earnings disregards: these allow claimants to earn low levels of income without affecting overall benefit payments. Means-tested benefits in the UK allow some income to be earned by either member of a couple before the benefit is reduced: in 1994–95 these were £10 per week for the claimant and £5 for a partner (and £25 for lone parents). Where both partners in a household are unemployed, given the relative earning power of men and women, it is more likely that the female partner will engage in low-paid work.

One recent study has proposed that, in the interests of women's financial independence, the earning disregards in social assistance benefits should be increased (Duncan *et al.*, 1994, pp.62–87). This proposal can be criticized on two grounds. First, unless disregards are increased dramatically, incentives would still remain for women to take employment which provides little income, and which, being under the national insurance threshold, cannot form the basis for building up personal entitlements to future social insurance benefits (including pensions). The second criticism relates to the aggregation rule in means-tested benefits which, as I have already argued, is a significant obstacle to women gaining independent income. As Luckhaus (1994) rightly points out, increasing disregards merely raises the level at which the taper to reduce the household benefit begins; it does not challenge the household basis of the means test nor its effects on women's choices.

It should be clear, therefore, that arguments concerning the dangers of not damaging women's employment incentives and proposals designed to counteract this, may be of a nature that reinforces the worst elements of the current system. It is certainly correct, in my opinion, that women's incentives to take up employment should not be undermined, but these should be incentives to take up the kind of employment that is likely to provide women with an adequate personal income.

To summarize, there is still a long way to go for women to achieve greater access to independent income from the benefit system. Directive 79/7/EEC has contributed to this process by demanding equality of access for women in relation to employment-related benefits, and this has brought benefits to women in all four countries. An equality principle which could contribute to the goal of women's financial independence would be ends-oriented and would explicitly recognize the existing inequality and disadvantage in the sphere of both paid and unpaid work. In the longest term caring should be included within the entitlement structures to adequate social insurance benefits in order to challenge women's lack of access to independent income from the social security system. But then, we may ask, why should we demand anything less?

NOTES

1   This effect may be of a lesser magnitude in Belgium because, first, social insurance schemes give benefits that are over the levels of social assistance benefits and, second, because unemployment insurance is given for an unlimited duration for certain categories of claimants (Oorschot and Schell, 1991, pp.206–7).

2   *R* v. *Secretary of State for Employment ex p. Equal Opportunities Commission* [1994] WLR 409 (HL).

3   The importance attached to not undermining women's employment incentives is a strong theme running through the Institute of Fiscal Studies' proposals regarding women and independent income (Duncan *et al.*, 1994).

References

ABFJ (Association Belge des Femmes Juristes) (1975), *Les inégalités entre l'homme et la femme en droit belge: bilan et options*, Brussels: Editions Créatif.

Alcock, Peter (1989), '"A Better Partnership Between State and Individual Provision": Social Security in the 1990s', *Journal of Law and Society*, **16**, 97–111.

Atkins, Susan (1981), 'Social Security Act 1980 and the EEC Directive on Equal Treatment in Social Security Benefits', *Journal of Social Welfare Law*, 16–20.

Atkins, Susan and Hoggett, B. (1984), *Women and the Law*, Oxford: Blackwell.

Atkins, Susan and Luckhaus, Linda (1987), 'The Social Security Directive and UK Law' in McCrudden, Christopher (ed.), *Women, Employment and European Equality Law*, London: Eclipse, 103–122.

Atkinson, A. (1993), *Beveridge, the National Minimum, and its Future in a European Context*, Discussion Paper WSP/85, London: London School of Economics.

Bacchi, Carol (1990), *Same Difference*, Sydney: Allen & Unwin.

Bacchi, Carol (1991a), 'Do Women Need Equal Treatment or Different Treatment?', Conference prepared for XVth World Congress of the International Political Science Association, 21–25 July 1991, Buenos Aires.

Bacchi, Carol (1991b), 'Pregnancy, the Law and the Meaning of Equality' in Meehan, Elizabeth and Sevenhuijsen, Selma (eds), *Equality, Politics and Gender*, London: Sage, 71–87.

Baldwin, Sally (1994), 'The Need for Care in Later Life: Social Protection for Older People and Family Caregivers' in Baldwin, Sally and Falkingham, Jane (eds), *Social Security and Social Change: New Challenges to the Beveridge Model*, Herts: Harvester Wheatsheaf, 180–95.

Ballestrero, Maria V. (1979), *Dalla tutela alla parità*, Bologna: Il Mulino.

Ballestrero, Maria V. (1989), *Parità e oltre*, Roma: Ediesse.

Ballestrero, Maria V. (1992a), 'L'eguaglianza: nozioni e regole. Un dibattito fra giurislavoristi e teorici del diritto', *Lavoro e Diritto*, **6**(2), 577–88.

Ballestrero, Maria V. (1992b), 'La nozione di discriminazione nella legge n. 125/91', *D & L, Rivista Critica di diritto del lavoro*, 773–84.

Banks, Karen (1991), 'Social Security – Objective Justification in the Context of Indirect Discrimination', *Industrial Law Journal*, 20, 220–3.

Barendrecht, Maurits and Van der Wal, Gerard (1986), 'Equality in Law Between Men and Women in the Netherlands' in Verwilghen, Michel (ed.), *L'égalité juridique entre femmes et hommes dans la Communauté européenne*, Vol. II, Louvain-la-Neuve: Presses Universitaires de Louvain, 321–33.

Barlow, J. and Lamb, P. (1990), 'Invalid Care Allowance and the Carer's Premium', *Legal Action*, December, 18–19.

Baudoux, C. and Zaidman, C. (1992), *Egalité entre les sexes*, Paris: Editions L'Harmattan.

Beveridge, W. (1942), *Social Insurance and Allied Services*, Cmnd 6404, London: HMSO.

Bieback, Karl-Jurgen (1992), 'Family Benefits: The New Legal Structures Subsidising the Family', *Journal of European Social Policy*, 2(4), 239–54.

Bieback, Karl-Jurgen (1993a), *Report on the EC Specialist Workshop on Indirect Discrimination in Social Security*, Brussels: Commission of the European Communities (V/6934/93-EN).

Bieback, Karl-Jurgen (1993b), 'The Protection of Atypical Work in the Australian, British and German Social Security Systems', *International Social Security Review*, 46(3), 21–42.

Blackwell, John (1994), 'Changing Work Patterns and their Implications for Social Protection' in Baldwin, Sally and Falkingham, Jane (eds), *Social Security and Social Change: New Challenges to the Beveridge Model*, Herts: Harvester Wheatsheaf, 79–99.

Blom, J. (1993), *Indirect Discrimination in EC Law*, European University Institute: Florence, unpublished masters dissertation.

Bock, G. and James, S. (1992), *Beyond Equality and Difference. Citizenship, feminist politics and female subjectivity*, London and New York: Routledge.

Bond, Larry (1993), 'Ireland in the European Community' in O Cinnéide, Seamus (ed.), *Social Europe: EC Social Policy and Ireland*, Dublin: Institute of European Affairs, 21–35.

Bradshaw, Jonathan (1985), 'Social Security Policy and Assumptions about Patterns of Work' in Klein, Renate and O'Higgins, Martin (eds), *The Future of Welfare*, Oxford: Blackwell, 204–15.

Brocas, Annemarie (1988), 'Equal Treatment of Men and Women in Social Security: An Overview' in International Social Security Association (ed.), *Equal Treatment in Social Security*, ISSA: Geneva, Studies and Research No. 27, 13–35.

Brocas, Annemarie *et al.* (1990), *Women and Social Security: Progress Towards Equality of Treatment*, Geneva: International Labour Organisation.

Bussemaker, Jet (1991), 'Equality, Autonomy and Feminist Politics' in Meehan, Elizabeth and Sevenhuijsen, Selma (eds), *Equality, Politics and Gender*, London: Sage, 52–70.

Bussemaker, Jet (1993), 'Intervention' in *Recherche sur L'Individualisation des Droits en Sécurité Sociale*, Brussels: Université des Femmes, 46–63.

Bussemaker, Jet (1994), 'Equality and Citizenship. Welfare Regimes and Gender Regimes in Some West European Countries', Conference Paper, presented to the ECPR Conference, April 1994, Madrid.

Bussemaker, Jet *et al.* (1993), 'Development and Debates on Women's Issues in the Dutch Welfare State', paper presented to the European Network on Theory and Research on Gender, Welfare and Citizenship, Canterbury, UK, September.

Buswell, Carol (1992), 'Training Women to be Low-Paid Women' in Glendinning, Caroline and Millar, Jane (eds), *Women and Poverty in Britain: the 1990s*, London: Harvester Wheatsheaf, 80–95.

Callender, Claire (1992), 'Redundancy, Unemployment and Poverty', in Glendinning, Caroline and Millar, Jane (eds), *Women and Poverty in Britain: the 1990s*, London: Harvester Wheatsheaf, 134–46.

Callender, Rosheen (1988), 'Ireland and the Implementation of Directive 79/7/EEC: The Social, Political and Legal Issues', in Whyte, Gerry (ed.), *Sex Equality, Community Rights and Irish Social Welfare Law*, Dublin: Irish Centre for European Law, 1–15.

Catasta, Anna (1993), 'Il Diritto Comunitario e le donne' in Franco, M.T. and Veglio, O. (eds), *Pari e dispari*, Milan: Franco Angeli, 9–16.

Chamberlayne, Prue (1991), 'New Directions in Welfare? France, West Germany, Italy and Britain in the 1980s', *Critical Social Policy*, **33**, 5–21.

Clarke, John and Langan, Mary (1993a), 'The British Welfare State: Foundation and Modernization' in Cochrane, Alan and Clarke, John (eds), *Comparing Welfare States: Britain in International Context*, London: Sage, 19–48.

Clarke, John and Langan, Mary (1993b), 'Restructuring Welfare: The British Welfare Regime in the 1980s' in Cochrane, Alan and Clarke, John (eds), *Comparing Welfare States: Britain in International Context*, London: Sage, 49–76.

Collin, Françoise (1991), 'Pluralité Différence Identité', *Présences 1991: Deux Sexes, C'est Un Monde*, 61–72.

Conroy Jackson, Pauline (1993), 'Managing the Mothers: The Case of Ireland' in Lewis, Jane (ed.), *Women and Social Policies in Europe: Work, Family and the State*, Aldershot: Edward Elgar, 72–91.

Cook, Geoff and McCashin, Anthony (1992), 'Inequality, Litigation and Policy Resolution: Gender Dependence in Social Security and Personal Income Tax in the Republic of Ireland', Conference paper presented to 'Social Security: Fifty Years After Beveridge', York, September 1992.

Cook, Juliet and Watt, Susan (1992), 'Racism, Women and Poverty' in Glendinning, Caroline and Millar, Jane (eds), *Women and Poverty in Britain: the 1990s*, London: Harvester Wheatsheaf, 11–23.

Cousins, Mel (1992a), 'The Personal and Temporal Scope of Directive 79/7/EEC', *European Law Review*, **17**, 55–65.

Cousins, Mel (1992b), 'Social Security and Social Assistance – The Final Round?', *European Law Review*, **17**, 533–9.

Cousins, Mel (1993), 'The Treatment of Households in the Irish Social Security Code', *Journal of Social Welfare Law*, 3–18.

Cousins, Mel (1994), 'Equal Treatment and Social Security', *European Law Review*, **19**(2), 123–45.

Cox, Robert (1993), *The Development of the Dutch Welfare State: From Workers' Insurance to Universal Entitlement*, Pittsburgh/London: University of Pittsburgh Press.

Coyle, Angela (1980), 'The Protection Racket?', *Feminist Review*, **4**, 1–12.

Curtin, Deirdre (1988), 'Equal Treatment and Social Welfare: The European Court's Emerging Case-law on Directive 79/7/EEC' in Whyte, Gerry (ed.), *Sex Equality, Community Rights and Irish Social Welfare Law*, Dublin: Irish Centre for European Law, 16–38.

Curtin, Deidre (1989), *Irish Employment Equality Law*, Dublin: Round Hall Press.

Curtin, Deirdre (1990), 'The Province of Government: Delimiting the direct effect of directives in a common law context', *European Law Review*, **15**, 195–223

Curtin, Deirdre (1992a), 'The Decentralised Enforcement of Community Law Rights. Judicial Snakes and Ladders' in Curtin, Deidre and O'Keeffe, David (eds), *Constitutional Adjudication in European Community and National Law*, London: Butterworths, 33–49.

Curtin, Deirdre (1992b), 'State Liability under Community Law: A New Remedy for Private Parties', *Industrial Law Journal*, **21**, 74–81.

Daly, Mary (1989), *Women and Poverty*, Dublin: Attic Press.

Daly, Mary (1992), 'Europe's Poor Women? Gender in Research on Poverty', *European Sociological Review*, **8**(1), 1–12.

Daly, Mary and Scheiwe, Kirsten (1991), *Time and Money: Models of Redistributing Resources Towards Women*, Working Paper ECS 91/4, Florence: European University Institute.

Davies, B. and Ward, S. (1992), *Women and Personal Pensions*, Manchester: Equal Opportunities Commission.

Deacon, Alan (1991), 'The Retreat from State Welfare' in Becker, Saul (ed.), *Windows of Opportunity*, London: Child Poverty Action Group, 9–19.

de Jong, P. *et al.* (1990), *Form and Reform of the Dutch Social Security System*, Deventer: Ministry of Social Affairs and Employment.

Denis, P. (1986), *Droit de la Sécurité Sociale*, Brussels: Larcier.

Department of Social Security (1995), *Piloting Change in Social Security: Helping People into Work*, London: HMSO.

De Vos, Dominique (1990a), 'Mise en Oeuvre en Belgique des Directives 79/7/CEE et 86/378/CCE relatives à l'égalité dans les régimes légaux et professionnels de la sécurité sociale', *Revue du Travail*, (4-6), 531–63.

De Vos, Dominique (1990b), 'Les pensions professionnelles ou l'art de l'interrogation', *Chroniques de Droit Social*, 357–63.

De Vos, Dominique (1994), 'Pensionable Age and Equal Treatment from Charybdis to Scylla', *Industrial Law Journal*, **23**, 175–180.

Dickens, L. (1992), *Whose Flexibility? Discrimination and Equality Issues in Atypical Work*, London: Institute of Employment Rights.

Dilnot, Andrew and Kell, Michael (1989), 'Male Unemployment and Women's Work' in Dilnot, Andrew and Walker, Ian (eds), *The Economics of Social Security*, Oxford: Clarendon, 153–68.

Dilnot, Andrew and Webb, Steven (1989), 'The 1988 Social Security Reforms' in Dilnot, Andrew and Walker, Ian (eds), *The Economics of Social Security*, Oxford: Clarendon, 239–67.

Docksey, Chris (1991), 'The Principle of Equality between Women and Men as a Fundamental Right under Community Law', *Industrial Law Journal*, **20**, 258–80.

Dominelli, Lena (1988), 'Thatcher's Attack on Social Security: Restructuring Social Control', *Critical Social Policy*, **23**, 46–61.

Döring, Diether *et al.* (1994), 'Old-Age Security For Women in the Twelve EC Countries', *Journal of European Social Policy*, **4**(1), 1–18.

Dowd, Nancy (1989), 'Work and Family: The Gender Paradox and the Limitations of Discrimination Analysis in Restructuring the Workplace', *Harvard Civil Rights Civil Liberties Review*, **24**(1), 79-172.

Duncan, Alan, Giles, Christopher and Webb, Steven (1994), *Social Security Reform and Women's Independent Incomes*, Manchester: Equal Opportunities Commission.

EC Commission of the European Communities (1983), *Interim Report on the Application of Directive 79/7/EEC of 19 December 1978 on the progressive implementation of the principle of equal treatment between men and women in matters of social security*, Brussels: EC Commission COM(83) 793 final.

EC Commission (1992), *The Position of Women on the Labour Market: Trends and Developments in the Twelve Member States of the European*

Community, Brussels: EC Commission, Women of Europe, Supplement No. 36.

Ellis, E. (1991), *European Community Sex Equality Law*, Oxford: Clarendon.

EOC (Equal Opportunities Commission) (1991), *Women and Men in Britain in 1991*, London: HMSO.

EOR (Equal Opportunities Review) (1993), 'Costs/Benefits of Extending Parents' Rights', *Equal Opportunities Review*, **48**, 6.

Esam, P. and Berthoud, R. (1991), *Independent Benefits for Men and Women*, London: Policy Studies Institute.

Eurostat (1992), *Women in the European Community*, Luxembourg: Official Publications of the European Community.

Ferrera, M. (1993), *Modelli di solidarietà: politica e riforme sociali nelle democrazia*, Bologna: Il Mulino.

Fitzgerald, Tony (1983), 'The New Right and the Family' in Loney, Martin *et al.* (eds), *Social Policy and Social Welfare*, Milton Keynes: Open University Press.

Fitzpatrick, Barry (1990), 'Dilemmas in Harmonizing Equality Upwards', unpublished mimeo.

Fitzpatrick, Barry (1991), 'Equality in Occupational Pensions – The New Frontiers After Barber', *Modern Law Review*, **54**(2), 271–80.

Fox Harding, Lorraine (1993), '"Alarm" versus "Liberation"? Responses to the Increase in Lone Parents – Part I', *Journal of Social Welfare and Family Law*, 101–12.

Fraser, N. (1989), *Unruly Practices: Power, Discourse and Gender in Contemporary Social Theory*, Cambridge: Polity Press.

Fredman, Sandra (1992), 'European Community Discrimination Law: A Critique', *Industrial Law Journal*, **21**, 119–34.

Frug, Mary Jo (1992), 'Sexual Equality and Sexual Difference in American Law' *New England Law Review*, **26**, 665–82.

Gaeta, L. and Zoppoli, L. (1992), *Il Diritto Diseguale. La Legge sulle azioni positive*, Turin: Giappichelli Editore.

Gianformaggio, Letitia (1992), 'Politica della differenza e principio di uguaglianza', *Lavoro e Diritto*, **6**(2), 187–204.

Gibson, Suzie (1989), 'The Structure of the Veil', *Modern Law Review*, **52**, 420–40.

Ginn, Jerry and Arber, Sara (1992), 'Towards Women's Independence: Pension Systems in Three Contrasting European Welfare States', *Journal of European Social Policy*, **2**(4), 255–77.

Ginn, Jerry and Arber, Sara (1993), 'Pension Penalties: The Gendered Division of Occupational Welfare', *Work, Employment and Society*, **7**(1), 47–70.

Ginn, Jerry and Arber, Sara (1994), 'Heading for Hardship: How the British

Pension System has Failed Women' in Baldwin, Sally and Falkingham, Jane (eds), *Social Security and Social Change: New Challenges to the Beveridge Model*, Herts: Harvester Wheatsheaf, 216–34.

Ginsburg, N. (1992), *Divisions of Welfare*, London: Sage.

Glendinning, Caroline (1990), 'Dependency and Interdependency: The Incomes of Informal Carers and the Impact of Social Security', *Journal of Social Policy*, **19**, 469–97.

Glendinning, Caroline (1992), 'Community Care: The Financial Consequences for Women' in Glendinning, Caroline and Millar, Jane (eds), *Women and Poverty in Britain: the 1990s*, London: Harvester Wheatsheaf, 162–75.

Glendinning, Caroline and Millar, Jane (1991), 'Poverty: The Forgotten Englishwomen' in Maclean, Mavis and Groves, Dulcie (eds), *Women's Issues in Social Policy*, London/New York: Routledge, 20–37.

Glendinning, Caroline and McLaughlin, Eugene (1993), *Paying for Care: Lessons from Europe*, London: HMSO: Social Security Advisory Committee.

Graham, Hilary (1983), 'Caring: A Labour of Love' in Finch, Janet and Groves, Dulcie (eds), *A Labour of Love: Women, Work and Caring*, London: Routledge and Kegan Paul, 13–30.

Gregory, J. (1987), *Sex, Race and the Law*, London: Sage.

Groves, Dulcie (1983), 'Members and Survivors: Women and Retirement Pensions Legislation' in Lewis, Jane (ed.), *Women's Welfare Women's Rights*, London: Croom Helm, 38–63.

Groves, Dulcie (1987), 'Occupational Pension Provision and Women's Poverty in Old Age' in Glendinning, Caroline and Millar, Jane (eds), *Women and Poverty in Britain*, Brighton: Wheatsheaf.

Groves, Dulcie (1991), 'Women and Financial Provision in Old Age' in Maclean, Mavis and Groves, Dulcie (eds), *Women's Issues in Social Policy*, London and New York: Routledge, 38–60.

Groves, Dulcie (1992), 'Occupational Pension Provision and Women's Poverty in Old Age' in Glendinning, Caroline and Millar, Jane (eds), *Women and Poverty in Britain: the 1990s*, London: Harvester Wheatsheaf.

Groves, Dulcie and Finch, Janet (1983), 'Natural Selection: Perspectives on Entitlement to the Invalid Care Allowance' in Finch, Janet and Groves, Dulcie (eds), *A Labour of Love: Women, Work and Caring*, London: Routledge and Kegan Paul.

Guastini, Riccardo (1992), 'La grammatica di "eguaglianza"', *Lavoro e Diritto*, **6**(2), 205–10.

Hakim, Catherine (1989), 'Workforce Restructuring, Social Insurance Coverage and the Black Economy', *Journal of Social Policy*, **18**, 471–503.

Harlow, Carol (1992), 'A Community of Interests? Making the Most of European Law', *Modern Law Review*, **55**, 331–50.

Herbert, Francis (1990), 'La Discrimination Indirecte', *Revue de Travail*, (4–6), 655–80.

Herbert, Francis (1994), 'Social Security and Indirect Discrimination', paper presented at a conference in Oxford, 'Equality in Treatment in Social Security Between Men and Women', 4-6 January 1994.

Hervey, Tamara (1991), 'Justification for Indirect Sex Discrimination in Employment: European Community and United Kingdom Law Compared', *International and Comparative Law Quarterly*, **40**, 807–26.

Hervey, Tamara (1992), 'Case-Note on Smithson', *Journal of Social Welfare and Family Law*, 461–5.

Hewitt, P. (1993), *About Time: The Revolution in Work and Family Life*, London: Rivers Oram Press.

Holtmaat, Rikki (1989), 'The Power of Legal Concepts: The Development of a Feminist Theory of Law', *International Journal of the Sociology of Law*, **17**, 481–502.

Holtmaat, Rikki (1993a), 'Intervention' in *Recherche sur L'Individualisation des Droits en Sécurité Sociale*, Brussels: Université des Femmes, 64–95.

Holtmaat, Rikki (1993b), 'Between Non-Responsibility and Care: New Rights for Women', Conference Paper presented to Critical Lawyers Conference, September, 1993, Oxford.

Hoskyns, Catherine (1985), 'Women's Equality and the European Community', *Feminist Review*, **20**, 71–88.

Hoskyns, Catherine (1986), 'Women, European Law and Transnational Politics', *International Journal of the Sociology of Law*, **14**, 299–315.

Hoskyns, Catherine (1992), 'The European Community's Policy on Women in the Context of 1992', *Women Studies International Forum*, **15**(1), 21–28.

Hoskyns, Catherine and Luckhaus, Linda (1989), 'The European Community Directive on Equal Treatment in Social Security', *Policy and Politics*, **17**(4), 321–55.

Hutton, Sandra (1994), 'Men's and Women's Incomes: Evidence from Survey Data', *Journal of Social Policy*, **23**(1), 21–40.

ISSA (International Social Security Association) (1973), *Women and Social Security*, ISSA: Geneva, Studies and Research No. 5.

Jacqmain, J. (1989), *L'égalité juridique entre femmes et hommes dans la Communauté Européenne: Recueil de Textes Nationaux: Droit Belge*, Louvain-la-Neuve: Presses Universitaires de Louvain.

Jarman, Jennifer (1991), 'Equality or Marginalisation: The Repeal of Protective Legislation' in Meehan, Elizabeth and Sevenhuijsen, Selma (eds), *Equality, Politics and Gender*, London: Sage, 142–53.

Joshi, Heather (1991) 'Sex and Motherhood as Handicaps in the Labour Market' in Maclean, Mavis and Groves, Dulcie (eds), *Women's Issues in Social Policy*, London and New York, 179–93.

Kaplan, G. (1992), *Contemporary Western European Feminism*, London: University College Press.

Kaufmann, Claudia (1991), 'Egalité des Droits et droits spécifiques pour les femmes, y a-t-il contradiction?', *Présences: Deux Sexes c'est un Monde*, 123–36.

Kidd, Tony (1989), 'Women and Welfare' in Reid, Ivan and Stratta, Erica (eds), *Sex Differences in Britain*, Aldershot: Gower, 75–102.

Kingdom, Elizabeth (1989), 'Birthrights: Equal or Special?' in Lee, Robert and Morgan, Derek (eds), *Birthrights: Law and Ethics at the Beginnings of Life*, London: Routledge, 17–36.

Kowarzik, Ute and Popay, Jennie (1989), *That's Women's Work. Report on Women's Unpaid Labour in the Home*, London: Employment and Training Group, London Research Centre.

Kravaritou-Manitakis, Y. (1988), *New Forms of Work: Labour Law and Social Security Aspects in the European Community*, Luxembourg: European Foundation for the Improvement of Living and Working Conditions.

Krieger, Linda and Cooney, Patricia (1983), 'The Miller–Wohl Controversy: Equal Treatment, Positive Action and the meaning of Women's Equality', *Golden Gate University Law Review*, **13**, 513–72.

Lacey, Nicola (1987), 'Legislation Against Sex Discrimination: Questions from a Feminist Perspective', *Journal of Law and Society*, **14**, 411–21.

Land, Hilary (1989), 'The Construction of Dependency' in Bulmer, Martin *et al.* (eds), *The Goals of Social Policy*, London: Unwin Hyman, 141–59.

Laurent, André (1979), 'Une Directive pour les années quatre-vingt: La Directive communautaire relative à la mise en oeuvre progressive du principe de l'égalité de traitement entre hommes et femmes en matière de sécurité sociale', *Droit Social*, 243–6.

Laurent, André (1986), 'Le Droit Communautaire et les droits des Etats Membres relatifs au principe de l'égalité de traitment en matière de sécurité sociale', in Verwilghen, Michel (ed.), *L'égalité juridique entre femmes et hommes dans la Communauté européenne*, **I**, Louvain-la-Neuve: Presses Universitaires de Louvain, 189–210.

Laurent, André (1987), 'Le principe de l'égalité de traitement entre homme et femme en matière de sécurité sociale et ses limites', *Il Diritto del Lavoro*, 510–524.

Law, Sylvia (1984), 'Rethinking Sex and the Constitution', *University of Pennyslvania Law Review*, **132**, 955–1040.

Leira, Arnlaug (1993), 'The "Woman-Friendly" Welfare State?: The Case of Norway and Sweden' in Lewis, Jane (ed.), *Women and Social Policies in Europe: Work, Family and the State*, Aldershot: Edward Elgar, 49–71.

Lewis, Jane (1983), 'Dealing with Dependency: State Practices and Social

Realities, 1870–1945' in Lewis, Jane (ed.), *Women's Welfare Women's Rights*, Kent: Croom Helm, 17–35.

Lewis, Jane (1992), 'Gender and the Development of Welfare Regimes', *Journal of European Social Policy*, **2**(3), 159–73.

Lewis, Jane and Davies, Celia (1991), 'Protective Legislation in Britain; 1870–1990: Equality, Difference and their Implications for Women', *Policy and Politics*, **19**, 13–25.

Lister, Ruth (1990), 'Women, Economic Dependency and Citizenship', *Journal of Social Policy*, 445–67.

Lister, Ruth (1991), 'Social Security in the 1990s', *Social Policy and Administration*, **25**(2), 91–107.

Lister, Ruth (1992), *Women's Economic Dependency and Social Security*, Manchester: Equal Opportunities Commission.

Loenen, T. (1992), *Verschil in gelijkheid. De conceptualisering van het juridische gelijkheidsbeginsel met betrekking tot vrouwen en mannen in Nederland en de Verenigde Staten*, Zwolle: Tjeenk Willink.

Lonsdale, Susan (1992), 'Patterns of Paid Work' in Glendinning, Caroline and Millar, Jane (eds), *Women and Poverty in Britain: the 1990s*, London: Harvester Wheatsheaf.

Luckhaus, Linda (1983), 'Social Security: The Equal Treatment Reforms', *Journal of Social Welfare Law*, 325–34.

Luckhaus, Linda (1986a), 'Severe Disablement Allowance: the Old Dressed Up as New', *Journal of Social Welfare Law*, 153–69.

Luckhaus, Linda (1986b), 'Payment for Caring: A European Solution', *Public Law*, 526–37.

Luckhaus, Linda (1987), 'Case Note on *Clarke* v. *Chief Adjudication Officer*', *Journal of Social Welfare Law*, 378–83.

Luckhaus, Linda (1988), 'Sex Discrimination in State Social Security Schemes: *Teuling*', *European Law Review*, **13**, 52–8.

Luckhaus, Linda (1990), 'Changing Rules, Enduring Structures', *Modern Law Review*, **53**, 655–68.

Luckhaus, Linda (1992a), 'New Disability Benefits: Beveridge Turned Upside Down', *Industrial Law Journal*, **21**, 237–44.

Luckhaus, Linda (1992b), 'Intentions and the Avoidance of Community Law', *Industrial Law Journal*, **21**, 315–22.

Luckhaus, Linda (1993), 'The Role of the "Economic" and the "Social" in social security and community law' in Weick, Gunther (ed.), *National and European Law on the Threshold of the Single Market*, Frankfurt: Peter Lang, 213–30.

Luckhaus, Linda and Dickens, L. (1991), *Social Protection of Atypical Workers in the United Kingdom*, a report prepared for the European Commission, Brussels.

McCashin, A. (1993), *Lone Parents in the Republic of Ireland: Enumeration, Description and Implications for Social Security*, Dublin: Economic and Social Research Institute.

McCrudden, Christopher (1982), 'Institutional Discrimination', *Oxford Journal of Legal Studies*, **2**, 303–67.

McCrudden, Christopher (ed.) (1987), *Women, Employment and European Equality Law*, London: Eclipse.

McCrudden, Christopher and Black, Julia (1994), 'Issues of Costs and Problems of Implementation, Including Retrospection', paper presented to conference 'Equality Between Men and Women in Social Security', Oxford, 4–6 January 1994.

McLaughlin, Eugene *et al.* (1989), *Work and Welfare Benefits*, Aldershot: Avebury.

McLaughlin, Eugene (1993), 'Ireland: Catholic Corporatism' in Cochrane, Alan and Clarke, John (eds), *Comparing Welfare States: Britain in International Context*, London: Sage, 205–37.

Maclennan, Emma and Weitzel, Renate (1984), 'Labour Market Policy in Four Countries: Are Women Adequately Represented?' in Schmid, Gunther and Weitzel, Renate (eds), *Sex Discrimination and Equal Opportunity: The Labour Market and Employment Policy*, Aldershot: Gower, 202–48.

MacKinnon, Catherine (1979), *Sexual Harassment of Working Women*, New Haven and London: Yale University Press.

MacKinnon, Catherine (1989), *Towards a Feminist Theory of the State*, Cambridge: Harvard University Press.

Magrez, Michel (1988), 'Les Plans de Réforme du Droit de la Sécurité Sociale', in Van der Vost, P. (1988), *Cent Ans de Droit Sociale Belge*, Brussels: Bruylant, 491–514.

Maier, Friederike (1991), 'Part-time work, Social Security Protections and Labour Law: An International Comparison', *Policy and Politics*, **19**, 1–11.

Majury, Diana (1987), 'Strategizing in Equality', *Wisconsin Women's Law Journal*, **3**, 169–87.

Mangan, Gerry (1993a), 'Social Protection: Common Problems' in O Cinnéide, Seamus (ed.), *Social Europe: EC Social Policy and Ireland*, Dublin: Institute of European Affairs, 36–45.

Mangan, Gerry (1993b), 'Social Protection in Ireland' in O Cinnéide, Seamus (ed.), *Social Europe: EC Social Policy and Ireland*, Dublin: Institute of European Affairs, 107–16.

Mangan, Ita (1993c), 'The Influence of EC Membership on Irish Social Policy and Social Services' in O Cinnéide, Seamus (ed.), *Social Europe: EC Social Policy and Ireland*, Dublin: Institute of European Affairs, 60–81.

Mazey, Sonia (1988), 'European Community Action on behalf of Women: the Limits of Legislation', *Journal of Common Market Studies*, **27**, 63–84.

Meehan, Elizabeth (1990), 'Sex Equality Policies in the European Community', *Révue d'intégration Européenne*, **13**, 185–96.

Micklewright, J. (1990), *Why Do Less than a Quarter of the Unemployed in Britain Receive Unemployment Insurance?*, Working Paper ECO No. 90/17, Florence: European University Institute.

Millar, Jane (1988), 'Barriers to Equal Treatment and Equal Outcome: Means-Testing and Unemployment' in International Social Security Association (ed.), *Equal Treatment in Social Security*, Geneva: International Social Security Association (Studies and Research No. 27), 149–60.

Millar, Jane (1989), 'Social Security, Equality and Women in the UK', *Policy and Politics*, **17**, 311–19.

Millar, Jane (1994), 'Lone Parents and Social Security Policy in the UK' in Baldwin, Sally and Falkingham, Jane (eds), *Social Security and Social Change: New Challenges to the Beveridge Model*, Herts: Harvester Wheatsheaf, 62–75.

Millar, Jane *et al.* (1989), 'The Employment Lottery: Risk and Social Security Benefits', *Policy and Politics*, **17**, 75–81.

Millar, J. *et al.* (1992), *Lone Parents: Poverty and Public Policy in Ireland*, Dublin: Combat Poverty Agency.

Mitchell, Juliet (1987), 'Women and Equality' in Phillips, Anne (ed.), *Feminism and Equality*, Oxford: Blackwell, 24–43.

More, Gillian (1993), '"Equal Treatment" of the Sexes in European Community Law: What Does "Equal" Mean?', *Feminist Legal Studies*, **1**(1), 45–74.

Morris, A. and Nott, S. (1991), *Working Women and the Law: Equality and Discrimination in Theory and Practice*, London: Routledge.

Morris, Lydia (1987), 'Constraints on Gender: The Family Wage, Social Security and the Labour Market; Reflections on Research in Hartlepool', *Work, Employment and Society*, **1**, 85–106.

Moss, P. (1990), *Childcare in the European Communities 1985–1990*, Women of Europe (Supplement No. 31), Brussels: Commission of the European Communities.

MSAE (Ministry of Social Affairs and Employment) (1990), *Social Security in the Netherlands*, Deventer: Kluwer.

Mückenberger, Ulrich (1989), 'Non Standard Forms of Work and the Role of Changes in Labour and Social Security Regulation', *International Journal of the Sociology of Law*, **17**(4), 381–402.

O'Donovan, K. and Szyszczak, E. (1988), *Equality and Sex Discrimination Law*, Oxford: Blackwell.

Ogus, A. and Barendt, E. (1988), *The Law of Social Security*, London: Butterworths.

Ogus, A. and Barendt, E. (1995), *The Law of Social Security*, London: Butterworths.

O'Kelly, Rory (1985), 'The Principle of Aggregation' in Silburn, Richard (ed.), *The Future of Social Security*, London: Macmillan, 73–85.

Oorschot, Wim van and Schell, John (1991), 'Means-testing in Europe: A Growing Concern' in Adler, Michael *et al.* (eds), *The Sociology of Social Security*, Edinburgh: Edinburgh University Press, 187–211.

Pahl, Jan (1984), 'The Allocation of Money Within the Household' in Freeman, Michael (ed.), *State, Law and the Family: Critical Perspectives*, London: Tavistock, 36–50.

Pahl, Jan (1989), *Money and Marriage*, London: Macmillan.

Pahl, Jan (1991), 'Money and Power in Marriage' in Abbott, P. and Wallace, C. (ed.), *Gender, Power and Sexuality*, Basingstoke: Macmillan, 41–57.

Pascall, G. (1986), *Social Policy: A Feminist Analysis*, London: Tavistock.

Peemans-Poullet, H. (1993), 'Enjeux et Principes de L'Individualisation des Droits', *Chronique Féministe*, **46**, 31–9.

Pieters, D. (1990), *Introduction into the Social Security Law of the Member States of the European Community*, Brussels: Bruylant.

Pillinger, J. (1992), *Feminising the Market: Women's Pay and Employment in the European Community*, Basingstoke: Macmillan.

Prechal, Sacha (1993), 'Combating Indirect Discrimination in a Community Law Context', *Legal Issues of European Integration*, 81–97.

Prechal, Sacha and Burrows, N. (1990), *Gender Discrimination Law of the European Community*, Aldershot: Dartmouth.

Reid, M. (1990), *The Impact of Community Law on the Irish Constitution*, Dublin: Irish Centre for European Law.

Rhode, Deborah (1989), *Justice and Gender*, Cambridge: Harvard University Press.

Rhode, Deborah (1990), 'Definitions of Difference' in Rhode, D. (ed.), *Theoretical Perspectives on Sexual Difference*, New Haven: Yale University Press, 197–212.

Rhode, Deborah (1992), 'The Politics of Paradigms: Gender Difference and Gender Disadvantage' in Bock, Gisela and James, Susan (eds), *Beyond Equality and Difference: Citizenship, Feminist Politics and Feminist Subjectivity*, London/New York: Routledge, 149–63.

Richards, Margaret (1979), 'A Study of the Non-Contributory Invalidity Pension for Married Women', *Journal of Social Welfare Law*, 66–75.

Roebroek, Joop (1993), 'Basic Schemes in the Netherlands' in Berghman, Jos and Cantillon, Bea (eds), *The European Face of Social Security*, Aldershot: Avebury, 239–60.

Roll, J. (1991), *What is a Family? Benefit Models and Social Realities*, London: Family Policy Studies Centre.

Room, Graham *et al.* (1989), '"New Poverty" in the European Community', *Policy and Politics*, 165–76.

Rubenstein, Michael (1990), 'Teorie sulla discriminazione', *Quaderni di Diritto del Lavoro e delle Relazioni Industriali*, **4**, 85–94.

Rutherford, Françoise (1989), 'The Proposal for a European Directive on Parental Leave: Some Reasons Why it Failed', *Policy and Politics*, **17**(4), 301–9.

Sainsbury, Diane (1993a), 'Dual Welfare and Sex Segregation of Access to Social Benefits: Income Maintenance Policies in the UK, the US, the Netherlands and Sweden', *Journal of Social Policy*, **22**, 69–98.

Sainsbury, Diane (1993b), 'Welfare State Restructuring? Gender Equality Reforms and their Impact', Conference Paper presented to 'Gender and Welfare', ECPR Workshop, April, Leiden.

Savy, Nicole (1990), 'La Mixité des Droits', *Hommes et Libertés*, 19–23.

Scales, Anne (1980), 'Towards a Feminist Jurisprudence', *Indiana Law Journal*, **56**, 375–444.

Scarponi, Stefania (1992), 'Le Nozione di Discriminazione' in Gaeta, Lorenzo and Zoppoli, Lorenzo (eds), *Il Diritto Diseguale. La legge sulle azioni positive*, Torino: Giappichelli Editore, 43–79.

Scheiwe, Kirsten (1990), *Report on the Implementation of the EC Equality Directives*, Brussels: EC Commission.

Scheiwe, Kirsten (1991), *Male Times and Female Times in the Law: Normative Models in Labour Law, Social Security Law and Family Law and their Impact on the Gendered Division of Labour*, Florence: European University Institute.

Scheiwe, Kirsten (1993), 'What do Institutions Contribute to Increase Mothers' Poverty Risk?', paper presented to the European Working Group on Poverty, Welfare and Gender, November, St Martins, Germany.

Scheiwe, Kirsten (1994), 'EC Law's Unequal Treatment of the Family: The Case Law of the European Court of Justice on Rules Prohibiting Discrimination on Grounds of Sex and Nationality', *Social and Legal Studies*, **3**, 243–65.

Scheiwe, Kirsten (1995), 'The Gender Dimension in German Labour Law: Time Revisited' in Kravaritou, Yota (ed.), *The Sex of Labour Law*, Deventer: Kluwer Law and Taxation.

Schunter-Kleeman, Suzanne (1992), 'The Implementation of the European Community Equality Directive on Social Security', *Review of Labour Economics and Industrial Relations*, **6**, 37–55.

Scott, Joan (1988), 'Deconstructing Equality-versus-Difference: Or, the Uses of Poststructuralist Theory for Feminism', *Feminist Studies*, **12**, 33–50.

SIPTU (Services Industrial Professional Technical Union) (1992), 'The "Equal Treatment" Changes', *Social Welfare Briefing*, (3), September 1992.

Sjerps, Ina (1988), 'Indirect Discrimination in Social Security in the Netherlands: Demands of the Dutch Women's Movement' in Buckley, Mary and Anderson, Malcolm (eds), *Women, Equality and Europe*, London: Macmillan, 95–106.

Smart, Carol (1987), 'Securing the Family? Rhetoric and Policy in the field of Social Security' in Loney, Martin *et al.* (eds), *The State or the Market*, London: Sage, 99–114.

Sohrab, Julia (1993a), 'Indirect Discrimination Against Women in Social Security: Directive 79/7/EEC, Additions for Dependent Spouses and Earnings Rules: Case-Note on *Molenbroek*', *Journal of Social Welfare and Family Law*, 355–59.

Sohrab, Julia (1993b), 'Linking Benefits to the Differential Pension Ages for Men and Women: The Principle of Equal Treatment in Social Security and the Derogation in Article 7(1)(a) Directive 79/7/EEC: Case-Note on *Secretary of State for Social Security* v. *Thomas et al.*', *Journal of Social Welfare and Family Law*, 359–63.

Sohrab, Julia (1993c), 'Avoiding the Exquisite Trap: A Critical Look at the Equal Treatment/Special Treatment Debate in Law', *Feminist Legal Studies*, **1**(2), 141–62.

Sohrab, Julia (1994), 'Women and Social Security: The Limits of EEC Equality Law', *Journal of Social Welfare and Family Law*, 5–17.

Stang Dahl, Tove (1984), 'Women's Rights to Money', *International Journal of the Sociology of Law*, **12**(2), 137–152.

Szyszczak, Erika (1990), 'European Court Rulings on Discrimination and Part-Time Working and the Burden of Proof in Equal Pay Claims', *Industrial Law Journal*, **19**, 114–20.

Szyszczak, Erika (1992a), 'European Community Law: New Remedies, New Directions?', *Modern Law Review*, **55**, 690–97.

Szyszczak, Erika (1992b), '*Emmott* v. *Chief Adjudication Officer*', *Common Market Law Review*, **29**, 604–14.

Taylor-Gooby, P. (1991), 'Welfare State Regimes and Welfare Citizenship', *Journal of European Social Policy*, **1**, 93–105.

Van Droogenbroeck, J. and Denis, Pierre (1986), 'L'égalité de l'homme et de la femme en droit belge de sécurité sociale' in Verwilghen, Michel (ed.), *L'égalité juridique entre femmes et hommes dans la Communauté Européenne*, Vol. II, Louvain-la-Neuve: Presses Universitaires de Louvain, 41–58.

Van Every, Jo (1992), 'Who is 'the Family'? The Assumptions of British Social Policy', *Critical Social Policy*, **33**, 62–75.

Van Gerven, Walter (1994), 'Introduction to Existing Community Law on Equality of Treatment Between Men and Women in Social Security as Interpreted by the European Court of Justice', paper presented to conference "Equality Between Men and Women in Social Security", Oxford, 4–6 January 1994.

Vogler, Carolyn and Pahl, Jan (1993), 'Social and Economic Change and the Organisation of Money Within Marriage', *Work, Employment and Society*, **7**, 71–95.

Ward, A. *et al.* (1992), *Women and Citizenship in Europe: Borders, Rights and Duties*, Stoke-on-Trent: Trentham Books and EFSF.

Ward, C. *et al.* (1993), *Income Dependency Within Couples, London: Social Statistics Research Unit*, City University, National Child Development Study (NCDS) (Working Paper 36).

Ward, P. (1990), *Financial Consequences of Marital Breakdown*, Dublin: Combat Poverty Agency.

Warde, A. and Hetherington, K. (1993), 'A Changing Domestic Division of Labour? Issues of Measurement and Interpretation', *Work, Employment and Society*, **7**(1), 23–45.

Warner, Harriet (1984), 'EC Social Policy in Practice: Community Action on Behalf of Women and its Impact in the Member States', *Journal of Common Market Studies*, **23**, 141–67.

Watson, P. (1980), *Social Security Law of the European Communities*, London: Mansell.

Webb, Steven (1993), 'Women's Incomes: Past, Present and Prospects', *Fiscal Studies*, **14**, 14–36.

Westen, Peter (1982), 'The Empty Idea of Equality', *Harvard Law Journal*, **85**, 537–95.

Whyte, Gerry (1988), 'Council Directive 79/7/EEC in Ireland: Background to the Implementation of the Directive in Ireland' in Whyte, Gerry (ed.), *Sex Equality, Community Rights and Irish Social Welfare Law*, Dublin: Irish Centre for European Law, 39–59.

Whyte, Gerry (1992), 'Report of the Review Group on the Treatment of Households in the Social Welfare Code: A legal perspective', *Administration*, **40**(2), 134–50.

Whyte, Gerry and O'Dell, Eolain (1992), 'Welfare, Women and Unjust Enrichment', *Industrial Law Journal*, **21**, 304–313.

Williams, Joan (1989b), 'Deconstructing Gender', *Michigan Law Review*, **87**, 797–845.

Williams, Wendy (1982), 'The Equality Crisis: Some Reflections on Culture, Courts and Feminism', *Women's Rights Law Reporter*, **7**, 175–200.

Williams, Wendy (1985), 'Equality's Riddle: Pregnancy and the Equal Treatment/Special Treatment Debate', *New York University Review of Law and Social Change*, **13**, 325–80.

Williams, Wendy (1987), 'American Equality Jurisprudence' in Martin, Sheila and Mahoney, Kathleen (eds), *Equality and Judicial Neutrality*, Toronto: Carswell, 115–27.

Wolgast, E. (1980), *Equality and the Rights of Women*, Ithaca: Cornell University Press.

Index